Digital Forensics with Kali Linux
Second Edition

Perform data acquisition, data recovery, network forensics, and malware analysis with Kali Linux 2019.x

Shiva V. N. Parasram

BIRMINGHAM—MUMBAI

Digital Forensics with Kali Linux
Second Edition

Commissioning Editor: Vijin Boricha
Acquisition Editor: Ankita Darad
Senior Editor: Arun Nadar
Content Development Editor: Pratik Andrade
Technical Editor: Sarvesh Jaywant
Copy Editor: Safis Editing
Project Coordinator: Neil Dmello
Proofreader: Safis Editing
Indexer: Tejal Daruwale Soni
Production Designer: Jyoti Chauhan

First published: December 2017
Second Edition: April 2020

Production reference: 2100620

Published by Packt Publishing Ltd.
Livery Place
35 Livery Street
Birmingham
B3 2PB, UK.
ISBN 978-1-83864-080-4

www.packt.com

Contributors

About the author

Shiva V. N. Parasram is the Executive Director and CISO of the Computer Forensics and Security Institute, which specializes in penetration testing, forensics, and advanced cybersecurity training. As the only Certified EC-Council Instructor (CEI) in the Caribbean, he has also trained hundreds in CCNA, CND, CEH, CHFI, ECSA, and CCISO, among other certifications. He has partnered with international companies including Fujitsu (Trinidad) and Take It To The Top LLC as the lead trainer for advanced cybersecurity courses. Shiva is also the author of two other books from Packt Publishing and has delivered workshops, lectures, and keynote speeches regionally for ISACA, universities, law associations, and other institutions.

I'd like to thank all the loving and amazing people in my life: my guru, Pundit Hardeo Persad; my brave mom and patient dad; my beautiful wife, bestie, and biggest supporter, Savi Parasram aka Pinky Mittens aka Cuddles Kapoor (love you, babe). The NAFAD boys and the always entertaining gentlemen at the TDP group. My good friend, Beth Montoya; all my students at CFSI; Mr. Bepnesh Goolcharran; and of course, my furry little love, Bindi. Love you all.

`Packt.com`

Subscribe to our online digital library for full access to over 7,000 books and videos, as well as industry leading tools to help you plan your personal development and advance your career. For more information, please visit our website.

Why subscribe?

- Spend less time learning and more time coding with practical eBooks and Videos from over 4,000 industry professionals

- Improve your learning with Skill Plans built especially for you

- Get a free eBook or video every month

- Fully searchable for easy access to vital information

- Copy and paste, print, and bookmark content

Did you know that Packt offers eBook versions of every book published, with PDF and ePub files available? You can upgrade to the eBook version at `packt.com` and as a print book customer, you are entitled to a discount on the eBook copy. Get in touch with us at `customercare@packtpub.com` for more details.

At `www.packt.com`, you can also read a collection of free technical articles, sign up for a range of free newsletters, and receive exclusive discounts and offers on Packt books and eBooks.

About the reviewers

Alex Samm has over 11 years' experience in the IT field, holding a B.Sc. in computer science from the University of Hertfordshire, England. His experience includes EUC support, Linux and UNIX, server and network administration, and security, among others.

He currently works at EY Trinidad and Tobago and lectures at the Computer Forensics and Security Institute on IT security courses, including ethical hacking and penetration testing.

Alex co-authored *Kali Linux 2018: Assuring Security by Penetration Testing* (Fourth Edition), and reviewed *Digital Forensics with Kali Linux* (First Edition) by Shiva V.N. Parasram, all from Packt Publishing.

> *I'd like to thank my parents, Roderick and Marcia, for their continued support; Shiva and Savi for their guidance and support; and all my past and present students. Cheers!*

Dale Joseph is a digital forensic expert with over 12 years' experience in high-technology investigations. He has over 21 years' Law Enforcement Investigative experience and has been involved in numerous technology-based projects. Dale is currently the Cybercrime Policy Specialist at CARICOM (Caribbean Community).

His areas of expertise are wireless and VOIP Investigations, investigative scripting, OSINT, cryptocurrency, deep and dark web investigations, network, computer, live data, mobile and malware forensics.

Dale is also a certified Digital Forensics Trainer and has conducted several workshops/seminars that have trained members of law enforcement, the private sector, and Government entities.

Packt is searching for authors like you

If you're interested in becoming an author for Packt, please visit `authors.packtpub.com` and apply today. We have worked with thousands of developers and tech professionals, just like you, to help them share their insight with the global tech community. You can make a general application, apply for a specific hot topic that we are recruiting an author for, or submit your own idea.

Table of Contents

Section 2: Forensic Fundamentals and Best Practices

3
Understanding Filesystems and Storage Media

4
Incident Response and Data Acquisition

Section 3:
Forensic Tools in Kali Linux

5

Evidence Acquisition and Preservation with dc3dd and Guymager

6

File Recovery and Data Carving with foremost, Scalpel, and bulk_extractor

7
Memory Forensics with Volatility

8
Artifact Analysis

Section 4: Automated Digital Forensic Suites

9

Autopsy

10

Analysis with Xplico

11

Network Analysis

Other Books You May Enjoy

Preface

In this second edition of this book, you'll find that the theory and methodologies have remained mostly the same, as the procedures and documentation are standard throughout the field; however, you'll find that the technical chapters contain new labs using new examples. I've also decided to include two completely new chapters that go into artifact analysis and network analysis, showcasing several tools with practicals that even beginners will find easy to follow. As much as we try to secure our data, systems, and networks to the best of our abilities, breaches occur. In an effort to understand what took place, we turn to the field of digital forensics. Although still a relatively new field, forensics has become just as important as security, especially considering the wealth of information available to anyone accessing the internet with the intent of carrying out malicious activity. Thankfully, digital fingerprints and artifacts are sometimes left behind, whether in a deleted or hidden file, an email, in someone's browsing history, a remote connection list, or even a mobile text message.

Who this book is for

This book caters to beginners and digital forensics novices, as the first five chapters serve to get the reader acquainted with the technologies used and also guide the reader through setting up Kali Linux before delving into forensic analysis and investigations.

What this book covers

Chapter 1, Introduction to Digital Forensics, introduces the reader to the world of digital forensics and forensic methodology, and also introduces the reader to various forensic operating systems.

Chapter 2, Installing Kali Linux, covers the various methods that can be used to install Kali Linux as a virtual machine or as a standalone operating system, which can also be run from a flash drive or SD card.

Chapter 3, Understanding Filesystems and Storage Media, dives into the realm of operating systems and the various formats for file storage, including secret hiding places not seen by the end user or even the operating system. We also inspect data about data, known as metadata, and look at its volatility.

Chapter 4, Incident Response and Data Acquisition, asks what happens when an incident is reported or detected? Who are the first responders and what are the procedures for maintaining the integrity of the evidence? In this chapter, we look at best practices and procedures in data acquisition and evidence collection.

Chapter 5, Evidence Acquisition and Preservation with dc3dd and Guymager, helps you to harness the power of DC3DD to acquire evidence, calculate and verify hashes, split images, and even forensically erase media. We'll also look at the Guymager GUI interface to acquire evidence and introduce Windows imaging tools such as FTK Imager and Belkasoft RAM Capturer.

Chapter 6, File Recovery and Data Carving with foremost, Scalpel, and bulk_extractor, covers tools that demonstrate that deleted data can be recovered using various file-carving methods.

Chapter 7, Memory Forensics with Volatility, demonstrates the importance of preserving volatile evidence such as the contents of the RAM and the paging file. Using Volatility and Evolve, we will identify and analyze running processes and network connections, and identify existing malware.

Chapter 8, Artifact Analysis, deals with tools that we can use to identify systems, processes, passwords, emails, and other artifacts that are useful to any investigator. We also perform artifact analysis of the WannaCry ransomware.

Chapter 9, Autopsy, The Sleuth Kit, revisits Autopsy (with new labs), which is recognized as one of the very few available tools to rival commercial forensic tools. This powerful tool takes forensic abilities and investigations to a professional level, catering for all aspects of full digital forensics investigations from hashing to reporting.

Chapter 10, Analysis with Xplico, investigates and analyzes captured network and internet traffic using this powerful tool.

Chapter 11, Network Analysis, continues with network artifact analysis by demonstrating how to create packet captures with Wireshark, and then quickly moves into automated analysis using offline and online tools such as Network Miner, PcapXray, and PacketTotal.

To get the most out of this book

Knowledge of networks, protocols, and the OSI and TCP/IP models may prove to be an asset.

Software/hardware covered in the book	OS requirements
VirtualBox 5.0 or later	Windows, macOS X, or Linux (any)
Rufus 3.0 or later	Windows 7 or later
Kali Linux 2019.4 or later	6 or more GB RAM, 50GB or more HDD space, 3.0GHz Dual-core CPU or better

If you are using the digital version of this book, we advise you to type the code yourself or access the code via the GitHub repository (link available in the next section). Doing so will help you avoid any potential errors related to copy/pasting of code.

Download the example code files

You can download the example code files for this book from your account at www.packt.com. If you purchased this book elsewhere, you can visit www.packtpub.com/support and register to have the files emailed directly to you.

You can download the code files by following these steps:

1. Log in or register at www.packt.com.
2. Select the **Support** tab.
3. Click on **Code Downloads**.
4. Enter the name of the book in the **Search** box and follow the onscreen instructions.

Once the file is downloaded, please make sure that you unzip or extract the folder using the latest version of:

- WinRAR/7-Zip for Windows
- Zipeg/iZip/UnRarX for Mac
- 7-Zip/PeaZip for Linux

The code bundle for the book is also hosted on GitHub at https://github.com/PacktPublishing/Digital-Forensics-with-Kali-Linux-Second-Edition. In case there's an update to the code, it will be updated on the existing GitHub repository.

We also have other code bundles from our rich catalog of books and videos available at https://github.com/PacktPublishing/. Check them out!

Download the color images

We also provide a PDF file that has color images of the screenshots/diagrams used in this book. You can download it from `https://static.packt-cdn.com/downloads/9781838640804_ColorImages.pdf`.

Conventions used

There are a number of text conventions used throughout this book.

`Code in text`: Indicates code words in text, database table names, folder names, filenames, file extensions, pathnames, dummy URLs, user input, and Twitter handles. Here is an example: "In this example, we have specified the `11-carve-fat.dd` file located on the desktop."

Any command-line input or output is written as follows:

```
$ volatility -f 0zapftis.vmem imageinfo
```

Bold: Indicates a new term, an important word, or words that you see onscreen. For example, words in menus or dialog boxes appear in the text like this. Here is an example: "To begin our Kali Linux installation, click on the **Kali Large 2019.3** entry to the left of the screen."

> Tips or important notes
> Appear like this.

Get in touch

Feedback from our readers is always welcome.

General feedback: If you have questions about any aspect of this book, mention the book title in the subject of your message and email us at `customercare@packtpub.com`.

Errata: Although we have taken every care to ensure the accuracy of our content, mistakes do happen. If you have found a mistake in this book, we would be grateful if you would report this to us. Please visit `www.packtpub.com/support/errata`, selecting your book, clicking on the Errata Submission Form link, and entering the details.

Piracy: If you come across any illegal copies of our works in any form on the Internet, we would be grateful if you would provide us with the location address or website name. Please contact us at `copyright@packt.com` with a link to the material.

If you are interested in becoming an author: If there is a topic that you have expertise in and you are interested in either writing or contributing to a book, please visit `authors.packtpub.com`.

Reviews

Please leave a review. Once you have read and used this book, why not leave a review on the site that you purchased it from? Potential readers can then see and use your unbiased opinion to make purchase decisions, we at Packt can understand what you think about our products, and our authors can see your feedback on their book. Thank you!

For more information about Packt, please visit `packt.com`.

Section 1: Kali Linux – Not Just for Penetration Testing

In our first section, we cover the fundamentals of digital forensics, various operating systems used in forensics, and repositories for forensics tools, and jump right into Kali Linux 2019.3. We'll also look at the various methods for installing Kali Linux on physical, virtual, and portable devices, and the various modes within Kali Linux.

This part comprises the following chapters:

- *Chapter 1, Introduction to Digital Forensics*
- *Chapter 2, Installing Kali Linux*

1
Introduction to Digital Forensics

Welcome to the second edition of *Digital Forensics with Kali Linux*. For those of you who may have purchased the first edition, the practical aspects of this book have been updated with new labs, and there are several new tools (with labs) for us to explore in this updated edition, starting with *Chapter 2, Installing Kali Linux*, where we will set up the latest version of Kali Linux (2019.3). For readers new to this book, I recommend starting here from the first chapter.

Digital forensics has had my attention for well over 13 years. Ever since I was given my first PC (thanks, Mom and Dad), I've always wondered what happened when I deleted my files from my massively large 2-**gigabyte** (**GB**) hard drive or moved (and, most times, hid) my files to a less-than-inconspicuous 3.5-inch floppy diskette that maxed out at 1.44 **megabytes** (**MB**) in capacity.

As I soon learned, hard disk drives and floppy disk drives did not possess the digital immortality I so confidently believed in. Sadly, many files, documents, and priceless fine art created in Microsoft Paint by yours truly were lost to the digital afterlife, never to be retrieved again. Sigh. The world will never know.

It wasn't until years later that I came across an article on file recovery and associated tools while browsing the magical **World Wide Web (WWW)** on my lightning-fast 42-**kilobits-per-second (Kbps)** dial-up internet connection (made possible by my very expensive USRobotics dial-up modem, which sang the tune of the technology gods every time I'd try to connect to the realm of the internet). This process involved a stealthy ninja-like skill that would make even a black-ops team envious, as it involved doing so without my parents noticing, as this would prevent them from using the telephone line to make or receive phone calls. (Apologies, dear Mother, Father, and older teenage sister.)

The previous article on data recovery wasn't anywhere near as detailed and fact-filled as the many great peer-reviewed papers, journals, and books on digital forensics widely available today. As a total novice (also referred to as a noob) in the field, I did learn a great deal about the basics of filesystems, data and metadata, storage measurements, and the workings of various storage media.

It was at this time that, even though I had read about the Linux operating system and its various distributions, I began to get an understanding of why Linux distributions were popular in data recovery and forensics.

At this time, I managed to bravely download the Auditor and Slax Linux distributions, again on a dial-up connection. Just downloading these operating systems was quite a feat, and it left me feeling highly accomplished as I did not have any clue as to how to install them, let alone actually use them. In those days, easy installation and **graphical user interfaces (GUIs)** were still under heavy development, as user friendly—or, in my case, user unfriendly—as they were at the time (mostly due to my inexperience, lack of recommended hardware, and, also, a lack of resources such as online forums, blogs, and YouTube, which I did not yet know about). I'll explain more about the Auditor and Slax operating systems in *Chapter 2, Installing Kali Linux*, including their role in the infamous **BackTrack**, and now Kali Linux, operating systems.

As time passed, I researched many tools found on various platforms for Windows, Macintosh, and many Linux distributions. I found that many of the tools used in digital forensics could be installed in various Linux distributions or flavors, and many of these tools were well maintained, constantly being developed, and were widely accepted by peers in the field. Kali Linux is a Linux distribution or flavor, but before we go any further, let me explain this concept. Consider your favorite beverage: this beverage can come in many flavors, some without sweeteners or sugar, in different colors, and even in various sizes. No matter what the variations, it's still the basic ingredients that comprise the beverage at the core. In this way, too, we have Linux, and then different types and varieties of Linux. Some of the more popular Linux distributions and flavors include Parrot OS, **Computer Aided INvestigative Environment** (**CAINE**), Red Hat, CentOS, Ubuntu, Mint, Knoppix, and, of course, Kali Linux. Kali Linux will be discussed further in *Chapter 2, Installing Kali Linux.*

For this book, we take a very structured approach to digital forensics, as we would in forensic science. We first stroll into the world of digital forensics, its history, and some of the tools and operating systems used for forensics, and immediately introduce you to the concepts involved in evidence preservation. As far as international best practices and guidelines go, I'd recommend reading up on the Council of Europe's Budapest Convention on Cybercrime (`https://rm.coe.int/CoERMPublicCommonSearchServices/DisplayDCTMContent?documentId=09000016800cce5b`) and the **Association of Chief Police Officers** (**ACPO**) Good Practice Guide for Digital Evidence (`https://www.digital-detective.net/digital-forensics-documents/ACPO_Good_Practice_Guide_for_Digital_Evidence_v5.pdf`) to get a better understanding of international frameworks and digital forensics best practices.

How about we kick things off? Let's get started!

This chapter gives an introduction to the various aspects of the science of digital forensics. The topics we are going to cover in this chapter are as follows:

- What is digital forensics?
- Digital forensics methodology
- A brief history of digital forensics
- The need for digital forensics as technology advances
- Operating systems and open source tools for digital forensics
- The need for multiple forensics tools in digital investigations
- Commercial forensics tools
- Anti-forensics – threats to digital forensics

What is digital forensics?

The first thing I'd like to cover in this chapter is an understanding of digital forensics and its proper practices and procedures. At some point, you may have come across several books, blogs, and even videos demonstrating various aspects of digital forensics and the different tools used. It is of great importance to understand that forensics itself is a science, involving very well-documented best practices and methods in an effort to reveal whether something exists.

Digital forensics involves the preservation, acquisition, documentation, analysis, and interpretation of evidence identified from various storage media types. It is not only limited to laptops, desktops, tablets, and mobile devices, but also extends to data in transit that is transmitted across public or private networks.

In some cases, digital forensics involves the discovery and/or recovery of data using various methods and tools available to the investigator. Digital forensics investigations include, but are not limited to, the following:

- **Data recovery**: Investigating and recovering data that may have been deleted, changed to different file extensions, and even hidden.

- **Identity theft**: Many fraudulent activities, ranging from stolen credit card usage to fake social media profiles, usually involving some sort of identity theft.

- **Malware and ransomware investigations**: To date, ransomware spread by Trojans and worms across networks and the internet are some of the biggest threats to companies, military organizations, and individuals. Malware can also be spread to, and by, mobile devices and smart devices.

- **Network and internet investigations**: Investigating **Denial-of-Service (DoS)** and **Distributed Denial-of-Service (DDoS)** attacks, and tracking down accessed devices, including printers and files.

- **Email investigations**: Investigating the email header, message IDs, source and **Internet Protocol (IP)** origins; attached content and geo location information can all be investigated, especially if there is a **business email compromise (BEC)**.

- **Corporate espionage**: Many companies are moving away from print copies and toward cloud and traditional disk media. As such, a digital footprint is always left behind; should sensitive information be accessed or transmitted?

- **Child pornography investigations**: Sadly, the reality is that children are widely exploited on the internet and within the deep web. With the use of technology and highly-skilled forensic analysts, investigations can be carried out to bring down exploitation rings by analyzing internet traffic, browser history, payment transactions, email records, and images.

Digital forensics methodology

Keeping in mind that forensics is a science, digital forensics requires appropriate best practices and procedures to be followed in an effort to produce the same results time and time again, providing proof of evidence, preservation, and integrity that can be replicated, if called upon to do so.

Although many people may not be performing digital forensics to be used as evidence in a court of law, it is best to practice in such a way as can be accepted and presented in a court of law. The main purpose of adhering to best practices set by organizations specializing in digital forensics and incident response is to maintain the integrity of the evidence for the duration of the investigation. In the event that the investigator's work must be scrutinized and critiqued by another or an opposing party, the results found by the investigator must be able to be recreated, thereby proving the integrity of the investigation. The purpose of this is to ensure that your methods can be repeated and, if dissected or scrutinized, produce the same results time and again. The methodology used, including the procedures and findings of your investigation, should always allow for the maintenance of the data's integrity, regardless of which tools are used.

The best practices demonstrated in this book ensure that the original evidence is not tampered with, or, in cases of investigating devices and data in a live or production environment, show well-documented proof that necessary steps were taken during the investigation to avoid unnecessary tampering of the evidence, thereby preserving the integrity of the evidence. For those completely new to investigations, I recommend familiarizing yourself with some of the various practices and methodologies available and widely practiced by the professional community.

As such, there exist several guidelines and methodologies that you should adopt, or at least follow, to ensure that examinations and investigations are forensically sound.

The three best practices documents mentioned in this chapter are as follows:

- The ACPO Good Practice Guide for Digital Evidence
- The **Scientific Working Group on Digital Evidence**'s (**SWGDE**) Best Practices for Computer Forensics
- The Budapest Convention on Cybercrime (CETS No. 185)

Although written in 2012, ACPO, now functioning as the **National Police Chiefs'
Council (NPCC)**, put forth a document in a PDF file called the *ACPO Good Practice
Guide for Digital Evidence* regarding best practices when carrying out digital forensics
investigations, particularly focusing on evidence acquisition. The *ACPO Good Practice
Guide for Digital Evidence* was then adopted and adhered to by law enforcement
agencies in England, Wales, and Northern Ireland, and can be downloaded in its entirety
at `https://www.npcc.police.uk/documents/FoI%20publication/`
`Disclosure%20Logs/Information%20Management%20FOI/2013/031%20`
`13%20Att%2001%20of%201%20ACPO%20Good%20Practice%20Guide%20`
`for%20Digital%20Evidence%20March%202012.pdf`.

Another useful and more recent document, produced in September 2014, on best
practices in digital forensics was issued by the SWGDE. The SWGDE was founded
in 1998 by the Federal Crime Laboratory Directors Group, with major members and
contributors including the **Federal Bureau of Investigation (FBI)**, **Drug Enforcement
Administration (DEA)**, **National Aeronautics and Space Administration (NASA)**,
and the **Department of Defense (DoD)** Computer Forensics Laboratory. Though this
document details procedures and practices within a formal computer forensics laboratory
setting, the practices can still be applied to non-laboratory investigations by those not
currently in, or with access to, such an environment.

The SWGDE's *Best Practices for Computer Forensics* sheds light on many of the topics
covered in the following chapters, including the following:

- Evidence collection and acquisition
- Investigating devices that are powered on and off
- Evidence handling
- Analysis and reporting

The SWGDE's *Best Practices for Computer Forensics Acquisitions* (April 2018) can be
viewed and downloaded directly from here: `https://www.swgde.org/documents/`
`Current%20Documents/SWGDE%20Best%20Practices%20for%20`
`Computer%20Forensic%20Acquisitions`

Important note

The SWGDE has a collection of 78 documents (at the time of this publication)
that detail the best practices of evidence acquisition, collection, authentication,
and examination, which can all be found at `https://www.swgde.org/`
`documents/Current%20Documents/ SWGDE%20Best%20`
`Practices%20for%20Computer%20Forensics`.

A brief history of digital forensics

Although forensic science itself (including the first recorded fingerprints) has been around for over 100 years, digital forensics is a much younger field as it relates to the digital world, which mainly gained popularity after the introduction of personal computers in the 1980s.

For comparative purposes in trying to grasp the concept of digital forensics as still being relatively new, consider that the first actual forensic sciences lab was developed by the FBI in 1932.

Some of the first tools used in digital forensic investigations were developed in FBI labs circa 1984, with forensic investigations being spearheaded by the FBI's specialized **Computer Analysis and Response Team** (**CART**), which was responsible for aiding in digital investigations.

Digital forensics as its own field grew substantially in the 1990s, with the collaboration of several law enforcement agencies and heads of divisions working together and even meeting regularly to bring their expertise to the table.

One of the earliest formal conferences was hosted by the FBI in 1993. The main focus of the event, called the International Law Enforcement Conference on Computer Evidence, was to address the need for formal standards and procedures with digital forensics and evidence acquisition.

Many of these conferences resulted in the formation of bodies that deal with digital forensics standards and best practices. For example, the SWGDE was formed by the Federal Crime Laboratory Directors in 1998. The SWGDE was responsible for producing the widely adopted best practices for computer evidence (discussed later in this chapter). The SWGDE also collaborated with other organizations, such as the very popular **American Society of Crime Laboratory Directors** (**ASCLD**), which was formed in 1973 and has since been instrumental in the ongoing development of best practices, procedures, and training as it relates to forensic science.

It wasn't until the early 2000s, however, that a formal **Regional Computer Forensic Laboratory** (**RCFL**) was established by the FBI. In 2002, the **National Program Office** (**NPO**) was established, and this acts as a central body, essentially coordinating and supporting efforts between RCFL's law enforcement.

Since then, we've seen several agencies, such as the FBI, **Central Intelligence Agency** (**CIA**), **National Security Agency** (**NSA**), and **Government Communications Headquarters** (**GCHQ**), each with their own full cybercrime divisions, full digital forensics labs, and dedicated onsite and field agents, collaborating assiduously in an effort to take on tasks that may be nothing short of Sisyphean, when considering the rapid growth of technology and easier access to the internet and even the Dark Web.

In the Caribbean and Latin America, there have also been several developments where cybercrime and security are concerned. The **Caribbean Community Implementation Agency for Crime and Security (CARICOM IMPACS)** has been formally established and has published the **CARICOM Cyber Security and Cybercrime Action Plan (CCSCAP)**, which seeks to address vulnerabilities within the CARICOM states and also provide guidelines for best practices that would aid in cybercrime detection and investigation. The CCSCAP can be downloaded at `https://www.caricomimpacs.org/Portals/0/Project%20Documents/CCSAP.pdf`.

With the advancement of technology, the tools for digital forensics must be regularly updated, not only in the fight against cybercrime, but in the ability to provide accountability and for the retrieval of lost data. We've come a long way since the days of floppy disks, magnetic drives, and dial-up internet access, and are now presented with **Secure Digital (SD)** cards, **solid-state drives (SSDs)**, and fiber-optic internet connections at gigabit speeds. More information on cybercrime can be found on Interpol's website, at `https://www.interpol.int/en/Crimes/Cybercrime`.

The need for digital forensics as technology advances

Some of you may be sufficiently young-at-heart to remember the days of Windows 95, 3.x, and even **Disk Operating System (DOS)**. Smart watches, calculators, and many **Internet of Things (IoT)** devices are today much faster than the first generation of personal computers and servers. In 1995, it was common to come across hard disk drives between 4 and 10 GB, whereas today, you can easily purchase drives with capacities of 2 **terabytes (TB)** and up.

Consider also the various types of storage media today, including flash drives, SD cards, CDs, DVDs, Blu-ray discs, hybrid drives, and SSDs, as compared to the older floppy disks, which, at their most compact and efficient, only stored 1.44 MB of data on a 3 ¼-inch disk. Although discussed in detail in a later chapter, we now have many options for not only storing data but also for deleting and even hiding data (through the art of steganography), especially as **Alternate Data Streams (ADS)**, which can be done on Windows **New Technology File System (NTFS)** media. Encryption using TrueCrypt, VeraCrypt, and BitLocker also add to the complexity and duration of forensics investigations today.

With the advancement of technology also comes a deeper understanding of programming languages, operating systems both average and advanced, and knowledge and utilization of digital devices. This also translates into more user-friendly interfaces that can accomplish many of the same tasks as with the **command-line interface (CLI)**, used mainly by advanced users. Essentially, today's simple GUI, together with a wealth of resources readily found on search engines, can make certain tasks such as hiding data far easier than before.

Hiding large amounts of data is also simpler today, considering that the speed of processors, combined with large amounts of **random-access memory (RAM)**, including devices that can also act as RAM far surpasses those of as recent as 5 years ago. Graphics cards must also be mentioned and taken into consideration, as more and more mobile devices are being outfitted with very powerful high-end onboard NVIDIA and ATI cards that also have their own separate RAM, aiding the process. Considering all these factors does lend support to the idea put forth by Gordon E. Moore in the 1970s, which states that computing power doubles every 2 years, commonly known as Moore's Law.

However, Jensen Huang, **Chief Executive Officer (CEO)** of NVIDIA, stated that Moore's Law is dying as **graphics processing units (GPUs)** will ultimately replace **central processing units (CPUs)** due to the GPUs' performance and technological advancements and abilities in handling **artificial intelligence (AI)**.

Huang's statement was also mirrored by ex-Intel CEO Brian Krzanich.

All things considered, several avenues for carrying out cybercrimes are now available, including malware and ransomware distribution, DoS and DDoS attacks, espionage, blackmail, identity theft, data theft, illegal online activities and transactions, and a plethora of other malicious activities. Many of these activities are anonymous as they occur over the internet and often take place using masked IP addresses and public networks, and so make investigations that much harder for the relevant agencies in pinpointing locations and apprehending suspects. For more of the latest threats and cybercrime news, have a look at this Trend Micro link: `https://www.trendmicro.com/vinfo/us/security/news/cybercrime-and-digital-threats`.

With cybercrime being such big business, the response from law enforcement officials and agencies must be equally impressive in their research, development, intelligence, and training divisions if they are to put up a fight in what may seem like a never-ending battle in the digital world.

Digital forensics not only applies to storage media but also to network and internet connections, mobile devices, IoT devices, and, in reality, any device that can store, access, or transmit data. As such, we have a variety of tools, both commercial and open source, available to us, depending on the task at hand.

Earlier in 2019, digital forensic solution provider Paraben hosted a blog on their site that mentioned the need for more advanced and complicated **Digital Forensics and Incident Response (DFIR)** plans and solutions, seeing that business models today include virtualized infrastructure and some type of cloud service or subscription package that has led to the need for **Forensics As A Service (FAAS)**, which encompasses the bundling of forensic skillsets (within the many areas of digital forensics), software, analysis, and the ability to respond to any types of threats, as a service.

Operating systems and open source tools for digital forensics

Just as there are several commercial tools available, there exist many open source tools available to investigators, amateur and professional alike. Many of these tools are Linux-based and can be found on several freely available forensic distributions.

The main question that usually arises when choosing tools is usually based on commercial versus open source. Whether using commercial tools or open source tools, the end result should be the same, with preservation and integrity of the original evidence being the main priority.

> **Important note**
> Budget is always an issue, and some commercial tools (as robust, accurate, and user friendly as they might be) cost thousands of dollars.

The open source tools are free to use under various open source licenses and should not be counted out just because they are not backed by enterprise developers and researchers.

Many of the open source tools are widely reviewed by the forensic community and may be open to more scrutiny, as they are more widely available to the public and are built in non-proprietary code.

Though the focus of this book is on the forensic tools found in Kali Linux, which we will begin looking at toward the end of this section and onward, here are some of the more popular open source forensic distributions available.

Each of the distributions mentioned in the following sections is freely available at many locations but, for security reasons, we will provide the direct link from their home pages. The operating systems featured in this section are listed only in alphabetical order and do not reflect any ratings, reviews, or even the author's personal preference. Please refer to the hash verification of these tools to ensure that the version downloaded matches the exact version uploaded by the developers and creators.

Digital Evidence and Forensics Toolkit (DEFT) Linux

DEFT Linux comes in a full version and a lighter version called **DEFT Zero**. For forensic purposes, you may wish to download the full version as the Zero version does not support mobile forensics and password-cracking features. You can refer to the following points for downloading them:

- **Download page for DEFT Linux 8**: `http://na.mirror.garr.it/mirrors/deft/iso/`

- **Download page for DEFT Linux Z (2018-2)**: `http://na.mirror.garr.it/mirrors/deft/zero/`

- **Based on**: Ubuntu Desktop

- **Distribution type**: Forensics and incident response

As with the other distributions mentioned in this list, DEFT, as shown in the following screenshot, is also a fully capable live-response forensic tool that can be used on the go in situations where shutting down the machine is not possible, and also allows for on-the-fly analysis of RAM and the swap file:

Figure 1.1 – The DEFT splash screen boot options

When booting from the DEFT Linux DVD, bootable flash, or other media, the user is presented with various options, including the options to install DEFT Linux to the hard disk, or use as a live-response tool or operating system by selecting the **DEFT Linux 8 live** option, as shown in the following screenshot:

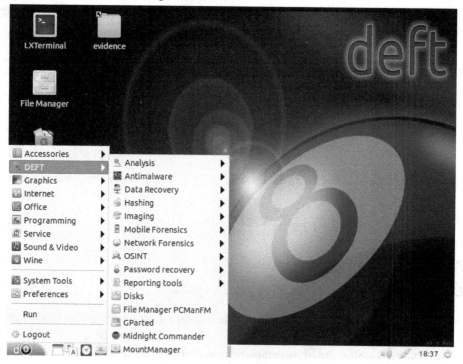

Figure 1.2 – The DEFT desktop environment and application menu

In the preceding screenshot, it can be seen that there are several forensic categories in DEFT Linux 8 such as **Antimalware**, **Data Recovery**, **Hashing**, **Imaging**, **Mobile Forensics**, **Network Forensics**, **Password recovery**, and **Reporting tools**. Within each category exist several tools created by various developers, giving the investigator quite a selection from which to choose.

CAINE

CAINE is a live-response bootable CD/DVD with options for booting in safe mode, text mode, as a live system, or in RAM, as shown in the following screenshot:

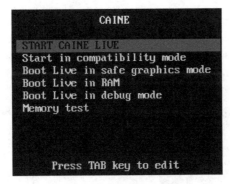

Figure 1.3 – The DEFT start up boot menu

- **Home page**: http://www.caine-live.net/

- **Based on**: GNU Linux

- **Distribution type**: Forensics and incident response

One of the most noticeable features of CAINE after selecting your boot option is the easy way to find the write-blocker feature, seen and labeled as an **UnBlock** icon, as shown in the following screenshot. Activating this feature prevents the writing of data by the CAINE operating system to the evidence machine or drive:

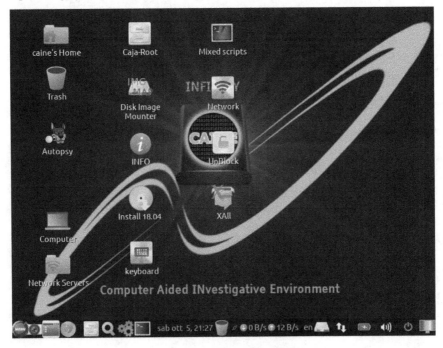

Figure 1.4 – The DEFT desktop

Forensic tools is the first menu listed in CAINE. As with DEFT Linux, there are several categories in the menu, as seen in the following screenshot, with several of the more popular tools used in open source forensics. Besides the categories, there are direct links to some of the more well-known tools, such as **Guymager** and **Autopsy**, which will both be covered in detail in later chapters:

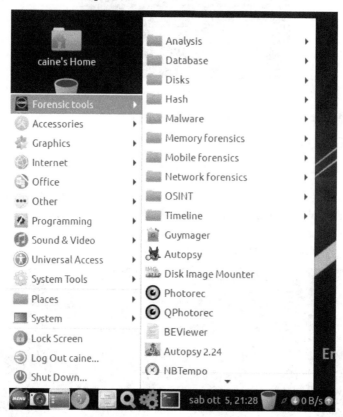

Figure 1.5 – The DEFT Forensic tools menu

For a full list of the features and packages included in CAINE at the time of this publication, please visit the following link:

`https://www.caine-live.net/page11/page11.html`

The latest version of CAINE 10.0 Infinity can be downloaded from `https://www.caine-live.net/page5/page5.html` in **International Organization for Standardization (ISO)** format, approximately 3.6 GB in size.

For installation on a **Universal Serial Bus (USB)** thumb drive, please ensure that the drive capacity is no less than 8 GB. A bootable CAINE drive can be created in an automated manner using the **Rufus** tool, which we will see in *Chapter 2, Installing Kali Linux.*

Kali Linux

Finally, we get to this lovely gem, Kali Linux, fully discussed in detail from its installation to advanced forensics usage in the next chapter and throughout this book. The basic points related to Kali Linux are listed here:

- **Home page:** https://www.kali.org/
- **Based on:** Debian
- **Distribution type:** Penetration testing, forensics, and anti-forensics

Kali Linux was created as a penetration testing, or pen-testing, distribution under the name BackTrack, which then evolved into Kali Linux, in 2015. This powerful tool is the definite tool of choice for penetration testers and security enthusiasts worldwide. As a **Certified EC-Council Instructor (CEI)** for the **Certified Ethical Hacker (CEH)** course, this operating system is usually the star of the class due to its many impressive bundled security programs, ranging from scanning and reconnaissance tools to advanced exploitation tools and reporting tools.

As with the previously mentioned tools, Kali Linux can be used as a live-response forensic tool as it contains many of the tools required for full investigations. Kali, however, can also be used as a complete operating system, as it can be fully installed to a hard disk or flash drive and also contains several tools for productivity and entertainment. It comes with many of the required drivers for successful use of hardware, graphics, and networking, and also runs smoothly on both 32-bit and 64-bit systems with minimal resources. It can also be installed on certain mobile devices, such as Nexus and OnePlus, and other phones and tablets.

Adding to its versatility, upon booting from a live CD/DVD or flash drive, the investigator has several options to choose from, including **Live (forensic mode)**, which leaves the evidence drive intact and does not tamper with it by also disabling any auto-mounting of flash drives and other storage media, providing integrity of the original evidence throughout the investigation.

When booting to Kali Linux from a DVD or flash drive, the user is first presented with options for a live environment and installation. Choosing the third option from the list carries us into **Live (forensic mode)**, as seen in the following screenshot:

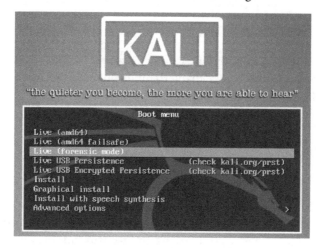

Figure 1.6 – The Kali Linux Boot menu

Once Kali **Live (forensic mode)** has booted, the investigator is presented with the exact same home screen as would be seen if using any of the GUIs in Kali, as shown in the following screenshot:

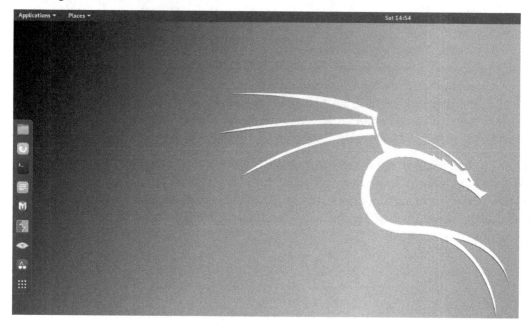

Figure 1.7 – The Kali Linux desktop environment

The Kali menu can be found at the top-left corner by clicking on **Applications**. This brings the user to the menu listing, which shows the forensics category lower down, as **11 - Forensics**. The following screenshot gives an idea of some of the forensic tools available in Kali that we'll be using later on in the book:

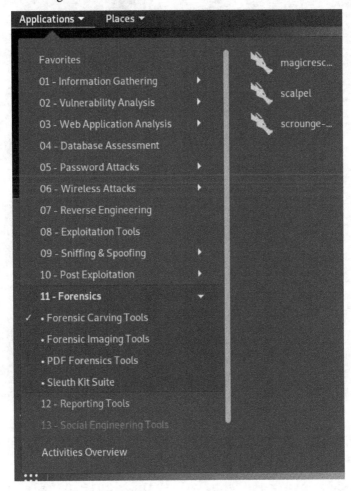

Figure 1.8 – The Kali Linux Applications menu

It should be noted that the tools listed are not the only tools available in Kali. There are several other tools that can be brought up via the Terminal, as we'll see in later chapters.

It's also noteworthy that, when in **forensic mode**, not only does Kali not tamper with the original evidence drive, but also does not write data to the swap file, where important data that was recently accessed and stored in memory may reside.

The following screenshot shows another view of accessing the forensic tools menu, using the last icon in the list on the sidebar menu (resembling nine dots in a square formation):

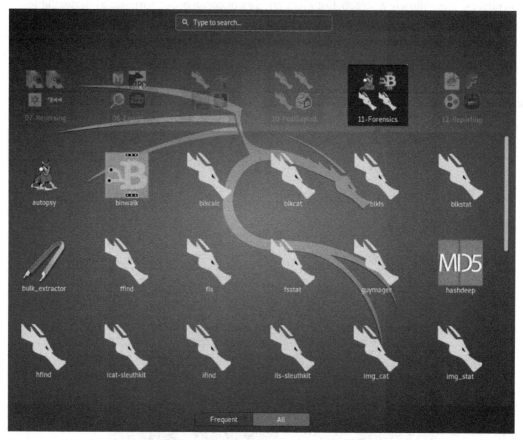

Figure 1.9 – The Kali Linux Forensics tool menu

For a full list of the features and packages included in the Kali Linux operating system at the time of this publication, please visit the following link:

```
https://www.kali.org/releases/kali-linux-2019-3-release/
```

Out of the three forensic distributions mentioned, Kali can operate as a live-response forensic tool, but can also be used as a full operating system, just like Windows, Mac, and Android, as it contains several built-in tools for productivity and everyday use. The fact that Kali can be installed to a hard disk means that several other tools can be downloaded and updated regularly, giving continuous access to all IT security and forensic tools, allowing the user to save progress as they use the tools and not have to worry too much about restarting their machine, should they decide to use it as a full operating system.

Using these open source forensic operating systems such as Kali gives us a range of tools to choose from and work with. There exist many tools for performing the same tasks within each category in the distributions. This is good, because our findings should be able to be replicated using different tools. This is especially good in instances where the investigator's work may be critiqued and the integrity of the case and evidence questioned and scrutinized; using multiple tools correctly will yield consistent results. Taking this into consideration, we can also look at the requirements and benefits of performing investigations within a forensic lab. Interpol has a very detailed document on *Global Guidelines for Digital Forensics Laboratories*, which can be downloaded at `shorturl.at/ikKR2`.

The need for multiple forensics tools in digital investigations

Preservation of evidence is of the utmost importance. Using commercial and open source tools correctly will yield results; however, for forensically sound results, it is sometimes best if more than one tool can be used and produces the same results.

Another reason to use multiple tools may simply be cost. Some of us may have a large budget to work with, while others may have a limited one or none at all. Commercial tools can be costly, especially due to research and development, testing, advertising, and other factors. Additionally, many commercial tools are now subscription-based, with yearly recurring renewal fees. Open source tools, while tested by the community, may not have the available resources and funding as with commercial tools.

So, then, how do we know which tools to choose?

Digital forensics is often quite time consuming, which is one of the reasons you may wish to work with multiple forensic copies of the evidence. This way, you can use different tools simultaneously in an effort to speed up the investigation. While fast tools may be a good thing, we should also question the reliability and accuracy of the tools.

The **National Institute of Standards and Technology** (**NIST**) has developed a **Computer Forensics Tool Testing** (**CFTT**) program that tests digital forensic tools and makes all findings available to the public. Several tools are chosen based on their specific abilities and placed into testing categories such as disk imaging, carving, and file recovery. Each category has a formal test plan and strategy for testing along with a validation report, again available to the public.

More on the CFTT program can be found at `https://www.cftt.nist.gov/disk_imaging.htm`. Testing and validation reports on many of the tools covered in this book can be found at `https://www.dhs.gov/science-and-technology/nist-cftt-reports`.

To re-enforce the importance of using multiple tools in maintaining the integrity of your investigations and findings, multiple tools will be demonstrated in the third and fourth sections of this book.

Commercial forensics tools

Although this book focuses on tools within the Kali Linux operating system, it's important to recognize the commercially available tools available to us, many of which you can download as trial or demo versions before determining a preference.

Because this book focuses primarily on open source tools, I'll just cover some of the more popular commercial tools available, along with their home pages. The tools are listed only in alphabetical order as follows, and do not reflect any ratings, reviews, or the author's personal preference:

Belkasoft Evidence Center (EC) 2020

Website: `https://belkasoft.com/`

Belkasoft EC is an automated incident response and forensic tool that is capable of analyzing acquired images of memory dumps, virtual machines, and cloud and mobile backups, as well as physical and logical drives.

Belkasoft EC is also capable of searching for, recovering, and analyzing the following types of artifacts:

- Office documents
- Browser activity and information
- Email
- Social media activity
- Mobile applications
- Messenger applications (WhatsApp, Facebook Messenger, and even BlackBerry Messenger)

Belkasoft also has a free acquisition tool and RAM Capturer tool, available along with a trial version of their Evidence Center, available at `https://belkasoft.com/get`

AccessData Forensic Toolkit (FTK)

Website: `https://accessdata.com/products-services/forensic-toolkit-ftk`

FTK has been around for some time and is used professionally by forensics investigators and law enforcement agencies worldwide. AccessData has also recently announced integration with Belkasoft for a better experience. Some features of FTK include the following:

- Fast processing with multi-core support using four engines
- Ability to process large amounts of data
- Indexing of data, to allow faster and easier searching and analysis
- Password cracking and file decryption
- Automated analysis
- Ability to perform customized data carving
- Advanced data recovery

The trial version of FTK can be downloaded at `https://accessdata.com/product-download/forensic-toolkit-ftk-international-version-7-0-0`. AccessData also has an image acquisition tool that is free to download and use, available at `https://accessdata.com/product-download/ftk-imager-version-4-2-1`.

EnCase Forensic

Website: `https://www.guidancesoftware.com/encase-forensic`

Created by Guidance Software, EnCase Forensic has also been at the forefront for many years and has been used internationally by professionals and law enforcement agencies alike for almost two decades. Much like FTK, EnCase comes with several solutions for incident response, e-discovery, and endpoint and mobile forensics.

Apart from being a full digital forensics solution and suite, some of the other features of EnCase include the following:

- The ability to acquire images from over 25 different types of mobile devices, including phones, tablets, and even **Global Positioning System** (**GPS**) devices

- Support for Microsoft Office 365

- Evidence decryption using Check Point **Full Disk Encryption** (**FDE**)

- Deep forensic and triage analysis

Other commercial tools also worth mentioning are the following:

- **Magnet Axiom**: `https://www.magnetforensics.com/computer-forensics/`

  Axiom is also one of the few tools to perform mobile and computer forensics along with memory analysis, which gives value for money compared to standalone analysis tools.

- **X-Ways Forensics**: `http://www.x-ways.net/forensics/index-m.html`

Many of the preceding commercial tools offer several (with many being proprietary) features, including the following:

- Write blocking

- Bit-by-bit or bit-stream copies and disk cloning/evidence cloning

- Forensically sound evidence acquisition

- Evidence preservation using hashes

- File recovery (hidden and deleted)

- Live and remote acquisition of evidence

- RAM and swap/paging file analysis

- Image mounting (supporting various formats)

- Advanced data and metadata (data about data) searches and filtering

- Bookmarking of files and sectors

- Hash and password cracking

- Automatic report generation

The main advantage of commercial tools is that they are usually automated and are actually a suite of tools that can almost always perform entire investigations, from start to finish, with a few clicks. Another advantage that I must mention is the support for the tools that are given with the purchase of a license. The developers of these tools also employ research and development teams to ensure constant testing and reviewing of their current and new products.

Anti-forensics – threats to digital forensics

As much as we would like the tasks involved in digital forensics to be as easy as possible, we do encounter situations that make investigations, and life as a forensics investigator, not so simple and sometimes stressful. People wishing to hide information and cover their tracks, and even those who have malicious intent or actually participate in cybercrimes, often employ various methods to try to foil the attempts of forensic investigators, with the intention of hampering or halting investigations.

In recent times, we've seen several major digital breaches online, especially from 2011 onward. Many of these attacks allegedly came from, or were claimed to be the work of, infamous hacker groups such as LulzSec, Anonymous, Lizard Squad, and many others, including individuals and hacktivists (people who hack for a specific cause or reason and are less concerned about doing time in prison). Some of these hacks and attacks not only brought down several major networks and agencies, but also cost millions in damages, directly and indirectly. As a result, the loss of public confidence in the companies concerned contributed to further increases in damages.

These daring, creative, and public attacks saw the emergence of many other new groups that learned from the mistakes of past breaches of Anonymous and others. Both social media and underground communication channels soon became the easiest forms of communication between like-minded hackers and hacktivists. With the internet and World Wide Web (WWW) becoming easily accessible, this also heralded competition not only between IPs, but also between private companies and corporations, which led to the creation of free wireless hotspots on almost every street with businesses, large or small.

The result of having internet access at just about every coffee shop enabled anyone with a smartphone, tablet, laptop, or other device to acquire almost unauthenticated access to the internet. This gave them access to hacker sites and portals, along with the ability to download tools, upload malware, send infected emails, or even carry out attacks.

The use of **Virtual Private Networks (VPNs)** also adds to the complexity of digital forensics investigations today. Many VPN providers do not keep logs of users and their activity for more than 7 days, allowing for the network communication logs of some cybercriminals to be deleted sometimes long before the incident has even been reported.

SSDs also employ newer TRIM technology that deletes data much more efficiently that older magnetic disks, as discussed in a later chapter.

Lastly, it has been my personal experience that in an environment without trained forensic personnel and those without any DFIR plans, policies, and implementations, breaches and incidents may go unnoticed for weeks or months at a time, allowing for important volatile evidence and artifacts that may have been stored in the memory (RAM) along with paging and swap files, to be lost once the systems have been restarted.

Encryption

Adding to this scenario is the availability of more user-friendly tools to aid in the masking of **Publicly Identifiable Information** (**PII**), or any information that would aid in the discovery of unveiling suspects involved in cybercrimes during forensic investigations. Tools used for encryption of data and anonymity, such as the masking of IP addresses, are readily and easily available to anyone, most of which were—and are—increasingly user friendly.

It should also be noted that many Wi-Fi hotspots themselves can be quite dangerous, as these can easily be set up to intercept personal data, such as login and password information together with PII (such as social security numbers, date-of-birth information, and phone numbers) from any user that may connect to the Wi-Fi and enter such information.

The process of encryption provides confidentiality between communication parties and uses technology in very much the same way we use locks and keys to safeguard our personal and private belongings. For a lock to open, there must be a specific matching key. So, too, in the digital world, data is encrypted or locked using an encryption algorithm and must use either the same key to decrypt or unlock the data. There also exists another scenario where one key may be used to encrypt or lock the data and another used to decrypt the data. A few such very popular encryption tools are TrueCrypt, VeraCrypt, BitLocker, and PGP Tool.

These encryption tools use very high encryption methods that keep data very confidential. The main barrier to forensics may be acquiring the decryption key to decrypt or unlock access to the data.

> **Important note**
> PGP Tool and VeraCrypt not only encrypt files but also encrypt folders, partitions, and entire drives!

Online and offline anonymity

Encryption, in particular, can make investigations rather difficult, but there is also the concept of anonymity that adds to the complexity of maintaining an accuracy of the true sources found in investigations. As with encryption, there exist several free and open source tools for all operating system platforms—such as Windows, Mac, Linux, and Android—that attempt and, most often, successfully mask the hiding of someone's digital footprint. This digital footprint usually identifies a device by its IP address and **Media Access Control** (**MAC**) address. Without going into the network aspect of things, these two digital addresses can be compared to a person's full name and home address, respectively.

Even though a person's IP address can change according to their private network (home and work) and public network (internet) access, the MAC address remains the same.

However, various tools are also freely available to spoof or fake your IP and MAC addresses for the purpose of privacy and anonymity. Adding to that, users can use a system of routing their data through online servers and devices to make the tracing of the source of the sent data quite difficult. This system is referred to as proxy chaining and does keep some of the user's identity hidden.

A good example of this would be the **Tor** browser; this uses onion routing and several proxies worldwide to route or pass the data along from proxy to proxy, making the tracing of the source very difficult, but not impossible. You can think of proxy chains as a relay race, but instead of having four people, one passing the baton to the next, the data is passed between hundreds of proxy devices, worldwide. Additionally, some hosting companies offer bulletproof hosting, which allows their users and clients to upload and distribute content that may not be allowed by others, allowing for spamming, different types of pornography, and other content that may not be legal, while offering a certain level of protection to customers' data and records.

Summary

Congratulations! You made it to the end of the first chapter. Before we jump into the second chapter, let's have a look at what was just covered.

We saw that digital forensics is still a relatively new field, although forensic science has been around for a very long time, as far back as the early 1900s. Although digital forensics may have only been on the scene since the early 2000s, as a science, we have certain best practices, procedures, and standards—such as those created by the ACPO, Budapest Convention, Interpol Guidelines, and the SWGDE—to adhere to. These maintain accuracy and the integrity of both the findings and the actual evidence when carrying out investigations, whether as an amateur or professional digital forensic investigator.

Some of the commercial tools mentioned were EnCase, FTK, and Magnet Forensics. Many of the open source tools available are made for Linux-based distributions and can be downloaded individually, but many are readily and easily available within certain forensic and security operating systems or distributions. These distributions include DEFT Linux, CAINE, and, of course, Kali Linux; all of these are freely available for download at the links provided.

I hope this introduction to digital forensics was informative and fun for you. Now that we've got a grounding in forensics, let's go deeper into Kali Linux as we learn how to download, install, and update Kali in *Chapter 2, Installing Kali Linux*. See you on the next page.

Further reading

Please refer to the following links for more information:

- Commercial forensic tools:
  `https://resources.infosecinstitute.com/category/computerforensics/introduction/commercial-computer-forensics-tools/`

- Top 20 free forensic tools:
  `https://techtalk.gfi.com/top-20-free-digital-forensic-investigation-tools-for-sysadmins/`

2
Installing Kali Linux

Here we are. Join me as we get started by installing Kali Linux. Some of our readers may already be familiar with the installation process, and perhaps even some of the advanced features, such as partitioning and networking. For the beginners and those new to Kali Linux, we encourage you to pay attention to this chapter as we begin from the absolute basics of downloading Kali Linux, working our way up to a successful installation.

The topics that we are going to cover in this chapter are as follows:

- Software version
- Downloading Kali Linux
- Installing Kali Linux
- Installing Kali Linux in VirtualBox

Software version

Kali Linux has been around for quite some time. Known previously as BackTrack, with releases from versions one to five, Kali Linux was first seen in 2015 and released as Kali 1.0. From 2016 onward, Kali Linux was then named according to the year of release. For instance, at the time of writing this book the version used is Kali 2019.4, released in November 2019.

For those running older versions of Kali, or purchasing this book at a later date when new versions of Kali Linux may be available, you can easily update your instance of Kali Linux by using the `sudo apt-get update distro` command, demonstrated toward the end of this chapter.

Downloading Kali Linux

For safety and security reasons, it is always best to download Kali Linux directly from the website of its creators, **Offensive Security**. The main reason for this is that the downloads of Kali Linux on other pages could possibly be fake, or worse, infected with malware such as Trojans, rootkits, and even ransomware. Offensive Security has also included hashes of all versions of Kali Linux downloads on their site, allowing users to compare the hash of their downloaded version of Kali Linux with what was generated and posted by Offensive Security on their website (`https://www.kali.org`). Once there, you can click on the **downloads** link, or go directly to the Kali Linux downloads page by visiting `https://www.kali.org/downloads/`.

Once on the downloads page, we can see nine instances of Kali Linux available for download, each with specific category information:

- **Image Name**: Specifies the name of the download as well as whether the operating system is 32-bit or 64-bit. Clicking on the image name also downloads that version in ISO format via the browser, which can then be saved to a location of your choice.

> Tip
> 32-bit operating systems are limited to utilizing only 4 GB of RAM. Should you have a system with more than 4 GB of RAM, you may wish to download the 64-bit version of Kali Linux.

> Important note
> ISO files (or ISO images, as they are commonly called) are exact copies of data used specifically when duplicating data.

- **Version**: Release details of this version of Kali Linux.

- **Size**: File size in GB.

- **SHA256Sum**: Command used in Linux to generate a checksum or digital output representing the existing data, which can then be used to compare against the checksum of the downloaded copy to ensure that no data or bits were changed or tampered with:

Image Name	Torrent	Version	Size	SHA256Sum
Kali Linux 32-Bit	Torrent	2019.3	2.9G	3fdf8732df5f2e935e3f21be93565a113be14b4a8eb410522df60e1c4881b9a0
Kali Linux 64-Bit	Torrent	2019.3	2.9G	d9bc23ad1ed2af7f0170dc6d15aec58be2f1a0a5be6751ce067654b753ef7020
Kali Linux Large 64-Bit	Torrent	2019.3	3.5G	dd44391927d38d91cae96ed1a8b918767d38bee2617761fab2d54ad8c77319ec
Kali Linux Light ARMhf	Torrent	2019.3	803M	9cee49c35400af04e127537a090b9b31b2440cac8cd2568bcaeeb6f4eb4e5a9d
Kali Linux Light 64-Bit	Torrent	2019.3	1.1G	b6e57c2d9a22cf73ead39d9d58033991bdaa4769c74e1a9d7174e574d1618af8

Figure 2.1 – Kali Linux versions available for download

For this book, we'll be using Kali Linux Large 64-Bit, downloaded as an ISO image, as in the following screenshot:

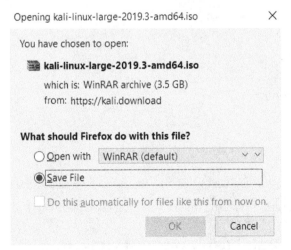

Figure 2.2 – Saving the Kali Linux ISO download file

- If downloading Kali Linux via torrent links, the use of torrent software will be required in order to download the .iso image. Once downloaded, let's begin the installation of Kali Linux.

Installing Kali Linux

As mentioned in *Chapter 1, Introduction to Digital Forensics*, Kali Linux can be used as a live-response operating system as well as a full operating system, installed and run from a hard disk. Tools such as **Rufus** and **UNetbootin** can also be used to install Kali Linux to removable storage media, including a flash drive, SD card, or external hard disk drive, depending on the user's preference.

For those who may not have the available resources to install Kali Linux on a brand new drive, there is also the option of installing Kali Linux within a virtual environment. Users can use virtualization technology, such as VMware and VirtualBox, to be able to run the Kali Linux operating system as a guest machine within their host machine.

Installing Kali Linux in VirtualBox

VirtualBox can run on many platforms, including Windows, macOS, Linux, and Solaris. In this section, we'll install **VirtualBox 6.0** on our host machine and take it from there.

VirtualBox can be found at `https://www.virtualbox.org/wiki/Downloads`:

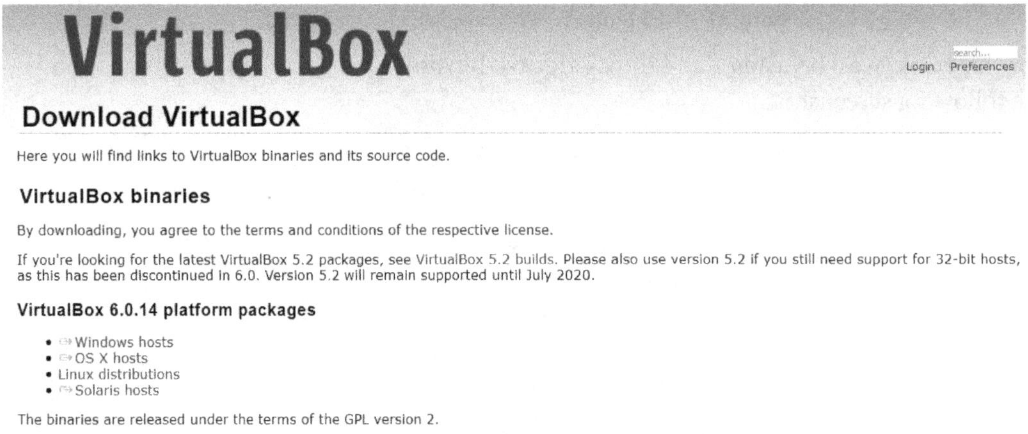

VirtualBox

Login   Preferences

Download VirtualBox

Here you will find links to VirtualBox binaries and its source code.

VirtualBox binaries

By downloading, you agree to the terms and conditions of the respective license.

If you're looking for the latest VirtualBox 5.2 packages, see VirtualBox 5.2 builds. Please also use version 5.2 if you still need support for 32-bit hosts, as this has been discontinued in 6.0. Version 5.2 will remain supported until July 2020.

VirtualBox 6.0.14 platform packages

- Windows hosts
- OS X hosts
- Linux distributions
- Solaris hosts

The binaries are released under the terms of the GPL version 2.

Figure 2.3 – VirtualBox download page displaying available packages

Depending on the operating system you are working on, download the respective package.

Preparing the Kali Linux virtual machine

Once VirtualBox has been downloaded, it can be installed and then configured to run Kali Linux and many other operating systems, depending on the amount of RAM available.

When setting up a new guest operating system or guest virtual machine, we first click on **New** and then fill in the following details:

- **Name**: Kali Large 2019.3 (or a name of your choice)
- **Type**: Linux
- **Version**: Debian (64-bit)

You can refer to the following image for the same details:

Figure 2.4 – VirtualBox operating system details

We then click **Next** and proceed to allocate RAM in the **Memory size** prompt:

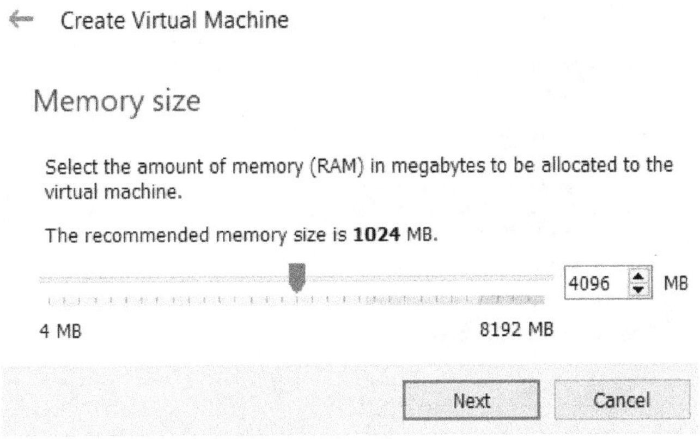

← Create Virtual Machine

Memory size

Select the amount of memory (RAM) in megabytes to be allocated to the virtual machine.

The recommended memory size is **1024** MB.

4 MB   8192 MB

4096 MB

Next   Cancel

Figure 2.5 – Virtual machine memory allocation

In the preceding screenshot, we can see the maximum RAM capacity to the right of the screen. The machine I used has 8192 MB (rounded off to 8 GB) of RAM. Although the recommended memory size for Kali Linux is a meager 1024 MB (1 GB), I do recommend at least 4 GB of RAM for smooth functionality when using the forensic tools. I have allocated 4096 MB of RAM for use on my virtual machine.

Next, we create a virtual machine by adding a virtual hard disk. I recommend starting with a new virtual hard disk, which is the second option in the selection. Click on **Create** to proceed, then choose **VDI (VirtualBox Disk Image)** as the **Hard disk file type**:

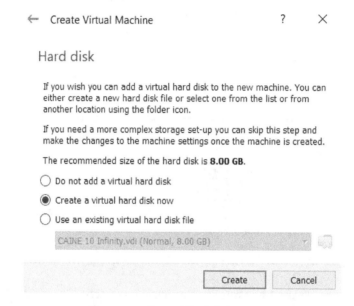

Figure 2.6 – Virtual hard disk creation

Select **VDI** and click **Next**:

Figure 2.7 – VirtualBox Disk Image (VDI) selection

Once **VDI** has been selected, choose the **Dynamically allocated** option to allow the virtual hard disk to be expanded, if the need arises:

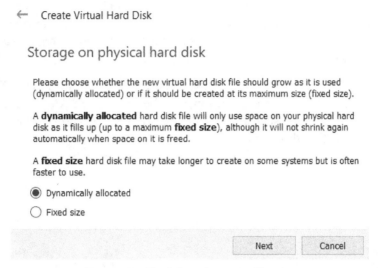

Figure 2.8 – Hard drive dynamic allocation

For the next step, we select the file location and the size of the virtual hard disk chosen. The recommended size for the Kali Linux VDI is 8 GB, but I've assigned an ample 32 GB. Once finished, click on **Create** to complete the creation of the virtual hard disk:

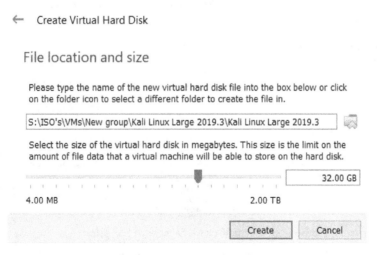

Figure 2.9 – Virtual machine location and size

This concludes the preparation of the virtual disk. Let's now install Kali Linux as a virtual machine.

Installing Kali Linux on the virtual machine

Once the virtual hard disk has been prepared and completed by following the steps from the previous section, we can then begin the actual Kali Linux installation process. In **Oracle VM VirtualBox Manager**, which is the main operating system management window for VirtualBox, we can see that the virtual machine has been prepared and we can now install Kali Linux.

To the middle of the screen, we can also see the resources assigned, such as the **Name** and **Operating System** type in the **General** section, and the amount of RAM assigned in the **System** section. Other settings, such as the **Video RAM (VRAM)** and **Display** settings can also be accessed within this section:

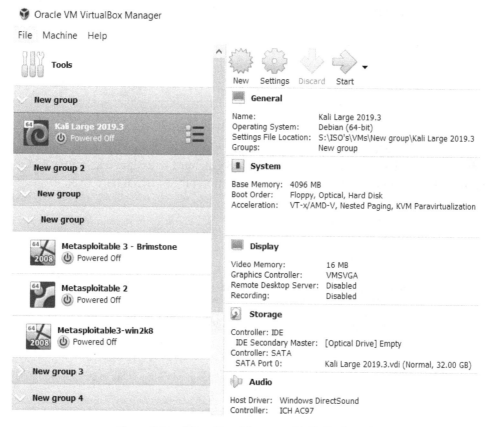

Figure 2.10 – VirtualBox Manager with Kali selected

1.   To begin our Kali Linux installation, click on the **Kali Large 2019.3** entry to the left and then click on the green **Start** arrow in the top-right corner:

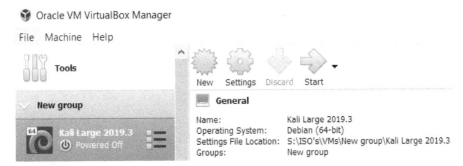

Figure 2.11 – VirtualBox Manager

2.   In the next step, we must locate the Kali Linux ISO image that we downloaded from the Offensive Security website. Click on the browse folder icon and navigate to the `Kali Linux 2019.3 iso` file you previously downloaded:

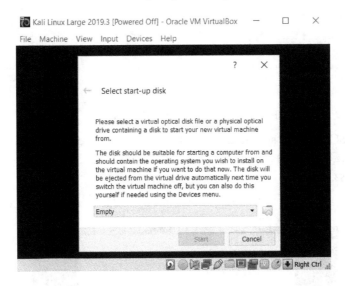

Figure 2.12 – VirtualBox start-up disk selection

3.   Once you've found the downloaded ISO, click on it, then select **Open**:

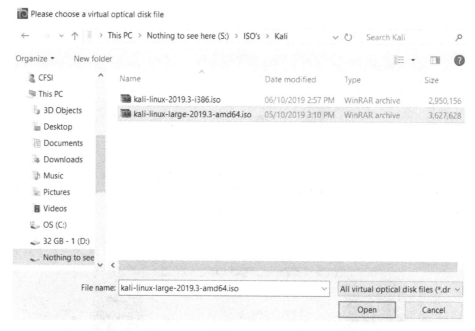

Figure 2.13 – Kali Linux ISO selection

4.   Once the ISO image is selected, you will notice the selected entry changes to `kali-linux-large-2019.3-amd64.iso (3.46 GB)`. Click on **Start** to begin the boot process:

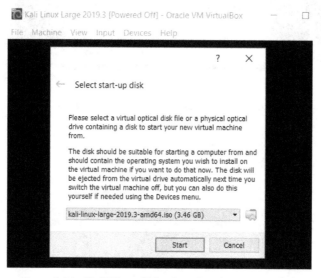

Figure 2.14 – Kali Linux ISO selected as the start-up disk

5. After clicking on **Start,** the boot menu displays the various options available, including the live versions of Kali. In this lab, we'll be choosing the **Graphical install** option to install Kali Linux on the virtual hard drive:

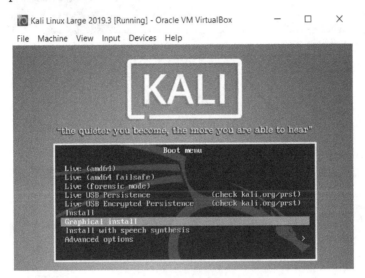

Figure 2.15 – Kali Linux Boot menu

Important note

As a side note, I should also draw your attention to the **Live (forensic mode)** option, which would be available to us when booting from a DVD, flash drive, or other removable storage media. It's a good idea to always have a copy of Kali Linux for situations where live forensics may be needed.

---

6. Okay, back to our installation. After clicking on the **Graphical install** option from the boot menu, we're prompted to choose our language and location:

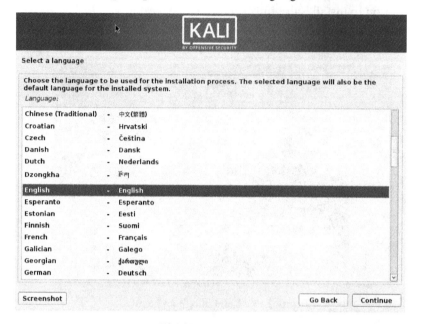

Figure 2.16 – Kali Linux Language selection menu

7. In the next step, we'll give our Kali Linux guest a hostname, which is the same as a username in a Windows environment:

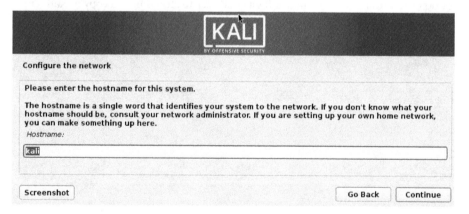

Figure 2.17 – Kali Linux Hostname details

8. I've left the **Domain name** area blank as I won't be joining this host machine to a domain:

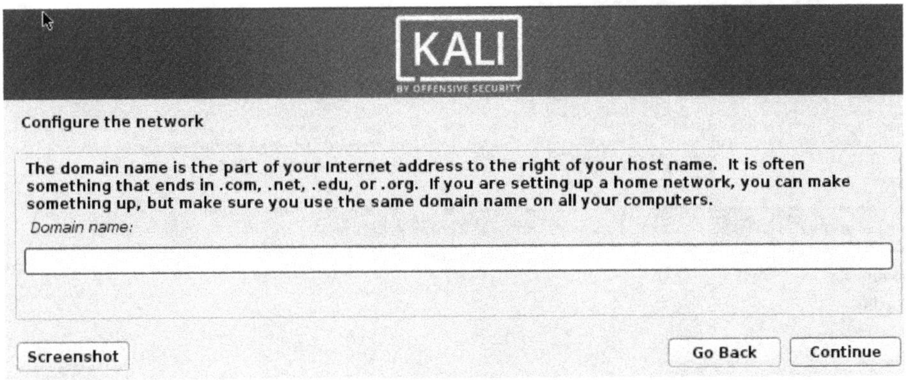

KALI
BY OFFENSIVE SECURITY
Configure the network
The domain name is the part of your Internet address to the right of your host name. It is often something that ends in .com, .net, .edu, or .org. If you are setting up a home network, you can make something up, but make sure you use the same domain name on all your computers.
Domain name:
Screenshot
Go Back
Continue

Figure 2.18 – Domain name details

9. When setting the password, be sure to use a complex string:

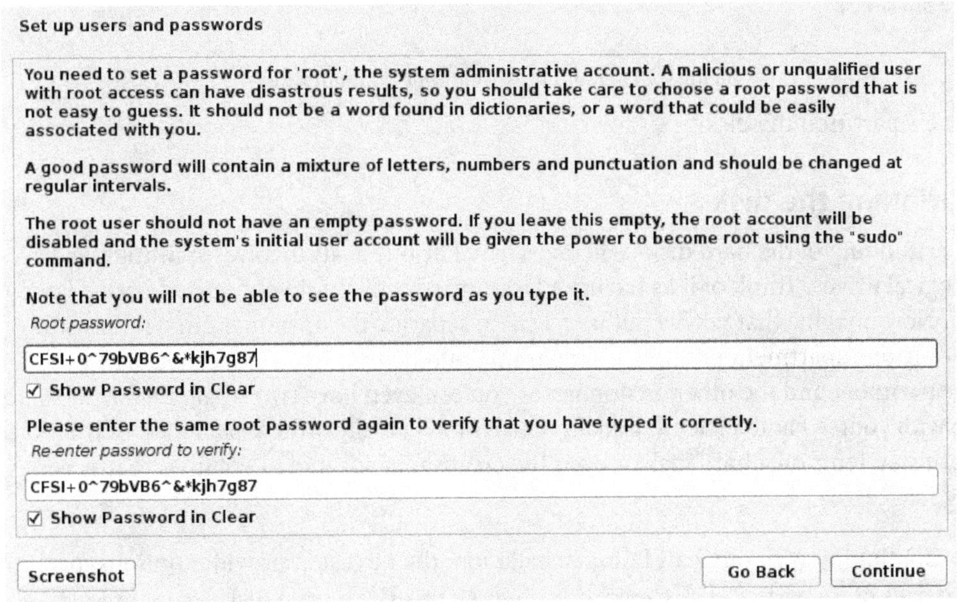

Set up users and passwords
You need to set a password for 'root', the system administrative account. A malicious or unqualified user with root access can have disastrous results, so you should take care to choose a root password that is not easy to guess. It should not be a word found in dictionaries, or a word that could be easily associated with you.
A good password will contain a mixture of letters, numbers and punctuation and should be changed at regular intervals.
The root user should not have an empty password. If you leave this empty, the root account will be disabled and the system's initial user account will be given the power to become root using the "sudo" command.
Note that you will not be able to see the password as you type it.
Root password:
CFSI+0^79bVB6^&*kjh7g87
Show Password in Clear
Please enter the same root password again to verify that you have typed it correctly.
Re-enter password to verify:
CFSI+0^79bVB6^&*kjh7g87
Show Password in Clear
Screenshot
Go Back
Continue

Figure 2.19 – Kali Linux password details

10. Configure the clock:

Configure the clock
Setting up the clock
Getting the time from a network time server...

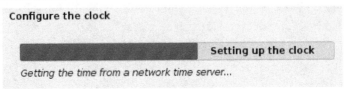

Figure 2.20 – Kali Linux clock configuration

11. Choose a time zone:

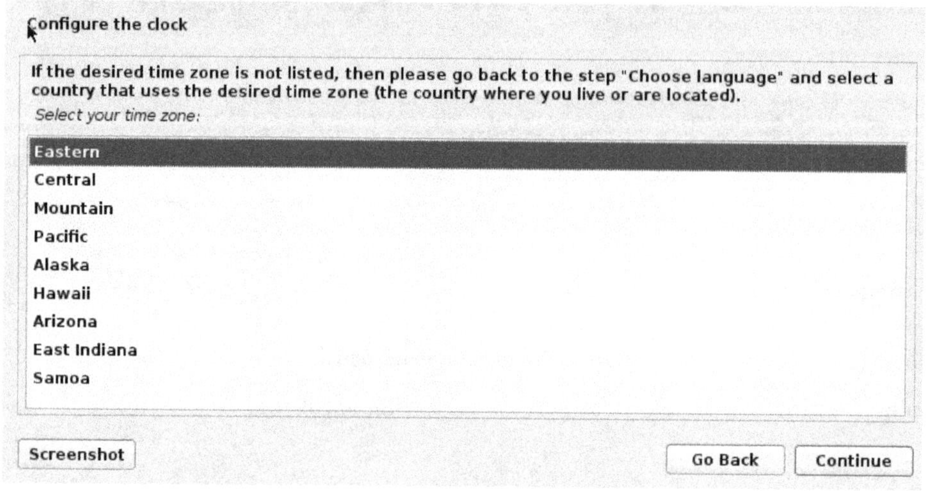

Configure the clock

If the desired time zone is not listed, then please go back to the step "Choose language" and select a country that uses the desired time zone (the country where you live or are located).

Select your time zone:

Eastern

Central

Mountain

Pacific

Alaska

Hawaii

Arizona

East Indiana

Samoa

Screenshot   Go Back   Continue

Figure 2.21 – Kali Linux time zone configuration

Let's now partition the disk.

Partitioning the disk

The partitioning of the hard disk (whether virtual or physical) involves splitting the drive into logical drives. Think of it as having a large apartment studio comprised of one large room. Now imagine that you've put up a wall to separate the apartment in half. It's still physically one apartment but now it's separated into two rooms. One can be used as the main apartment and the other as storage, or you can even have two smaller apartments to share with yourself and a friend. Equally, a partition can allow the installation of multiple operating systems on a hard disk or even the creation of additional volumes to use as storage space:

1. Continuing with our Kali Linux installation, the next step provides options for the usage of the virtual disk for partitioning. As this is a virtual disk, I recommend using the **Guided - use entire disk** partitioning method. This method is very simple and uses all the available allocated space assigned to the virtual disk in the preceding steps. Firstly, let's select the recommended partitioning method:

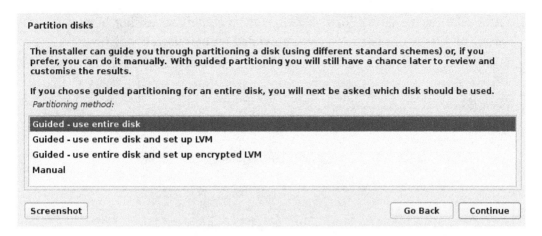

Figure 2.22 – Kali Linux disk partitioning method selection

> **Important note:**
> The other options in the preceding screenshot present the user with options
> for setting up **Logical Volume Manager** (**LVM**) and encrypted LVM. LVM
> manages logical partitions and can create, resize, and delete Linux partitions.

2. The prompt may warn you that all data (if any) on the disk will be erased if choosing
    this option. However, this is a new virtual disk with no existing data on it so we can
    continue with our installation:

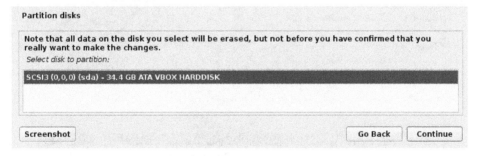

Figure 2.23 – Kali Linux virtual disk selection

3. After selecting the VirtualBox disk, as in in the preceding screenshot, be sure to select **All files in one partition (recommended for new users)**:

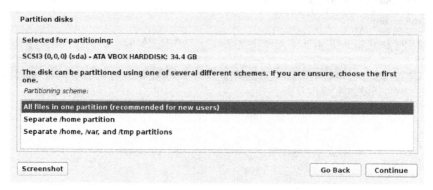

Figure 2.24 – Kali virtual disk partitioning

4. As we continue the partitioning process, I recommend choosing the **Guided partitioning** option because it does the partitioning automatically. From here, we simply choose the last available option, **Finish partitioning and write changes to disk**, then click **Continue**:

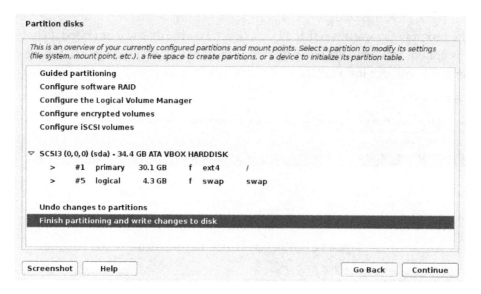

Figure 2.25 – Kali disk partitioning details

5. The last step in the partitioning process asks for confirmation to write the specified configurations and changes to the disk. Be sure to choose **Yes** before clicking on **Continue**:

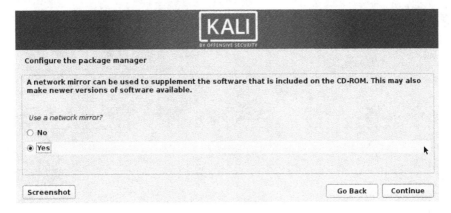

Figure 2.26 – Kali disk partition creation

We're now just a few clicks away from having our Kali Linux virtual machine installed and operational.

6. After the installation is complete, the package manager prompts us to choose a network mirror, which allows us to access newer versions of the software. Although the **Yes** option is selected by default, as in the following screenshot, I'd advise skipping this step by selecting **No** as we will soon be installing our updates for Kali Linux manually once we're up and running:

Figure 2.27 – Kali Linux package manager configuration

7. One of the last steps to take in the installation process is to install the GRUB boot loader on a hard disk. Without going into too much detail, the **GRand Unified Bootloader (GRUB)** allows for a multi-boot environment by allowing the user to safely have and choose between operating systems on the boot screen, preserving the boot entries for each installed OS.

8. Select the **/dev/sda** option and click on **Continue**:

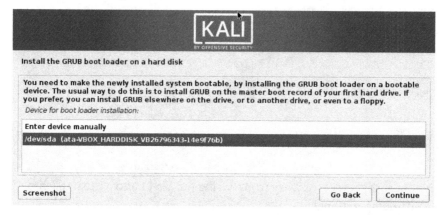

Figure 2.28 – Kali Linux GRUB boot loader selection

9. A couple more minutes and the installation will be complete. After clicking on **Continue**, the installation completes and boots into Kali Linux:

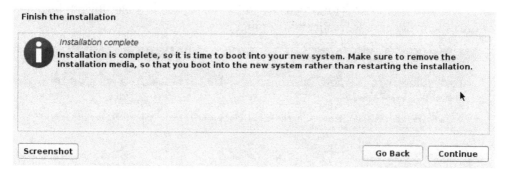

Figure 2.29 – Kali Linux installation completion confirmation

10. Should you have an error stating that `VirtualBox Failed to open a session for the virtual machine upon startup`, you may need to change the USB controller setting to **USB 1.1 (OHCI) Controller** by clicking on **Settings** and **USB**:

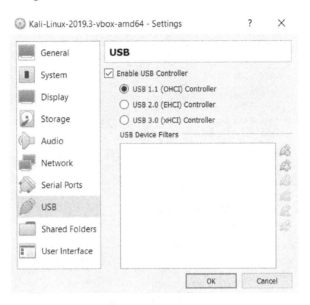

Figure 2.30 – VirtualBox USB settings

This concludes our Kali Linux installation within a virtual machine. Before we get started using it, however, let's look at another installation method by installing Kali Linux on a portable drive.

Creating a bootable Kali Linux portable drive

As I mentioned earlier in this chapter, it is always a good idea to have an installation of Kali Linux on a forensically sound device, such as a flash drive or SD card, to aid in live incident response.

For best results, I recommend using a USB 3.0 (32 GB) flash drive or thumb drive and, if using an SD card, I recommend using a Class 10 (32 GB) card:

1. To create our bootable drive, we'll be using the popular Rufus tool, which can be downloaded free of charge at `https://rufus.ie/`.

2. Once downloaded, run Rufus and select the device to load the Kali Linux operating system onto and select the ISO image of Kali Linux you wish to run via the flash drive or SD card. You can also select a persistent partition size to allow the saving of files and the loading of programs or updates to the Kali Linux OS:

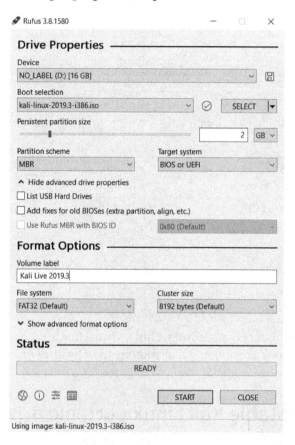

Figure 2.31 – Rufus bootable media creation interface

3. Once all of the previous options have been specified, click on **START**.

4. A warning alerts us that all data on the device will be destroyed. Click **OK** to continue:

Figure 2.32 – Rufus creation confirmation prompt

Thus begins the formatting process:

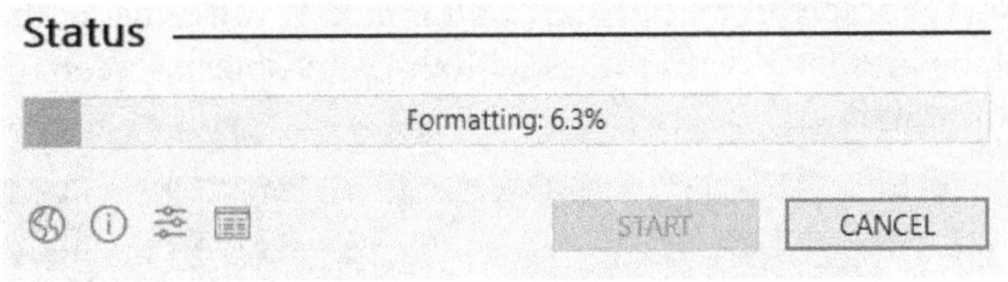

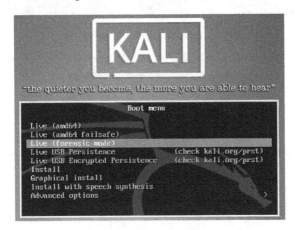

Figure 2.33 - Rufus status bar

Once the process has completed, the green status bar displays **READY**:

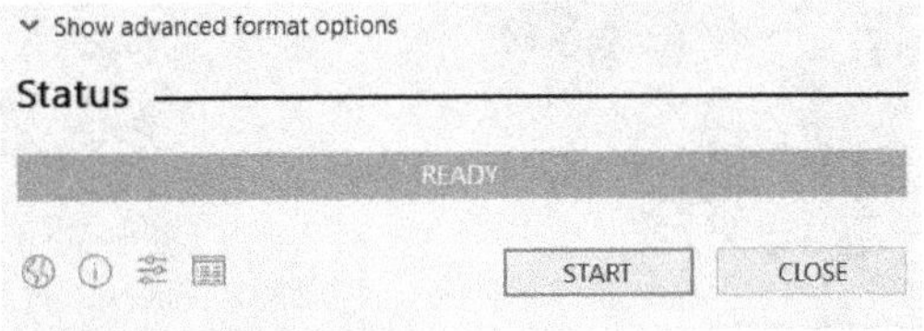

Figure 2.34 – Rufus status bar completion

5. When restarting your machine and booting from your bootable drive, you will be presented with the following **Boot menu**, which consists of various modes, including **Live (forensic mode)**, specifically made for incident response and forensics as it makes very minimal changes to the device during investigations:

Figure 2.35 – Kali Linux boot menu

Regardless of the method chosen to install Kali Linux, let's now move on to exploring the Kali Linux interface.

Exploring Kali Linux

Once our installation is complete, we can start Kali Linux. If you're using the VirtualBox installation, you will be presented with the usual Kali Linux splash screen. Choose the ***Kali GNU/Linux** option:

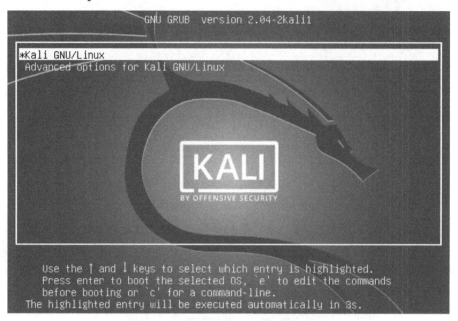

Figure 2.36 – Kali Linux OS selection

To log in, enter root as the username and the password you previously configured:

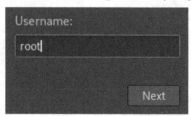

Figure 2.37 – Kali Linux Username field

This brings us to our Kali Linux desktop:

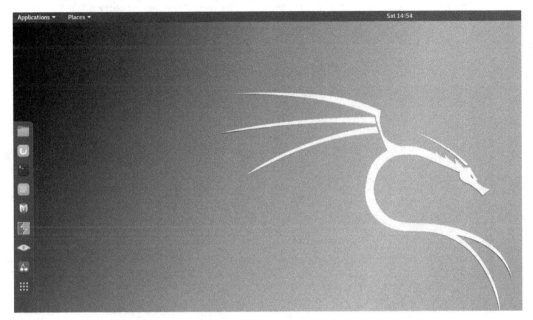

Figure 2.38 – Kali Linux desktop

When logged in, one of the first things we should do is enter three commands in the terminal to update Kali.

To get to the terminal, which is the equivalent of Command Prompt in Windows, click on **Applications | Terminal**.

With the terminal open, enter the following commands so that Kali Linux can check for package updates, software upgrades, and distribution updates:

- `apt-get update`
- `apt-get upgrade`

The apt-get command is used to install software (and can also be used to uninstall software). The apt-get update command checks for new versions of software and packages while the apt-get upgrade command actually upgrades the software and packages to the latest versions:

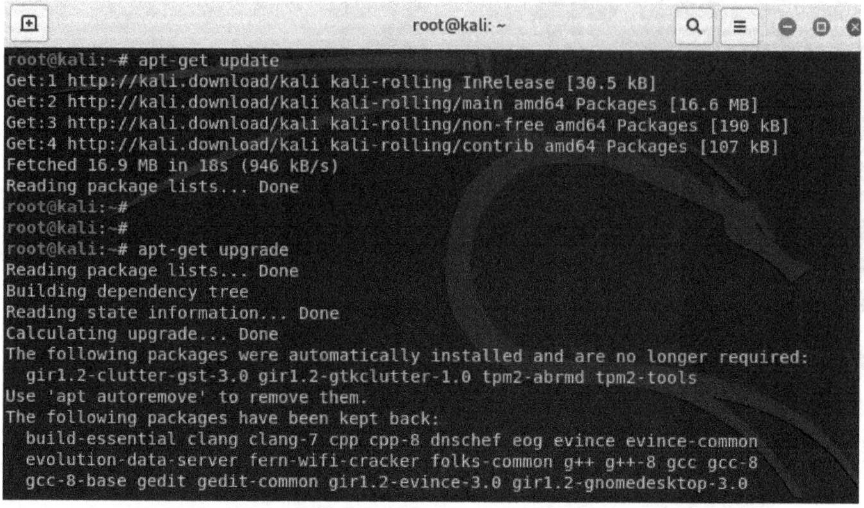

Figure 2.39 – Updating Kali Linux

At this point, we have a successfully updated installation of Kali Linux, which now contains the latest versions of tools as well as specific forensic repositories that contain the tools that we will be using. As this book deals with digital forensics in Kali Linux, we can dive right in by taking a look at some of the tools for forensics available on the Forensics menu in the main application menu.

There are two ways to get to the **Forensics** menu in Kali Linux:

1. The first is to click on **Applications**, then move down to menu item **11 - Forensics**, as in the following screenshot:

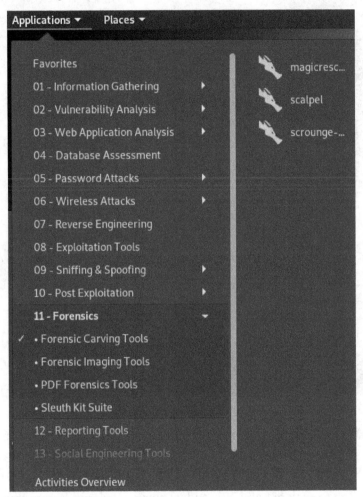

Figure 2.40 – Kali Linux main menu

2. For the second method, simply click on the **Show Applications** item (the last icon in the floating side menu) and choose **Forensics**:

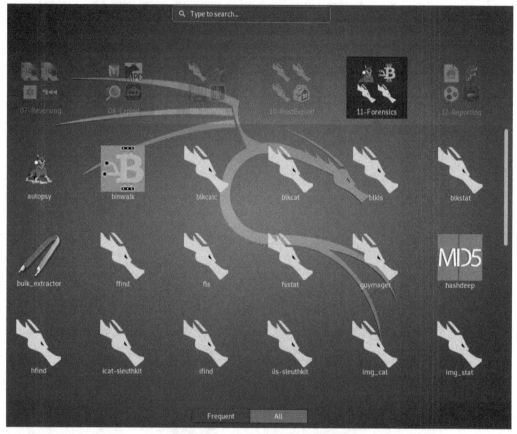

Figure 2.41 – Kali Linux Forensic tools

You'll notice that there are more tools available in this second option. This isn't to say that these are all the forensics tools available to us in Kali Linux. Many are available via the terminal, some of which will be accessed in this manner in later chapters.

I also encourage you to explore Kali Linux and its many wonderful features that also make it a fully functional operating system, not just for use in forensics and penetration testing.

> **Important note:**
>
> Should you be interested in discovering more about Kali Linux as a penetration-testing (pen-testing) distribution, Packt Publishing has many detailed books on Kali Linux, which I wholeheartedly endorse. I own many of them in paperback and use them regularly on the job as well as for preparing my lectures.

Summary

In this chapter, we dived into the technical aspect of Kali Linux and discovered the types of modes available to us via the Kali Linux ISO image, whether running it from a live environment or installing it in a virtual environment. Kali Linux can also be installed on removable storage, such as a flash drive or SD card. Being such a versatile operating system, we can also install Kali Linux as a full-fledged operating system.

We also looked in depth at installing Kali Linux in a virtual environment using VirtualBox. For beginners, I'd recommend this method of installation, as it allows trial and error within an isolated environment. Be sure to allocate enough RAM and remember that the 32-bit version of Kali Linux only allows up to 4 GB of RAM to be recognized and utilized. As a reminder, I once again suggest that you have access to both a Kali Linux live medium (created using Rufus) as well as an installation of the OS, whether physical or virtual, to ensure that all bases are covered.

Understanding the forensics tools used in Kali Linux is an excellent way to go about your investigations but we also need to understand the workings of storage media, filesystems, data types, and locations. Join me in the next chapter, as we continue our journey into digital forensics by first understanding these fundamental concepts.

You may want to consider keeping a log of tests, which ensures that tools were tested prior to investigation in the event that you are called upon to verify or defend your findings.

Section 2: Forensic Fundamentals and Best Practices

In this section, we gain an understanding of filesystems, data storage and media, hard drive technologies and **random access memory** (**RAM**), and also look at common and best practices for forensic imaging and acquisition.

This part comprises the following chapters:

- *Chapter 3, Understanding Filesystems and Storage Media*
- *Chapter 4, Incident Response and Data Acquisition*

3
Understanding Filesystems and Storage Media

It takes a lot more than just technical know-how to be a digital forensic investigator. There's a lot of research, processes, and analytics that also go into the case itself. Consider a scenario where you need to build a house. Sure, we need wood, nails, cement, metal, glass, and all the other raw materials, and we also require the skilled laborers and contractors to construct the structure and piece it together. Apart from the materials, tools, and resources, we would have also done our research to ensure that we understood what is needed for this to be a successful project.

For instance, we would have had to obtain permits to build, performed a soil analysis, considered the weather, and then chosen the types of materials based on the weather, location, soil type, and so on. It goes without saying that there must be an understanding of fundamental concepts in the field in order to efficiently carry out the task. In the same way, we need to have an understanding of the filesystems, operating systems, data types, and locations, as well as a thorough understanding of the methods and procedures for preserving data, storage media, and general evidence.

In this chapter, we will learn about the following topics:

- The history of storage media

- Filesystems and operating systems

- What about the data?

- Data volatility

- The paging file and its importance in digital forensics

The history of storage media

The end result of any investigation is to prove whether something exists or took place. In laptops, desktops, mobile devices, and smart devices, data has to be stored somewhere, even if it's just temporarily. Most of us may be familiar with hard disk drives within laptops, desktops, mobile devices, and so on, but we also need to focus on removable and portable storage devices. These include DVDs, portable drives, thumb or flash drives, SD and microSD cards, older media such as CDs and floppy disks, and countless more.

We should also consider that many portable flash drives come in many interesting shapes and sizes as novelty items and may not take the usual shape of the ordinary rectangular-shaped drive. Another issue to consider is that many of these storage media devices have changed in size over the years and may be smaller in size, usually as a result of evolving technology.

Cloud storage has also cemented its place as a common and cost-effective solution, with many companies offering free cloud storage solutions between 2 GB and 15 GB to the average user, with the option to pay for more storage. Although not a new concept, cloud storage is here to stay and with it also comes some challenges to data recovery and forensics as we do not have access to the physical storage servers. Fortunately, many cloud storage providers, such as Google, Dropbox, and Microsoft, offer a service of temporarily holding deleted files in the event that they were mistakenly deleted or need to be recovered.

IBM and the history of storage media

There can never be a story, journal, book, or even discussion on the history of hard drives and storage media without mentioning three letters: IBM. We're all familiar with this well-known tech giant, but we might not all be familiar with some of its great achievements.

International Business Machines (**IBM**, as we know it), has been around for quite some time. Known as the **Computing-Tabulating-Recording Company** (**CTR**) back in the early 1900s, IBM is better known for building the very first hard disk drive, the first PC, its servers, desktops, and laptops.

Between the years 1956 and 1957, IBM made major inroads with the development and release of the 305 **Random Access Method of Accounting and Control** (**RAMAC**), which utilized the first disk storage technology. This revolutionary technology weighed in at approximately one ton and was roughly 16 square feet in size. The disk space capacity of this behemoth, however, was only 5 MB (megabytes – yes, I said *megabytes*) in size.

Although 5 MB by today's standard is roughly the size of a high-definition photo taken with a mobile device, all things considered, this really was a monumental achievement for its time. Before IBM's invention, data was stored on punch cards, which could amount to as many as millions of cards just to hold a few megabytes.

A major issue faced back then with the introduction of this digital storage was the size of the device. Transportation by plane and truck may not have been an option for many and the space to store this would also have been an issue.

As technology progressed, IBM announced a much more portable computer in 1975, released as the IBM 5100 Portable Computer. In the 1980s, specifically 1981, we saw the birth of the IBM Personal Computer. Weighing in at much less than its predecessor, this portable computer also had a much more affordable price tag of between $8,000 and $20,000.

It wasn't until 1981, when IBM released the first personal computer, that the portability of computers was becoming an actual reality. With a price tag of $1,565, owners were afforded a keyboard and mouse, with options for a monitor, printer, and floppy drives. Apart from the floppy drives, this is the standard for today's personal computers.

Along with this newer and more portable technology, there were also improvements in data storage media over the years, which saw advancements from magnetic tape storage, to floppy disks and diskettes, CDs, DVDs, Blu-ray disks, and, of course, mechanical and **solid-state drives** (**SSDs**).

Removable storage media

Continuing on our topic of storage media, I'd first like to start by discussing removable storage media, as they play a role just as important as that of fixed storage media in today's world.

Magnetic tape drives

Introduced by IBM in the 1950s, **magnetic tape** was an easy and very fast way to store data at a speed equal to its processing time. The IBM 726 magnetic tape reader and recorder was one of the first devices to offer this storage, with a capacity or tape density of 100 bits per linear inch of tape. *Inch of tape* should give an indicator of the size of the tape, which was wound on a large wheel, similar to an old film roll movie tape.

With magnetic tape media, data is written across the width of the magnetic-coated plastic strip in frames separated by gaps consisting of blocks. Magnetic tape is still very much used today and, like many other storage media types, has significantly decreased in size while increasing in capacity and speed.

To give an idea of how far magnetic tape storage has come, in 2017, IBM developed newer tape storage media with a tape density of 200 Gbps per inch on a single cartridge, which can hold up to 333 GB of data. These cartridges (for older folks like myself) are the size of a cassette tape, or (for the younger ones) not much smaller than the average smartphone, which fits in your hand. As of 2019, Fujifilm released the Fujifilm **Linear Tape-Open Ultrium 8 (LTO-8)** magnetic tape cartridge with a native capacity of 12 TB (terabytes) and a data rate of 360 Mbps. 30 TB of compressed data can fit on this single 12 TB cartridge.

Floppy disks

The **floppy disk**, introduced yet again by IBM, was first seen along with its floppy disk drive in 1971. Although mainframe computers back then already had hard drives and magnetic tape storage media, there was a need for a simple and cheaper means of saving and passing on software and instructions to the mainframes, previously done using the much slower punch cards.

At the core of the floppy disk was a small magnetic disk, which, although far more portable than magnetic tape storage and hard disk drives at the time, stored much less data than other media we've mentioned.

Evolution of the floppy disk

Size: 8-inch
Year introduced: 1971
Maximum capacity: 80 kilobytes (KB)

Size: 5.25-inch
Year introduced: 1976
Maximum capacity: 360 KB

Size: 3.5-inch
Year introduced: 1984
Maximum capacity: 1.2 megabytes (MB)

> **Important note:**
> In 1986, the capacity of the floppy was increased to 1.44 MB, which remained as such until it was discontinued by Sony (the last remaining manufacturer of the floppy) in 2011.

Optical storage media

Optical storage media is so-called because of the way in which data is written to the various media types, involving the use of different types of lasers on the surface of the disk itself.

Although it may be somewhat difficult to distinguish various optical disks if there are no default labels on them, they do have slight differences in color and hue due to the size of the lasers used to write data to them.

Compact disks

Compact disks (**CDs**) are made of pits and lands, noticeable as bumps on the underside of the disk, coated with a thin layer of aluminum, which results in a reflective surface. Data is written in concentric circles, further split up into sectors of 512 bytes, each known as **tracks**, on the CD from the inside to the outside (or edge) of the disk:

- **Diameter**: 120 millimeters (mm)
- **Type of laser used to write data**: 780 nanometer (nm) infrared laser
- **Maximum capacity of a CD**: 650-700 MB

The various types of CDs are as follows:

- **Compact Disk – Read-Only Memory (CD-ROM)**: This disk comes with data on it in the form of programs, games, music, and so on, and can only be read from.
- **Compact Disk Recordable (CD-R)**: Data can be written to this disk, but only once.
- **Compact Disk – ReWritable (CD-RW)**: Data can be written to this disk many times.

Digital versatile disks

Digital Versatile Disks (DVDs), although the same size in diameter, can store much more data than CDs:

- **Diameter**: 120 mm (same as a CD)

- **Type of laser used to write data**: 650 nm red laser

- **Maximum capacity of a DVD**: 4.7 gigabytes (GB) and 15.9 GB (dual-layer DVD)

The various types of DVDs are as follows:

- **Digital Versatile Disk – Read-Only Memory (DVD-ROM)**: The DVD comes with data already written to it, much like a CD-ROM.

- **Digital Versatile Disk – Recordable (DVD-R)**: Data can be written once to the DVD.

- **Digital Versatile Disk + Recordable (DVD+R)**: Data can be written once to the DVD. +R DVDs utilize more advanced error detection and management technology.

- **Digital Versatile Disk – ReWritable (DVD-RW)**: Data can be written to the DVD several times. The DVD-RW disk differs from the DVD+RW disk in that the DVD-RW disk may be written-to a bit faster and may also be compatible with a larger variety of DVD players.

- **Digital Versatile Disk – Recordable Dual Layer (DVD-R DL)**: The DVD contains dual layers resulting in higher storage capacities of between 7.95 GB on a DVD-9 disk and 15.9 GB on a DVD-18 disk.

- **Digital Versatile Disk – Recordable Dual Layer (DVD+R DL)**: Same as the DVD-R DL, but has been argued as having a more efficient format, resulting in fewer errors.

- **Digital Versatile Disk – Random-Access Memory (DVD-RAM)**: Mainly used in video recording equipment due to its resiliency (lasting up to two decades) and the ability to rewrite data onto it. This disk is more expensive than other DVD formats and is also not compatible with many common DVD drives and players.

Blu-ray disk

The current standard for removable disk media, the **Blu-ray disk,** gets its name from the color of the laser used to read from and write to the disk. Due to the high-capacity storage of Blu-ray disks, **high definition (HD)** content can easily be stored on Blu-ray disks without a loss in quality:

- **Diameter**: 120 mm (same as a CD and DVD)

- **Type of laser used to write data**: 405 nm blue laser

- **Maximum capacity of a DVD**: 27 GB and 50 GB (double-layer Blu-ray)

Flash storage media

Flash memory is so named because the data is written to, and erased from, using electrical charges. You may have perhaps heard someone say that they've had to *flash* their mobile device. This is quite similar to erasing flash storage media on smartphones and smart devices, except devices with operating systems such as Android and iOS require a much more extensive procedure for flashing and reinstalling their operating systems. The end result, however, is very much the same in that the memory and storage areas are reset or wiped.

Flash storage chips come in two types, known as NAND and NOR flash memory, and are responsible for high-speed and high-capacity storage of data on flash storage media. They are newer types of **Electrically Erasable Programmable Read-Only Memory (EEPROM)** chips, and instead can wipe blocks of data or the entire drive, rather than just one byte at a time, as with the slower EEPROM. This type of flash memory chip is non-volatile, meaning the data is still stored on the chip even after power to the chip is lost. Data is erased when specific instructions are sent to the chip in the form of electrical signals via a method known as **in-circuit writing**, which alters the data accordingly.

The following photo shows one of my old 1 GB flash drives with a Samsung NAND chip, which stores the data. If you'd like to get down into the technical details of the chip, you can have a look at the datasheet PDF at `https://www.datasheet.directory/ index.php?title=Special:PdfViewer&url=https%3A%2F%2Fpdf. datasheet.directory%2F5164321c%2Fsamsung.com%2FK9K4G08U0M-PCB00.pdf`:

Figure 3.1 – A flash drive with the NAND chip exposed

Flash media storage has so far become the ultimate in portability, with many types ranging from the size of your thumb to the size of the nail on your little finger. The lifespan of flash storage all depends on the usage as they all have an average read-write usage, sometimes displayed on the packaging of the device. The read-write speeds are also some of the fastest at this point, which is why hard disk drives have moved away from the traditional mechanical disk mechanism to a solid-state one. SSDs will be discussed further later in this chapter.

> **Important note:**
> With flash storage media capacities ranging from 2 GB to 256 GB, particularly on SD, microSD and flash drives, these can now act as very fast removable drives with operating systems installed on them, and can even be partitioned using various tools. Yes, indeed, Kali Linux most certainly can be installed onto a flash drive, SD, or microSD card (and be made bootable) with as little as 8 GB of storage space.

USB flash drives

The **Universal Serial Bus** (**USB**) port, or interface, released in 1995, has become the standard for all devices, replacing older devices that would have been connected to specific parallel ports on a computer. It's quite common to see almost any device or peripherals connected to a computer via a USB connection, including mice, keyboards, flash drives, printers, scanners, cameras, mobile devices, and just about every other device.

The evolution of the USB port is shown here:

USB version	Released year	Data transfer speed
USB 1.0 and 1.1	1995	12 Mbps
USB 2.0	2000	480 Mbps
USB 3.0	2008	5 Gbps
USB 3.1	2013	10 Gbps
USB 3.2	2017	20 Gbps
USB 4	2020/2021	40 Gbps

USB flash drives come in all shapes and sizes today, from the standard rectangular to any shape imaginable. USB flash drives use NAND EEPROM chips to store their data, and today are available in various versions that define the read/write speeds of the flash drive.

The following photo shows various flash drives ranging from the oldest to the newest, left to right. The first drive is a USB 2.1 drive, the middle is a 32 GB USB 3.0 drive, and the last (right-side) is a significantly smaller 64 GB USB 3.2 drive:

Figure 3.2 – USB 2.1, 3.0, and 3.2 flash drives

> **Important note:**
> I should give a special mention to the elephant in the room here, the novelty flash drive, which can easily pass as a keychain or toy and may actually pose a threat to organizations that do not allow employees to bring to work or leave with flash drives due to the sensitive nature of the data within the organization.

Flash memory cards

Like flash drives, **flash memory cards** (or memory cards, as they are fondly referred to) also use NAND flash memory, which, as we previously learned, is a non-volatile, solid-state memory. Unlike USB flash drives, however, these cards do not come with a USB interface and must be used with either an adapter or memory card reader.

Over the years and decades, we've had several formats of memory cards grace our desktops, laptops, mobiles, and other devices, including cameras, MP3 players, and even toys. Although I'll only cover some of the more popular cards used today, it is important that you are at least familiar with memory cards and are also able to identify them.

The flash memory card types we will look at are as follows:

- Memory Stick PRO Duo (MSPD, proprietary card developed by Sony)
- Secure Digital (SD)
- Secure Digital High Capacity (SDHC) – 2–32 GB capacity
- Mini SDHC
- Micro SDHC
- Secure Digital eXtended Capacity (SDXC) – 32 GB–2 TB capacity
- CompactFlash (CF)
- MultiMediaCard (MMC)
- xD-Picture (xD)
- Smart Media (SM)

Of the aforementioned card types, I've opted to show three from my collection in the following photo. The card to the left is a Sony Memory Stick PRO Duo, the card in the middle is an SD card that has a sliding lock to the side, used to prevent data from being overwritten, and the card to the right is the more common card of today, the microSD:

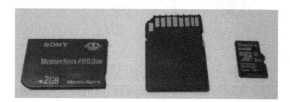

Figure 3.3 – Sony Pro Duo, SD, and micro-SD cards

I'd like to do a brief comparison of these three cards. Developed at least a decade apart, the older PRO Duo card is larger, with a capacity of 2 GB. Although not seen on the SD card, its capacity is 4 GB, and the smallest and newest card to the right (microSD) actually has a whopping 64 GB of storage capacity.

Have a look at the following photo to see a close-up of the microSD card. It shows the capacity of 64 GB, and also the class of the microSD card (class 10). 64 GB of data on something as small as a fingernail! Still, microSD cards are being developed with even larger capacities of 128 GB and even 256 GB:

Figure 3.4 – Class 10 microSD card

The various classes of microSD cards identify their read/write speeds and suggested uses. I do suggest getting a **class 10 (C10)** microSD card if purchasing one, as the C10 is much faster than the other classes (2, 4, and 6) and supports constant HD and even 4k video recording.

Classes 2, 4, 6, and 10 support speeds of up to 2 MBps, 4 MBps, 6 MBps, and 10 MBps, respectively, and are known as SD Speed Class. Class 1 and class 3 are known as the UHS Speed Class and support speeds of up to 10 MBps and 30 Mbps, respectively. The newer Video Speed Class, which is recommended for HD video in 4K and 8K, supports much faster speeds. The V10, V30, V60, and V90 cards support speeds of up to 10 MBps, 30 MBps, 60 MBps, and 90 MBps, respectively.

As mentioned earlier, flash memory cards require card readers, which connect to laptops, desktops, and other media players using USB ports. The following photo shows one of my many card readers, which supports CompactFlash, Memory Stick PRO Duo, Secure Digital, and even the Smart Media cards:

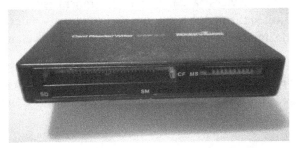

Figure 3.5 – USB multi-card reader

I'd suggest getting yourself a few USB card readers that support the various card types to easily access cards (whether for ordinary use or data recovery) as most newer laptops, desktops, and devices may only support SD card slots and USB interfaces.

Hard disk drives

Now that we've had a good look at non-volatile storage, including tape and flash storage, let's go a bit deeper into the world of **hard disk drives** (HDDs), which serve as fixed storage media. I'll try to keep things simple and short by focusing mainly on the knowledge necessary for forensics investigators in particular.

HDD technology has certainly come a long way from the monstrous storage devices first seen in IBM mainframes and is now more compact, fast, and affordable, with capacities in the terabytes.

Although the newer solid-state drives use the same type of memory found in flash memory devices, they are still a bit costly when compared to mechanical drives. This may be, perhaps, one of the contributing factors to why older mechanical drive technology is still being used. Mechanical drives consist of moving parts, including platters, an actuator arm, and a very powerful magnet. Although it is very common to still find these mechanical HDDs in today's laptops and hard drives, they are much slower than the newer solid-state drives, which have no moving parts and look very similar to the chipset of a USB flash drive.

In your forensics investigations and adventures, you may come across or be presented with older HDDs that can have different interfaces and use different cable technologies to connect to motherboards. Let's have a look, shall we?

IDE HDDs

Many of the first PCs in the mid-1980s were outfitted with hard drives that used **Parallel Advanced Technology Attachment** (**PATA**) and **Integrated Drive Electronics** (**IDE**) technology. As with all older devices back then, parallel transmission was the order of the day, allowing for very limited throughput. An easy way to identify older IDE drives is to simply have a look at the interface where the data and power cables connect to the drive.

These older drives, as in the following photo, have four pins for power, which connect to a Molex connector separated by eight pins used to set the device as a master or slave device, and then 40 pins for the IDE data cable, which transmits the data to the motherboard:

Figure 3.6 – An older 40-pin EIDE hard disk drive

In 1994, advancements in technology led to the release of **Enhanced Integrated Drive Electronics (EIDE)**, which saw an increase in the number of pins for the data cable from 40 to 80, also increasing the transmission speeds from 4 Mbps to a possible 133 Mbps.

IDE/EIDE was still, however, limited to a maximum of four IDE/EIDE drives per computer, as the jumper pins on the drive only allowed for two primary and two secondary drives, set in a master/slave configuration. Consideration also had to be given to the fact that CD-ROM and RW devices, and DVD-ROM and RW devices, were also using IDE/EIDE technology at that time.

SATA HDDs

In 2002, Seagate released an HDD technology called **Serial Advanced Technology Attachment (SATA)**, which used serial transmission instead of slower parallel transmission. While PATA drives speeds of 33/66/133 Mbps, SATA boasts speeds of 150/300/600 Mbps. This meant that the lowest SATA transmission speed of 150 Mbps was faster than the highest PATA speed of 133 Mbps.

The connector interfaces of the SATA drives were also different, but it was common at the time to see SATA drives with connectors for both SATA and PATA power cables for backward compatibility.

SATA data cables are much thinner than PATA cables, as they only contain seven wires connecting to seven pins. SATA devices use one cable per drive, unlike PATA devices, which connect two drives on one IDE/EIDE cable connected in a master/slave configuration.

The following photo shows an older SATA drive with SATA data and power connectors to the right and a legacy IDE Molex power cable (four pins) to the left:

Figure 3.7 – A SATA hard disk drive

SATA still continues to be the standard today for drive technology for both desktops and laptops and has had several revisions, as listed here. Speeds listed are in MBps (megabytes per second) and not Mbps (megabits per second):

- **SATA 1**: 150 MBps

- **SATA 2**: 300 MBps

- **SATA 3**: 600 MBps

The following photo shows two SATA laptop 2.5-inch drives. The one to the left is damaged and has been opened for us to see the circular platter at the middle with the actuator arm at the top, slightly positioned over the platter. At the end of the actuator arm is a read/write head, which actually does the reading and the writing of data to the platter.

The drive on the right-hand side in the photo is actually a hybrid drive, or a **Solid-State Hybrid Drive (SSHD)**. This is actually a mechanical drive like the one to the left, but also has flash memory in it to allow for faster access to the data on the platters:

Figure 3.8 – A mechanical laptop drive with platters exposed

Solid-state drives

As briefly mentioned before, SSDs are non-volatile storage media and use NAND flash memory in an array to hold data. SSDs have been around for quite some time. However, mainstream use would have been greatly hampered by the high cost of the drive. Samsung first released a 32 GB SSD with a PATA interface in 1996, followed by SanDisk's 32 GB SSD, but with a SATA interface.

Although SSD drives use flash memory, the materials used are more high-end than that found in flash drives, which makes it the much preferred option for use as a hard drive, but again contributes to the very high cost.

Some advantages of SSDs come from the fact that there are no moving parts in an SSD. No moving parts make the SSD more durable in the event of a fall or swift foot to the PC tower as there are no platters or actuator arms to be scratched or struck. Also, the faster read/write speeds and access times greatly reduce the time taken for the device to boot or start, and even gives an enhanced experience when using resource-intensive software and games.

As far as digital forensics goes, SSDs are still a relatively new technology that will be constantly improved upon for some time to come. It's important to remember that you are not dealing with a mechanical drive and that data on an SSD, much like a flash drive or memory card, can be lost or wiped within minutes or even seconds. Although traditional tools can be used to image and recover data from SSDs, I strongly suggest researching any SSD drive before performing any forensic activities to get a better understanding of its workings and complexities, such as de-chipping and wear-leveling algorithms.

More information on the reasons for the wearing out of SSDs, as well as wear-leveling, can be found at `https://www.dell.com/support/article/en-tt/sln156899/hard-drive-why-do-solid-state-devices-ssd-wear-out?lang=en`.

Here's a photo of a 250 GB SSD:

Figure 3.9 – An M2 NVMe Solid State Drive (SSD)

Take note of the pin layout interface for the SSD connector (left side), which connects to a PCIe interface on the board instead of the usual SATA connectors. The connector in the preceding photo is an M.2 **Non-Volatile Memory express** (**NVMe**) SSD connector type, but there are other types as well. When performing forensic acquisitions on SSDs, which may require the use of a USB adapter, be sure you know which connector you are working with.

Different SSD interface types include the following:

- SATA 3.0 (up to 6 Gb/s bandwidth)
- mSATA (up to 6 Gb/s bandwidth) – found in older computers
- M.2 SATA (up to 32 Gb/s bandwidth)
- M.2 NVMe (up to 32 Gb/s bandwidth)
- U.2 (up to 32 Gb/s bandwidth but not very common)

Filesystems and operating systems

Now that we've covered the physical, let's get logical! Any and every type of storage media needs to be formatted with a particular filesystem. The filesystem chosen will also determine which operating system can be installed on the medium, along with file and partition sizes.

A simple way to think of this is to imagine a blank sheet of paper as any type of new or wiped storage media. We can put several types of information on this piece of paper, but we'll probably first want to organize or prepare the sheet of paper in a way that makes our data easy to understand, access, and even store. We can choose to write on it from left to right in sentences and paragraphs in English, or we can perhaps create tables using rows and columns. We can even use printed slides to display our data, or even use images, graphs, and flowcharts. Additionally, we can format our storage media in a way that best suits the data that will be stored and used.

Filesystems ensure that the data is organized in such a way that it can be easily recognized and indexed. Consider the storage space within a filing cabinet with multiple compartments. Some may be used specifically for storing files in alphabetical order, others in chronological order, some compartments for stationery supplies, miscellaneous, and even random items. Although all are used for storing different items, they can all be labeled and easily recognized, and also organized in such a way that the contents of each compartment can be easily accessed or even removed.

To install any operating system on a hard drive or removable storage media, the device must first be formatted and prepared for the operating system by choosing the appropriate filesystem. Windows, macOS, Android, Kali, and so on all have filesystems that organize the storage medium so that the operating system can be successfully installed.

Some of the more popular operating systems and their filesystems are as follows.

Microsoft Windows:

- **Filesystem: Net Technology File System (NTFS)**

- **Supported versions**: Server 2019, Server 2016, Server 2012, Server 2008, Windows 10, 8, 7, Vista, XP, 2000, NT

- **Maximum volume size**: 256 TB (although listed as theoretically 16 Exabytes, or 16 EiB)

- **Maximum supported file size**: 256 TB (using a 64 KB cluster size)

- **NTFS features**: Compression, EFS (Encrypted File System), disk quotas

> **Important note:**
>
> Older versions of Microsoft Windows supported the **File Allocation Table** (**FAT**) filesystem by default. Newer versions of Windows also support FAT and FAT32, but with drive size limitations (8 TB) and file size limitations (4 GB). exFAT was created to remove the limitations of FAT32, but may not be as widely supported as FAT32.

Macintosh (macOS):

- **Filesystem**: HFS+ (Hierarchical File System)

- **Supported versions**: macOS up to version 10

- **Maximum volume size**: 2 TB

- **Maximum supported file size**: 8 EB

> **Important note:**
>
> In 2017, Apple advanced to a newer filesystem called **Apple File System** (**APFS**) to replace HFS+, optimized specifically for SSDs. APFS is available as the default filesystem for macOS High Sierra and anything newer, and also for iOS 10.3 and anything newer.

Linux:

- **Filesystem**: Ext4 (Fourth Extended File System). Several filesystems are available for Linux, but I recommend this one if you are uncertain as to which should be used.

- **Supported versions**: Red Hat, Kali, Ubuntu, and so on.

- **Maximum volume size**: 1 EB.

- **Maximum supported file size**: 16 TB.

> **Important note:**
> Many open source operating system distributions are based on Linux, including Kali Linux and Android, so use the ext2/ext3/ext4 filesystems. They are also able to use the FAT32 filesystem.
> FAT32 can be used across any platform, including older versions of Windows, Mac, and Linux, and is supported by almost any device with a USB port.

What about the data?

In this chapter so far, we've looked at the various media for storing data. Now, I'd like to talk about the actual data itself, some of its states, and what happens when it's accessed.

Data states

Firstly, there's **data in transit**, also called **data in motion**. These states describe data on the move, perhaps traversing across the network between devices or even between storage media, actively moving between locations.

Then there's **data in use**. Data in this state is currently being accessed by a user or processed by a CPU. When data is accessed from the hard drive, it is temporarily stored in RAM, which is much faster than the hard drive (particularly mechanical drives) and stored there for as long as the user accesses it and there is power to the device.

When data is not in motion, transit, or in use, it is described as **data at rest**. In this state, the data *rests* or resides on non-volatile media such as hard drives, optical media, flash drives, or memory cards.

Metadata

Metadata is simply data about data. Take an item such as a laptop stored in a warehouse, for example. Somewhere in the warehouse (and also, possibly, in other locations such as the cloud), there may be several pieces of information about that laptop, which can be referred to as data about the laptop, or even laptop metadata, such as:

- Location of the laptop within the warehouse
- Laptop brand and model
- Manufacture date
- Warranty dates and information

- Hardware and software specs
- Color and size

Additionally, data may have at least some basic information pertaining to it, whether it be at rest or in motion. At rest, data may be indexed on a hard drive in the file table to identify the location of the data and whether it may be available to the user or is waiting to be overwritten. Data in transit will also contain header information (which will be discussed in later chapters), which gives information about source and destination addresses and the size of the data, to name just a few aspects.

Slack space

Clusters are the smallest amount of disk space or allocation units on storage media that store data. When formatting drives, we need to define the size of these allocation units, or we can use the default cluster size of 4 KB. This is where slack space comes in.

Slack space (also referred to as **file slack**) is the empty and unused space within clusters that contain data but are not completely filled with data. To fully understand this, we first need to understand default cluster sizes specified by operating systems. A drive formatted using NTFS (for Windows) has a default cluster size of 4 KB. Let's say that you've saved a text file to your disk with a file size of 3 KB. This means that you still have 1 KB of unused or slack space within that cluster.

Slack space is of particular interest to a forensic investigator as data can be easily hidden inside it. Lucky for us, we have several tools available, such as **Sleuth Kit** and **Autopsy**, within Kali Linux, to help investigate slack space and find hidden files.

Data volatility

In this section, we will take a look at why data is lost when power to the volatile memory is lost.

Data can exist as long as the media it is stored on is capable of storing the data. Hard drives (mechanical and solid-state), flash drives, and memory cards are all non-volatile storage media. Although SSDs have made, and continue to make, drastic improvements in data access times, RAM thus far remains the faster type of memory, typically referred to only as **memory**, inside devices.

RAM, however, is **volatile memory**. Unlike non-volatile memory found in hard drives and flash drives, data stored in RAM is kept there temporarily, only for as long as there is an electrical current being provided to the chips. There are two types of RAM that we need to be aware of: **Static RAM (SRAM)** and **Dynamic RAM (DRAM)**.

SRAM is superior to DRAM but is far more costly because of the expensive materials used in building the chips. SRAM is also physically much larger than DRAM. SRAM can be found in the CPU cache (**L1** or **Level 1**) and, on some chips, on the motherboard (**L2/L3**), although in very small sizes (KB) due to the cost and physical size.

Although DRAM is slower, it is much cheaper and remains one of the reasons for its usage as the main memory in devices. What makes RAM volatile is its components, such as **transistors** and **capacitors**. Some of you may already be familiar with this topic from certification courses such as **A+**, but for the benefit of all our readers, allow me to go into a bit more detail.

DRAM uses capacitors, which store electrical charges temporarily as part of a refresh circuit. The chips need to be constantly refreshed in order to hold the data while being accessed. However, between refreshes, a wait state is created, which makes DRAM slower when compared to SRAM as it uses transistors instead of capacitors, which do not have wait states.

Over the decades, there have been many types of DRAM or memory sticks in slightly varying sizes and increased pins with which to make contact with the motherboard. Some of the RAM types, in order of age, are as follows:

- **Extended Data Output RAM (EDO RAM)**: One of the earlier types of DRAM.

- **Synchronous Dynamic RAM (SDRAM)**: Began synchronizing itself with the CPU clock speed. Had a maximum data rate of 166 MT/s (millions of transfers per second). Labeled as PC100, PC133, and PC166. SDRAM had a maximum transfer rate/speed of 1.3 GB/s.

- **DDR-SDRAM/DDR 1 (Double Data Rate – SDRAM)**: Effectively doubled the transfer rate of SDRAM. Had a maximum transfer rate of 400 MT/s and the maximum transfer speed was 3.2 GB/s.

- **DDR2**: Had a maximum transfer rate and speeds of 800 MT/s and 6.4 GB/s, respectively.

- **DDR3**: Consumes up to a third less power than DDR2. Had a maximum transfer rate and speeds of 1,600 MT/s and 14.9 GB/s, respectively.

- **DDR4**: Had a maximum transfer rate and speeds of 3,200 MT/s and 21 GB/s, respectively.

- **Graphics Double Data Rate Synchronous Dynamic RAM (GDDR SDRAM)**: GDDR is used in graphic cards for video graphics rendering.

In today's laptops and desktops, you will mainly come across DDR3 and DDR4, but it may not be uncommon to run into a legacy machine, such as an older server with DD2. The following photo shows different RAM types, **Dual Inline Memory Modules (DIMM)**. From top to bottom, we have SDRAM, DDR1, DDR2, and, lastly, DDR3:

Figure 3.10 – Various desktop RAM form factors

> **Important note:**
> Laptops also use DDR RAM but are available in a more compact size called **Small Outline DIMM (SODIMM)** modules.

The paging file and its importance in digital forensics

Operating systems have the ability to use a portion of the hard disk as an extension of RAM. This is referred to as **virtual memory** and is usually a good idea if a computer or laptop has limited RAM. Although the hard drive is much slower than the RAM, the swap or paging file on the disk can store files and programs that are being accessed less, leaving the RAM available to store data that is being frequently accessed. This process involves the operating system swapping pages of data that are less frequently used and moving data to the dedicated paging file area on the hard drive.

The paging file is very important to us in forensics investigations. Although not as volatile as RAM itself, due to being stored on the hard disk, it is a hidden file in Windows called pagefile.sys, and should always be inspected using tools of your choice as this file may reveal passwords for encrypted areas, information from sites visited, documents opened, logged-in users, printed items, and so on.

Data on mechanical drives, in particular, is stored in a fragmented manner. However, the advantage of the paging or swap file is that the data can be stored in a contiguous manner, one piece after the next, allowing for faster access times.

It is recommended that the size of the paging file is set to 1.5 times the amount of memory and that it also be stored on a separate drive if possible, not just a separate partition.

> **Important note:**
>
> `Pagefile.sys` can be located in the Windows registry path: `HKEY_LOCAL_MACHINE\SYSTEM\CurrentControlSet\Control\Session Manager\Memory Management`

Summary

In this chapter, we took the time to cover some of the basics of non-volatile storage media, which stores data even after there is no power supplied to the medium. Non-volatile media includes different types of HDDs, such as mechanical and solid-state PATA, as well as SATA drives, flash drives, and memory cards.

Newer storage media devices, including SSDs, use a special type of flash memory called NAND flash to store data. This flash memory is significantly faster and more durable than traditional mechanical drives as the devices contain no moving parts. However, they are still quite costly for now.

We also had a look at various filesystems associated with various operating systems and saw that the smallest allocation of data is called a cluster, in which slack space can reside. Slack space is the unused space within a cluster in which data can be hidden. Data itself has different states and can be at rest, in motion, or in use. Regardless of the state of the data, there always resides some information about the data itself, called metadata.

Any data accessed by the user or operating system is temporarily stored in volatile memory or RAM. Although data can be stored for lengthy periods on non-volatile memory, it is lost when electrical charges to volatile memory (RAM) are also lost. An area of the hard disk called the paging file can act as virtual RAM, allowing the computer to think it has more RAM than installed.

I do encourage you to do more research and expand your knowledge on these topics, allowing you to gain a greater understanding of what has been covered. Let's now move on to the next chapter, where we'll learn about investigative procedures and the best practices for incident response, such as acquiring volatile data and procedures for working with and analyzing live machines.

4
Incident Response and Data Acquisition

It's sometimes difficult to ascertain exactly what qualifies as evidence, especially at the exact start of an investigation, when all the facts on what occurred may not have yet been collected or stated. In any investigation, we should be aware of and follow the guidelines, practices, and procedures for acquiring evidence in such a way that it is not altered or, in a worst-case scenario, lost.

At the scene of a crime, let's say a robbery, there are specific items that may immediately qualify as evidence. The physical evidence is easily collected, put into evidence bags, labeled, and then shipped off to the labs and secure storage areas for safekeeping. This evidence may include spent bullet casings, a gun, fingerprints, and blood samples. Let's not forget witness statements and **Closed Circuit Television** (**CCTV**) footage, also. It's also of interest to consider the individuals from law enforcement agencies that would be at the scene and the order in which they may have arrived. Seems simple enough, right?

However, when a breach or crime involving a computer or smart device is reported, collecting the evidence is sometimes not as simple, as there are many factors to consider before labeling any items as evidence.

If a desktop was involved in the act, for example, do we take the tower alone or do we also seize the monitor, keyboard, mouse, and speakers? What about the other peripherals, such as printers and scanners? Are there any additional fixed or removable storage media at the scene and do we also seize them? We must also consider the handling and storage of evidence by first responders, which includes anti-static and stronghold bags for evidence storage, along with forensically sound media for the cloning of hard disks and other media that must be acquired for analysis. If the first responders are to examine the internal components of systems, anti-static wrist-bands should also be worn to avoid electrostatic discharge, which may damage components such as RAM and thereby compromise the investigation.

This chapter answers all these questions and provides guidelines and the best practices for incident response, evidence acquisition, and other topics, including the following:

- Digital evidence acquisition and procedures

- Documentation and evidence collection

- Preserving evidence integrity

- Write blocking and hashing

- Live acquisition versus post-mortem acquisition

- Live acquisition best practices

- Data imaging and hashing the chain of custody

Digital evidence acquisition and procedures

As we covered in the last chapter, data can be stored on both fixed and removable storage media. Data, however, can easily be deleted or completely lost depending on a multitude of factors that must be considered if we are to ensure the preservation of data. It might even be argued that there are more threats to digital than paper-based storage. The following are threats to paper-based storage:

- Water

- Fire and humidity

- Bugs

- Age

- Natural disasters—floods, earthquakes, tornadoes, hurricanes, and so on

The following are threats to data on storage media:

- Human error and negligence
- Magnetism and electromagnetic fields
- Water and condensation
- Heat
- Dust
- Physical impacts
- Voltage
- Static electricity
- Natural disasters—floods, earthquakes, tornadoes, hurricanes, and so on

When exactly does data become evidence?

Specific data may have a value that is relative to an investigation when considering the events that transpired.

Incident response and first responders

Preserving evidence does not begin only at the acquisition of data, but as early on as the physical viewing of the suspect device. There should be some kind of structured response to the suspected crime or breach in the same way as with a crime reported to the police. A person makes a call to the emergency services who then dispatch the police, fire services, and ambulance personnel, and other first responders who may then escalate the issue to the FBI or other agencies. There should also be a similar chain of command when dealing with reports that require digital investigation.

There are many sources for guidelines, best practices, and cybersecurity strategies, which you should familiarize yourself with. I'd suggest researching your local **Computer Emergency Response Team (CERT)** and/or **Computer Security Incident Response Team (CSIRT)** to begin with, such as the US-CERT (`https://www.us-cert.gov/resources`) and the European Union Agency for CyberSecurity (ENISA), which has all the national cybersecurity strategies for EU member states, available at `https://www.enisa.europa.eu/topics/national-cyber-security-strategies/ncss-map/national-cyber-security-strategies-interactive-map`.

The **Cybersecurity and Infrastructure Security Agency (CISA)** also has publicly available resources, which provide information on reporting vulnerabilities and also provide alerts and bulletins on security activity and new vulnerabilities. The **Scientific Working Group on Digital Forensics (SWGDE)** also has individual best practices guidelines for evidence collection, acquisition, and much more, all publicly available at https://www.swgde.org/.

When a breach or crime is discovered or suspected, there should be a dedicated first responder who is alerted and called to the scene. This person usually has some knowledge or understanding of the workings of devices, networks, and even of the IT infrastructure in the organization, if applicable.

First responder personnel can include the following:

- Systems administrators
- Network administrators
- Security administrators
- IT managers

While the people in the preceding roles may not be skilled in digital forensics or digital investigations, they will be responsible for securing the scene and ensuring that the data, peripherals, equipment, and storage are not used, tampered with, removed, or compromised by unauthorized individuals. First responder roles must be clearly defined prior to any investigation or examination at the scene so as not to compromise the investigation or tamper with evidence.

The duties of first responders include the following:

- Being the first to respond to the scene (as the name suggests) and making an initial assessment
- Documenting the scene and room fully in a circular fashion, using the center of the room as a focal point
- Securing the scene by not allowing unauthorized users or suspects to access the devices or area and especially to volatile data and storage media
- Preserving and packaging evidence for transportation and ensuring the use of the **Chain of Custody (CoC)** forms

You may wish to refer to the *Electronic Evidence – A Basic Guide for First Responders* document from ENISA, which outlines evidence collection, first responder roles and toolkits, and evidence acquisition and examination, and can be downloaded at `shorturl.at/aksy7`.

Documentation and evidence collection

Documentation of the scene should also be done by the first responders to aid in investigations. Documentation of the scene should include photographs, video, voice recording, and manual documentation of the following:

- The room where the device is located (desk, ceiling, entrance/exit, windows, lighting, electrical outlets, and data drops)
- The state of the device (on, off, power light blinking)
- The screen contents and whether the device is on (operating system, running programs, date and time, wired and/or wireless network connectivity)
- Books, notes, and pieces of paper
- Connected and disconnected cables

Once the scene has been secured and documented by the first responders, the forensic investigator should also be called in, if not already alerted.

If the first responder has been trained in evidence collection and preservation, they can also begin the process of acquiring what can be considered as physical evidence.

Examples of physical evidence include the following:

- Computer system units
- Laptops
- Tablets
- Fixed and removable storage media
- Cables and chargers

Physical evidence collection and preservation

Consideration should be given to the physical aspect of the evidence collection phase. Like any other investigation, documentation, collection, and preservation should be done while following proper guidelines and best practices by ENISA, SWGDE, CERT, and local CSIRTs, as mentioned in the previous section, to ensure the integrity of the investigation. At a crime scene, for example, evidence has to be properly identified, labeled, and handled by authorized staff, who are trained in investigative procedures that can be scrutinized in a court of law.

A first responder toolkit should contain the following items in preparation for documentation, evidence collection, and preservation at the scene:

- Protective clothing, including eyewear and gloves

- An anti-static mat or wristbands

- Identification label tags, stickers, and portable labeling devices (if available)

- Various pens and markers for easy identification

- Cable ties

- A toolkit with various sizes of Phillips, flathead, Torx, and specialized screwdrivers or heads

- A flashlight and magnifying glasses

- Seizure and CoC forms

- Containers, boxes, and packaging materials, including anti-static and stronghold bags

- Write-blocking hardware

- Portable imaging and acquisition devices

Here's an affordable but portable and very well-organized screwdriver kit, which I keep in my first responder toolkit. It has all the attachments for opening desktops, laptops, tablets, and for removing and even opening removable storage media, such as hard disk drives, optical drives, and even floppy drives, if I encounter them:

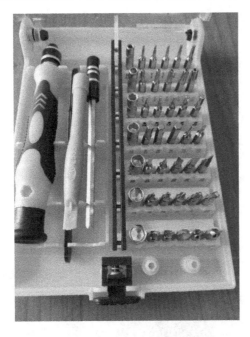

Figure 4.1 – A portable screwdriver kit

Let's now take a look at the other tools required for the physical acquisition of forensic evidence.

Physical acquisition tools

We've looked at the tools necessary for the collection and acquisition of physical evidence, but what tools do we need for the acquisition and extraction of digital evidence? Remember when we covered the different types of storage media back in *Chapter 3, Understanding Filesystems and Storage Media*? We saw that many of them had their own connectors as they were of various sizes.

Here's a list of some of the equipment required when acquiring data from evidence:

- A write blocker (can also be software-based)
- A card reader
- Various adapters (USB to SATA and EIDE, USB to various types of USB)
- Device cables, such as power, SATA, EIDE, HDMI, and VGA
- Networking cables, such as straight-through, crossover, and console

The following photo shows a collection of various USB adapters, all costing under $10 and available on Amazon:

Figure 4.2 – Various USB adapters

For laptop drives, I also use an SATA to USB 3.0 adapter, such as the one seen here:

Figure 4.3 – A USB 3.0 to SATA drive adapter

For connecting to routers and switches, console cables and serial to USB cables can also be included in your kit, such as the ones seen here:

Figure 4.4 – Serial to RJ-45 and Serial to USB cables

All mobile devices, including phones and tablets, can also connect to laptops and desktops via USB ports. The following image shows an On-The-Go (OTG) cable, which can connect a USB device to phones or tablets with OTG capabilities:

Figure 4.5 – USB OTG cable

In the following image, we have a USB 3.0 type C adapter:

Figure 4.6 – USB to USB type-C adapter

The guidelines for physical collection and preservation are as follows:

- Label all cables and connectors.

- Use labeled evidence collection bags as needed.

- Special stronghold bags may have to be used when storing devices with wireless and radio capabilities, preventing communication with other devices.

- Store sensitive equipment, such as hard drives and flash drives, in anti-static bags and protective casings.

- Label containers used for storage during transportation.

- Maintain the CoC forms when passing evidence from one person/handler to another (this is discussed later in this chapter).

Order of volatility

When collecting evidence, we should keep in mind the volatility of data. As mentioned earlier in this chapter, data can be easily lost or destroyed. As such, when collecting data, a well-documented and common best practice would be to collect evidence in the order of most to least volatile, if possible.

The **Scientific Working Group on Digital Evidence (SWGDE)** Capture of Live Systems document lists the order of volatility from most to least volatile and crucial as follows:

- RAM
- Running processes
- Active network connections
- System settings
- Storage media

With this in mind, it is essential to acquire the contents of the memory and the paging file first as they are the most volatile and can be easily lost, resulting in the loss of very useful information, including unencrypted passwords, user and program information, network connection information, and other types of useful data.

Chain of custody

CoC is a form that legally ensures the integrity of evidence as it is exchanged between individuals, and so it also provides a level of accountability as personal identification is required when completing the forms. This form gives an exact log and account of the transportation and the exchange between parties, from collection at the scene to a presentation in a court.

Some of the typical fields on the CoC form are as follows:

- Case number offence
- Victim and suspect names
- Date and time seized:

  a) Location where seized

  b) Item number

  c) Description of item

  d) Signatures and IDs of individuals releasing and receiving the items

- Authorization for disposal
- Witness to destruction of evidence
- Release to lawful owner

A sample CoC form can be downloaded directly from the **National Institute of Standards and Technology (NIST)**, at `https://www.nist.gov/document/ sample-chain-custody-formdocx`.

Live acquisition versus post-mortem acquisition

When investigating devices that are powered on and powered off, special consideration must be given to the volatility of data. Booting, rebooting, or shutting down a device can cause data to be written to the hard drive, resulting in data (deleted files) in unallocated space being overwritten.

Powered-on devices

Before we begin any examination of live systems, it is of high importance that all steps be thoroughly documented, particularly if the report and evidence are to be presented in court. Investigating a live system means that logs and timestamps will be generated while the system is being examined. Therefore, thorough documentation will justify the actions taken by the forensic examiner and not be viewed as evidence tampering.

When investigating a powered-on device, the following precautions should be taken:

- Move the mouse or glide your fingers across the touchpad if you suspect the device may be in a sleep state. Do not click on the buttons as this may open or close programs and processes.

- Photograph and record the screen and all visible programs, data, time, and desktop items.

- Unplug the power cord on desktops and remove the battery, if possible, on portables.

It is of the utmost importance that data stored in RAM and paging files be collected with as little modification to the data as possible. More on this will be covered in later chapters using imaging tools such as **Guymager** and **dc3dd** in Kali Linux. Other live acquisition tools such as **Computer Aided INvestigative Environment (CAINE)** and **Helix** can also be used for acquiring RAM and the paging file.

There are quite a few reasons for imaging and acquiring the RAM. As mentioned in the previous chapter, data that may have been encrypted by the user may be stored in an unencrypted state in the RAM. Logged-in users, opened programs, accessed files, and running processes can all be extracted and analyzed if the RAM and paging file are analyzed.

However, if the device is switched off or rebooted, this data and evidence can easily be lost.

For powered-on portable devices (such as laptops and mobile), the battery can be removed, if possible. Some devices, however, may not have a removable battery. In these cases, the power button should be held down for 30 to 40 seconds, which forces the device to power off.

Powered-off devices

Powered-off devices should never be turned on unless done so by the forensic investigator. Special steps must be taken to ensure that existing data is not erased and that new data is not written.

Before examining the system, you may want to consider using a pair of latex gloves, to avoid leaving additional fingerprints on the system and components. Devices can often appear as if they are off but they can be in a sleep or hibernate state. As a simple test, the mouse can be moved and monitors (if any) can be switched on to determine whether they are, in fact, in either of those states. Even if they are in an off state, one should still photograph the screen and ports.

When investigating portable and mobile devices in an already off state, it is suggested that the battery is removed (if possible) and placed in an evidence bag to ensure that there will be no way of accidentally turning on the device once unplugged. The device should also be switched to airplane mode to avoid any further connections and communications. According to the *NIST.SP.800-101r1—Guidelines on Mobile Forensics* documentation, it should be noted that removing the battery can alter the contents in the volatile memory, even when in an off state.

Write blocking

Once our evidence has been properly documented and collected, we can begin working on acquiring the actual digital evidence. I'll mention this a couple times in an effort to drive home the point, but the original evidence should only be used to create forensic copies or images, which will be discussed further on in this chapter and again in other chapters.

Working on the original evidence can, and usually will, modify the contents of the medium. For instance, booting a seized laptop into its native OS will allow data to be written to the hard drive and may also erase and modify the contents contained in RAM and the paging file.

To prevent this from happening, the use of a write blocker must be employed. Write blockers, as the name suggests, prevent data from being written to the evidence media. Write blockers can be found in both hardware and software types. If a hardware write blocker is not available, software versions are readily available as standalone features in forensic operating systems, including C.A.I.N.E, as mentioned in *Chapter 1*, *Introduction to Digital Forensics*, and also as a part of some commercial and open source tools, such as EnCase and Autopsy.

Again, it is of high importance that a write blocker is used in investigations to protect and preserve the original evidence from being modified. It is also important that you test hardware and software write blockers to ensure that they are functional and do not lead to the compromise of the evidence. The following image shows a cost-effective and efficient portable SATA and IDE adapter with write-blocking switches, used in drive acquisition and recovery:

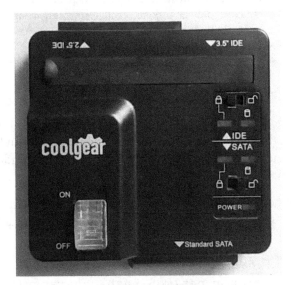

Figure 4.7 – Portable Coolgear Write Blocker

Be sure to choose a write blocker based on functionality, not just cost.

Data imaging and hashing

Imaging refers to the exact copying of data either as a file, folder, partition, or entire storage media or drive. When doing a regular copy of files and folders, not all files may be copied due to their attributes being set to the system or even hidden. To prevent files from being left out, we perform a special type of copy where every bit is copied or imaged exactly as it is on the current medium as if taking a picture or snapshot of the data.

Creating a copy of each bit of data exactly is referred to as creating a **physical image**. Performing a **bit-stream copy** ensures the integrity of the copy. To further prove this, a hash of the original evidence and the physical image are calculated and compared. A hash can be compared to a digital fingerprint of the data whereby an algorithm such as MD5, SHA1, SHA-256, or even SHA-512 can be run against the evidence data to produce a unique output. If one bit changes in the evidence and the hash is again calculated, the output string of characters drastically changes. Hashes are used to verify that the evidence was not tampered with or modified after the evidence was acquired.

> Tip:
> The original evidence should only be handled by qualified and authorized professionals and should also only be used to create forensically sound physical images. The original evidence should otherwise never be used as this compromises the integrity of the investigation.

Message Digest hash

Hash values are produced by specific algorithms and are used to verify the integrity of the evidence by proving that the data was not modified. Hash values can be thought of as digital fingerprints in that they are unique and play a major role in the identification of evidence and physical images.

One such algorithm, although older and containing vulnerabilities, is the **Message Digest (MD5)** cryptographic hashing algorithm, which produces a 128-bit hexadecimal output value.

For a working example, let's open a browser and head over to `http://passwordsgenerator.net/md5-hash-generator/`.

This site creates hashes of words and sentences as strings. For this example, I've entered the string `Digital Forensics with Kali Linux`. The MD5 value, which was automatically calculated, was displayed as **7E9506C4D9DD85220FB3DF671F09DA35**, as in the following screenshot:

Figure 4.8 – Hash calculation of a text phrase

By removing the K from the Kali in the same string, which now reads as Digital Forensics with ali Linux, the MD5 now reads **7A4C7AA85B114E91F247779D6A0B3022**, as in the following screenshot:

Figure 4.9 – Changes in hash output

As a quick comparison, we can see that just removing K from Kali yields a noticeably different result.

I encourage you to try this yourself and perhaps add a comma or period to the string to further compare hash values.

Secure Hashing Algorithm (SHA)

Another cryptographic hash algorithm commonly used in forensics and also used in the next chapter is SHA1. The **Secure Hashing Algorithm-1 (SHA1)** is more secure than MD5 as it produces a 160-bit output instead of a 128-bit output as with MD5. Due to known collision attacks against both MD5 and SHA-1, the safer and more robust option for hashing is now the **Secure Hashing Algorithm-2 (SHA-2)**.

SHA-2 is actually a group of hashes, not just one, as with SHA-1, with the most common bit-length being SHA-256, which produces a 256-bit output. The alternate bit-length algorithms of SHA-2 are SHA-224, SHA-384, and SHA-512.

The stronger the cryptographic algorithm used, the less chance of it being attacked or compromised. This means that the integrity of the evidence and physical images created remain intact, which will prove useful in forensic cases and expert testimony.

More on creating hashes will be demonstrated in *Chapter 5, Evidence Acquisition and Preservation with dc3dd and Guymager*.

Device and data acquisition guidelines and best practices

While I've tried to give you a general and summarized overview of the procedures when collecting and preserving evidence, there are several official documents that I highly recommend you read and become familiar with, as they all give good details and guidelines on the documentation of the scene, evidence collection, and data acquisition.

SWGDE Best Practices for Digital Evidence Collection, Version 1.0, published in July 2018, outlines the best practices for computer forensics in the following areas:

- Evidence collection and handling
- Documentation

The full SWGDE best practices for computer forensics document can be downloaded from `https://www.swgde.org/documents/Current%20Documents/SWGDE%20 Best%20Practices%20for%20Digital%20Evidence%20Collection`.

The *SWGDE Best Practices for Computer Forensics Acquisitions* document, version 1.0, released in April 2018, provides guidelines on evidence collection and acquisition, types of acquisitions, verification, and documentation.

This document is only 11 pages long and can be downloaded from `https://www. swgde.org/documents/Current%20Documents/SWGDE%20Best%20 Practices%20for%20Computer%20Forensic%20Acquisitions`.

In July 2019, SWGDE also released the *Best Practices for Mobile Device Evidence Collection & Preservation, Handling, and Acquisition* document, detailing guidelines on scene documentation, iOS and Android preservation processes, extraction methods, and other topics for mobile evidence handling and acquisition.

The full eighteen-page document can be downloaded at `https://www.swgde.org/documents/Current%20Documents/SWGDE%20Best%20Practices%20for%20Mobile%20Device%20Evidence%20Collection%20and%20Preservation,%20Handling,%20and%20Acquisition`.

The *NIST Guidelines on Mobile Device Forensics* documentation, although older, is also another very useful document, which applies specifically to mobile devices. Revision one of this document, released in 2014, goes into great detail about the different aspects of mobile forensics investigations. Its content includes the following:

- Mobile and cellular characteristics
- Evaluation and documentation of the scene
- Device isolation and packaging
- Device and memory acquisition
- Examination, analysis, and reporting

The full document can be downloaded from `http://nvlpubs.nist.gov/nistpubs/SpecialPublications/NIST.SP.800-101r1.pdf`

Summary

If there was only one thing that I'd like you to take away from this chapter, it would be to remember that the original evidence, particularly hard drives, storage media, and RAM images, should only be used to create forensically sound bit-stream copies. The original evidence is never to be worked on.

To recap, when a breach is reported there should be an established first responder who, as per protocol, performs the tasks of documenting and securing the scene as well as collecting and preserving the evidence. The first responder should have a toolkit with various tools and items for the acquisition of evidence and, when handing over the evidence to other parties, ensure that the chain of custody is maintained.

We also had a look at the various procedures and best practices when investigating devices that are powered on and powered off, and also discussed the importance of using a write blocker to prevent the original evidence from being tampered with and then using a hashing tool for integrity verification purposes.

The *best evidence rule* of law is a legal term that states that the original evidence must be provided unless unavailable. Forensic acquisition may involve the acquisition of volatile and temporary data, such as data stored in RAM and the paging file, which are lost once power to the device is disrupted or lost. Forensic imaging and hashing of the volatile data provides a bit-by-bit or bit-stream copy of the evidence, which can then be submitted as evidence.

Admissibility of digital evidence can be a challenge also when best practices and official procedures are not adhered to in the data collection or storage and preservation phases.

You've come this far and I know it must have been a bit of an information overload, but now we can get to the practical section of this book where we can begin our investigation using digital forensics tools in Kali Linux. We'll continue our journey by using two tools called DC3DD and Guymager to perform forensic acquisitions (imaging) of evidence drives. Let's go!

Section 3: Forensic Tools in Kali Linux

Let's get to the good stuff. In this section, we will have a detailed look at the tools for acquiring forensic images, data recovery and memory dump analysis, and ransomware detection and analysis.

This part comprises the following chapters:

- *Chapter 5, Evidence Acquisition and Preservation with dc3dd and Guymager*
- *Chapter 6, File Recovery and Data Carving with foremost, Scalpel, and bulk_extractor*
- *Chapter 7, Memory Forensics with Volatility*
- *Chapter 8, Artifact Analysis*

5
Evidence Acquisition and Preservation with dc3dd and Guymager

In the previous chapter, we learned that documentation and proper procedures are key in any investigation. These ensure the integrity of the investigation by providing proof of data authenticity and preservation of the original evidence and documentation, which can be used to achieve the same exact results if the usage of tools and methods are repeated.

In this chapter, we will demonstrate forensically sound techniques for the acquisition of data using bitstream copies, including creating data hashes, in keeping with best practices.

In this chapter, we will cover the following topics:

- Device identification in Linux
- Creating MD5 and SHA hashes
- Using dc3dd for data acquisition

- Erasing drives with dc3dd
- Using DD for data acquisition
- Using the Guymager GUI for data acquisition

The first tool we will use for acquisition is called **Department of Defense Cyber Crime Center Data Dump (dc3dd)**. dc3dd is a patch of the very popular **Data Dump (DD)** tool used for forensic acquisition and hashing.

Drive and partition recognition in Linux

Users new to Kali Linux or any Linux variations may find that the drive, partition recognition, and naming in Kali Linux are different from that of Windows devices.

A typical device in Linux can be addressed or recognized as /dev/sda, whereas drives in Windows are usually recognized as Disk 0, Disk 1, and so on:

- /dev: Refers to the path of all devices and drives, which can be read from or written to, recognized by Linux

- /sda: Refers to the **Small Computer System Interface (SCSI)**, SATA, and USB devices

The **sd** stands for **SCSI Mass-Storage Driver**, with the letter after it representing the drive number:

- **sda**: Drive 0, or the first drive recognized
- **sdb**: The second drive

While Windows recognizes partitions as primary, logical, and extended, Linux partitions are recognized as numbers after the drive letter:

- **sda1**: Partition 1 on the first disk (sda)
- **sda2**: Partition 2 on the first disk
- **sdb1**: Partition 1 on the second disk (sdb)
- **sdb2**: Partition 2 on the second disk

Device identification using the fdisk command

For the exercises in this chapter, I'll be using an old 2 GB flash drive for the acquisition process using dc3dd. At this point, we should consider attaching our media to a write blocker before examining it. It's also important to remember to continue using your write blocker when acquiring and creating forensic images of evidence and drives, in order to not write data to the drives or modify the original evidence files.

To list your devices and ensure that you are aware of them before performing any acquisition operations, the fdisk -l command should be run before any other. The sudo fdisk -l command may have to be used if the previous one does not work. The sudo command allows the user to run the command as root, which is similar to the **Run as Administrator** feature in Windows.

The fdisk-l command has been executed in the following screenshot. Then, the 2 GB flash drive is attached. There is one hard disk listed as sda. The primary partition is listed as sda1, with the Extended and Linux swap partitions listed as sda2 and sda5, respectively:

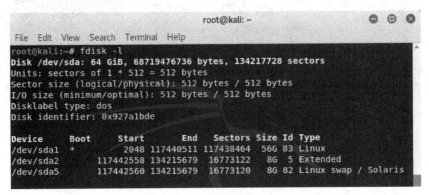

Figure 5.1 – Using the fdisk command to identify devices and partitions in Kali

After attaching the 2 GB flash drive for acquisition, the fdisk -l command was run yet again and can be seen in the following screenshot with these details:

- **Disk**: sdb
- **Size**: 1.9 GB
- **Sector size**: 512 bytes

- **Filesystem:** FAT32

```
root@kali:~# fdisk -l
Disk /dev/sda: 64 GiB, 68719476736 bytes, 134217728 sectors
Units: sectors of 1 * 512 = 512 bytes
Sector size (logical/physical): 512 bytes / 512 bytes
I/O size (minimum/optimal): 512 bytes / 512 bytes
Disklabel type: dos
Disk identifier: 0x927a1bde

Device     Boot      Start        End   Sectors Size Id Type
/dev/sda1  *          2048  117440511 117438464  56G 83 Linux
/dev/sda2        117442558  134215679  16773122   8G  5 Extended
/dev/sda5        117442560  134215679  16773120   8G 82 Linux swap / Solaris


Disk /dev/sdb: 1.9 GiB, 2003795968 bytes, 3913664 sectors
Units: sectors of 1 * 512 = 512 bytes
Sector size (logical/physical): 512 bytes / 512 bytes
I/O size (minimum/optimal): 512 bytes / 512 bytes
Disklabel type: dos
Disk identifier: 0x00e9f1d3

Device     Boot Start       End Sectors  Size Id Type
/dev/sdb1  *       32   3901439 3901408  1.9G  b W95 FAT32
root@kali:~#
```

Figure 5.2 – Full output of the fdisk command in Kali Linux

As seen in the preceding screenshots (and also explained earlier in this chapter), Kali Linux recognizes two devices:

- sda: Primary hard disk with three partitions
- sdb: Flash drive to be forensically acquired or imaged

Now that we've distinguished and become certain of which drive is to be imaged (sdb), we can begin the forensic imaging using dc3dd.

> **Important note**
> Although I have used an older 2 GB flash drive to demonstrate the usage of dc3dd, you can use any drive (portable or otherwise) to practice using the tools in this chapter. Be sure to use the fdisk -l command to identify your drives and partitions.

Maintaining evidence integrity

In order to provide proof that the evidence was not tampered with, a hash of the evidence should be provided before and during, or after, an acquisition.

In Kali Linux, we can use the md5sum command, followed by the path of the device, to create an MD5 hash of the evidence/input file – for example, md5sum /dev/sdx.

You may also try the command with superuser privileges by typing in sudo md5sum / dev/sdx.

For this example, the 2 GB flash drive that I'll be using (named test_usb) is recognized as sdb and the command I will be using is shown in the following screenshot:

```
root@kali:~# md5sum /dev/sdb
9f03801715e000c68cc319251301c7d3   /dev/sdb
```

Figure 5.3 – Creating an MD5 hash using md5sum

In the previous example, the output of the md5sum command of the 2 GB flash drive is displayed as 9f038....1c7d3/dev/sdb. When performing the acquisition or forensic imaging of the drive using dc3dd, we should also have that exact result when hashing the created image file output to ensure that both the original evidence and the copy are exactly the same, thereby maintaining the integrity of the evidence.

I've also created an SHA-1 hash (which will be used for comparative purposes) using the following syntax:

```
root@kali:~# sha1sum /dev/sdb
0d5021a1abf889e4663b145f701b6e48e69e374a   /dev/sdb
```

Figure 5.4 – Creating an SHA1 hash using sha1sum

Now that we can identify our devices and create MD5 and SHA-1 hashes in Kali Linux, let's move on to using dc3dd in the next section.

Using dc3dd in Kali Linux

Before we get started using dc3dd, I need to again draw your attention to one of the features of DD: being able to wipe data, partitions, and drives. Hence, you may find that DD is sometimes also fondly referred to as the **Data Destroyer**. Be sure to always first identify your devices, partitions, input and output files, and parameters when using DD and dc3dd.

These are the features of DD:

- Bitstream (raw) disk acquisition and cloning

- Copying disk partitions

- Copying folders and files

- Hard disk drive error checking

- Forensic wiping of all data on hard disk drives

dc3dd was developed by the Department of Defense Cyber Crime Center and is updated whenever DD updates. dc3dd offers the best of DD with more features, including the following:

- On-the-fly hashing using more algorithm choices (MD5, SHA-1, SHA-256, and SHA-512)

- Hash verification

- A meter to monitor progress and acquisition time

- Writing of errors to a file

- Splitting of output files (mix split and unsplit outputs)

- Verification of files

- Wiping of output files (pattern wiping)

> **Important note**
>
> Although we'll only be looking at DD and dc3dd there is also another tool called dcfldd, which can be installed on Linux-based systems.
>
> dc3dd is a patch of DD and is regularly updated whenever there are updates to DD. dc3dd offers more features than DD, which is why we'll be using it.

Unlike previous versions of Kali Linux, dc3dd must now be installed manually in Kali Linux 2019.3. First, we'll update our version of Kali Linux by using the `apt-get update` command:

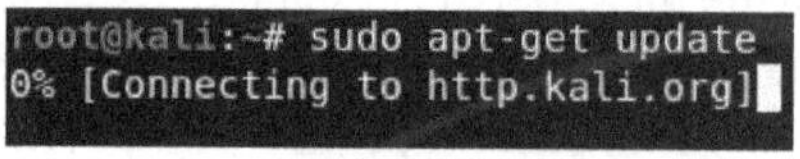

Figure 5.5 – Updating Kali Linux

Once Kali Linux updates, you can manually install dc3dd by typing in the sudo apt-get install dc3dd command. It is recommended to install dc3dd on your flash drive or SD card before performing any live acquisitions and not do so at the time of acquisition, which may tamper with the investigation:

```
root@kali:~# sudo apt-get install dc3dd
Reading package lists... Done
Building dependency tree
Reading state information... Done
The following NEW packages will be installed:
  dc3dd
0 upgraded, 1 newly installed, 0 to remove and 1068 not upgraded.
Need to get 119 kB of archives.
After this operation, 486 kB of additional disk space will be used.
Get:1 http://kali.download/kali kali-rolling/main amd64 dc3dd amd64 7.2.646-3 [119 kB]
Fetched 119 kB in 2s (77.8 kB/s)
Selecting previously unselected package dc3dd.
(Reading database ... 353343 files and directories currently installed.)
Preparing to unpack .../dc3dd_7.2.646-3_amd64.deb ...
Unpacking dc3dd (7.2.646-3) ...
Setting up dc3dd (7.2.646-3) ...
Processing triggers for man-db (2.8.6.1-1) ...
root@kali:~#
```

Figure 5.6 – Installing dc3dd in Kali Linux

dc3dd is a CLI tool and can be easily run in Kali Linux by first opening a Terminal and typing in dc3dd. To start with, I recommend using the dc3dd --help command, which lists the available parameters used with dc3dd:

```
root@kali:~#
root@kali:~# dc3dd --help
------
usage:
------


        dc3dd [OPTION 1] [OPTION 2] ... [OPTION N]

               *or*

        dc3dd [HELP OPTION]

        where each OPTION is selected from the basic or advanced
        options listed below, or HELP OPTION is selected from the
        help options listed below.


--------------
basic options:
--------------

        if=DEVICE or FILE    Read input from a device or a file (see note #1
                             below for how to read from standard input). This
                             option can only be used once and cannot be
                             combined with ifs=, pat=, or tpat=.
        ifs=BASE.FMT         Read input from a set of files with base name
                             BASE and sequential file name extensions
                             conforming to the format specifier FMT (see note
                             #4 below for how to specify FMT). This option
                             can only be used once and cannot be combined with
                             if=, pat=, or tpat=.
        of=FILE or DEVICE    Write output to a file or device (see note #2
                             below for how to write to standard output). This
                             option can be used more than once (see note #3
                             below for how to generate multiple outputs).
        hof=FILE or DEVICE   Write output to a file or device, hash the
                             output bytes, and verify by comparing the output
                             hash(es) to the input hash(es). This option can
                             be used more than once (see note #3 below for
                             how to generate multiple outputs).
```

Figure 5.7 – Viewing the dc3dd help options

> **Important note**
> When copying an image to a drive, the destination drive size should be of equal size or larger than the image file.

As seen in the preceding screenshot, when using the `dc3dd --help` command, the typical usage looks as follows:

```
dc3dd [option 1] [option 2] ... [option n]
```

In our previous example, I've used the following options:

```
root@kali:~# dc3dd if=/dev/sdb hash=md5 log=dc3ddusb of=test_usb.dd
```

Figure 5.8 – Using dc3dd to create an MD5 hash and bit-stream copy of SDB

The code terms used here are:

- `if`: Specifies the input file, which is the device we will be imaging.

- `hash`: Specifies the type of hash algorithm we will be using for integrity verification. In this case, I have used the older MD5 hash.

- `log`: Specifies the name of the log file that logs the details of the device and the acquisition, including errors.

- `of`: Specifies the output filename of the forensic image created by dc3dd. Although a `.dd` image file type was specified in this example, other formats are also recognized by dc3dd, including `.img`, as seen in a later example.

The device size (in sector and bytes) should be noted and later compared to the **output results for device** field.

The last line also displays the progress and status of the acquisition process, showing the amount of data copied, the elapsed time in seconds, and the speed of the imaging process in Mbps:

```
root@kali:~# dc3dd if=/dev/sdb hash=md5 log=dc3ddusb of=test_usb.dd

dc3dd 7.2.646 started at 2019-11-03 06:23:25 -0400
compiled options:
command line: dc3dd if=/dev/sdb hash=md5 log=dc3ddusb of=test_usb.dd
device size: 3913664 sectors (probed),    2,003,795,968 bytes
sector size: 512 bytes (probed)
 1590591488 bytes ( 1.5 G ) copied ( 79% ),    97 s, 16 M/s
```

Figure 5.9 – Output of the dc3dd command

> **Important note**
>
> The larger the drive or file to be acquired, the lengthier the time taken to do so. Might I suggest you get yourself a cup of coffee or other refreshing beverage, or even have a look at some other wonderful titles available from Packt Publishing at https://www.packtpub.com/.

Once the acquisition process has been completed, the input and output results are displayed as follows:

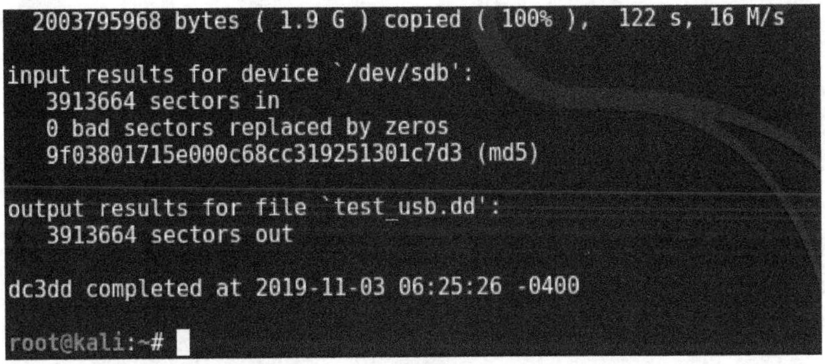

```
 2003795968 bytes ( 1.9 G ) copied ( 100% ),   122 s, 16 M/s

input results for device `/dev/sdb':
   3913664 sectors in
   0 bad sectors replaced by zeros
   9f03801715e000c68cc319251301c7d3 (md5)

output results for file `test_usb.dd':
   3913664 sectors out

dc3dd completed at 2019-11-03 06:25:26 -0400

root@kali:~#
```

Figure 5.10 – Output of the dc3dd command displaying the MD5 hash

Analyzing the results, we can see that the same amount of sectors (3913664) have been imaged, with no bad sectors being replaced by zeros. We can also see that the exact MD5 hash was created for the image, assuring us that an exact copy was created without modification.

In the Terminal, we can also use the ls command to list the directory contents to ensure the dc3dd output file (test_usb.dd) and log (dc3ddusb) have been created:

```
root@kali:~# ls
cfsi       desktop    Documents  Images  Pictures  Templates    Videos
dc3ddusb   Desktop    Downloads  Music   Public    test_usb.dd
root@kali:~#
```

Figure 5.11 – Output of the ls command

To access our forensic image and log file, we can go to our /home directory by clicking on places (top-left corner) and then **Home**.

Within my **Home** folder, the first file, 2GBdcedd.dd, is the output image created by dc3dd using the of=test_usb.dd command. The last file, dc3ddusb, is the log file, created when we used the log=dc3ddusb command:

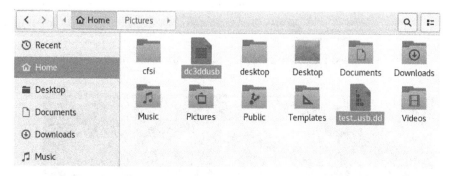

Figure 5.12 – Screenshot of the output file location

It's important to keep this log file to have a record of the acquisition process and its results, which are displayed on-screen upon completion:

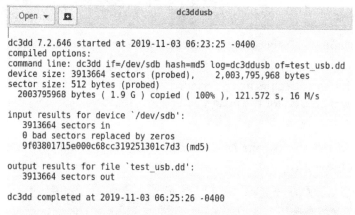

Figure 5.13 – Screenshot of the log file generated by dc3dd

In future chapters, we will be analyzing acquired forensic images using various tools. However, the image can also be copied or directly cloned to another device if the investigator so wishes.

As an example, we could clone the forensic image acquired previously (test_usb.dd) onto a new drive recognized as sdc. The command used to perform this task is as follows:

```
dc3dd if=test_usb.dd of=/dev/sdc log=drivecopy.log
```

In keeping with proper and formal case management, the names of the image file and log file should be unique to the investigator and the investigation for easy reference, as you may find yourself with multiple images and log files later on. The location of the images should also be stored on forensically sound or sanitized drives and labeled accordingly.

File-splitting using dc3dd

Depending on the size of the evidence, manageability and portability can become an issue. dc3dd has the ability to split forensically acquired images into multiple parts.

This is accomplished using the ofsz and ofs options:

- ofsz specifies the size of each output file part.
- ofs specifies the output files with numerical file extensions, typically .000, .001, .002, and so on.

> **Tip**
> Always ensure that you have specified enough zeros for the file extension. Logically, .000 allows for more parts than .00.

For this example, I've used the same 2 GB flash drive as before. However, for demonstrative purposes, you'll notice two changes.

Instead of using the MD5 hash, I've specified that SHA-1 be used and the output file type will be .img instead of the previously used .dd.

In this instance, the imaged 2 GB flash size will instead be split into multiple parts (four in total) of 500 MB each using ofsz=500M with the parts named as 2GBdc3dd2.img.000, 2GBdc3dd2.img.001, 2GBdc3dd2.img.002, and 2GBdc3dd2.img.003.

The command used to achieve this is as follows:

```
dc3dd if=/dev/sdb       hash=sha1    log=dd_split_usb  ofsz=500M
ofs=split_test_usb.img.000
```

In the following screenshot, we can see the command as well as the output and status of the process:

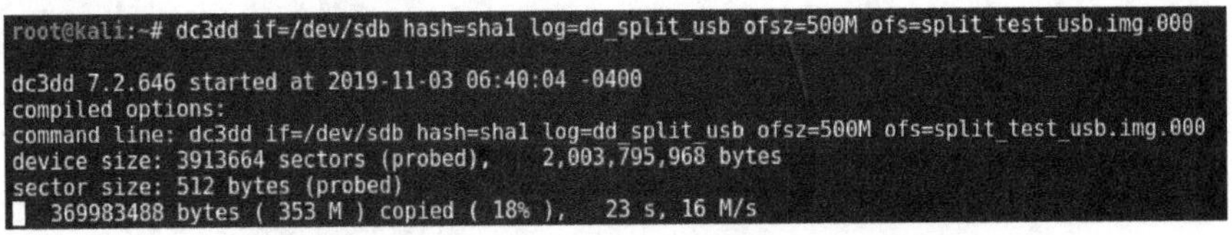

Figure 5.14 – The command used to split the acquired file size

Once completed, the input results for the device show the SHA-1 hash output and also display the first part of the split image files:

```
2003795968 bytes ( 1.9 G ) copied ( 100% ),  123 s, 15 M/s

input results for device `/dev/sdb':
   3913664 sectors in
   0 bad sectors replaced by zeros
   0d5021a1abf889e4663b145f701b6e48e69e374a (sha1)

output results for files `split_test_usb.img.000':
   3913664 sectors out

dc3dd completed at 2019-11-03 06:42:07 -0400

root@kali:~#
```

Figure 5.15 – The output of the sha1sum option using dc3dd

Using the `ls` command once more, we can see that the extensions of each of the four split output files are all in numerical format, from `.000` to `.003`:

```
root@kali:~# ls
cfsi            Desktop     Images     Public                     split_test_usb.img.002   Videos
dd_split_usb    Documents   Music      split_test_usb.img.000     split_test_usb.img.003
desktop         Downloads   Pictures   split_test_usb.img.001     Templates
root@kali:~#
```

Figure 5.16 – The output of the ls command showing created acquisition images

All split parts of the image file can be found in the **Home** folder along with the log file:

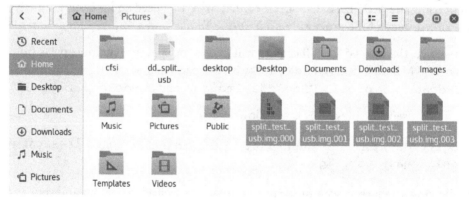

Figure 5.17 – Screenshot of the folder location containing the created acquisition images

Now that we have successfully created bitstream copies of the evidence, let's look at verifying the integrity of the forensic acquisitions using hash verification.

Hash verification

Double-clicking on the `.info` file in the **Image directory** location allows us to inspect a variety of details about the acquisition process from start to completion, including the hashed outputs.

This `.info` file contains much more data than the log file produced by dc3dd, including the case management details:

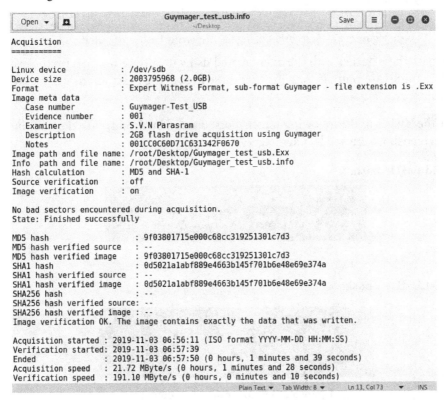

Figure 5.18 – Screenshot of the log file displaying hash values

Let's have a closer look at the hash details within the `.info` file.

We can see that the MD5 and SHA-1 hashes have been created and verified and, as stated in the last line of the following screenshot, **Image verification OK. The image contains exactly the data that was written**:

```
MD5 hash                   : 9f03801715e000c68cc319251301c7d3
MD5 hash verified source   : --
MD5 hash verified image    : 9f03801715e000c68cc319251301c7d3
SHA1 hash                  : 0d5021a1abf889e4663b145f701b6e48e69e374a
SHA1 hash verified source  : --
SHA1 hash verified image   : 0d5021a1abf889e4663b145f701b6e48e69e374a
SHA256 hash                : --
SHA256 hash verified source: --
SHA256 hash verified image : --
Image verification OK. The image contains exactly the data that was written.
```

Figure 5.19 – Screenshot of log file displaying hash verification

If we compare these hashes with the ones created using dc3dd we would have the exact same MD5 and SHA-1 outputs, proving that these images are exact forensic copies of the original evidence.

Compare the hashes in the following screenshots, created by dc3dd, with the ones in the previous screenshots, created by Guymager:

- **dc3dd MD5 hash**:

```
9f03801715e000c68cc319251301c7d3 (md5)

output results for file `test_usb.dd':
   3913664 sectors out
```

Figure 5.20 – MD5 calculation output

- **dc3dd SHA-1 hash**:

```
0d5021a1abf889e4663b145f701b6e48e69e374a (sha1)

output results for files `split_test_usb.img.000':
   3913664 sectors out

dc3dd completed at 2019-11-03 06:42:07 -0400
```

Figure 5.21 – SHA-1 calculation output

If we look at the preceding hashes and compare them with the ones created by Guymager in the .info file, we can see that the SHA-1 hash contains more characters than the MD5 hash, as the MD5 (although faster) has a 128-bit output whereas the SHA-1 has a 160-bit output. I'd highly recommend using SHA-1 or SHA256 instead of MD5 as MD5 is outdated and no longer used as it was proven to be vulnerable to hash collision attacks, where different sets of hashed data can produce the same output, rendering it invalid. More on MD5 collisions can be found in this document, written by the researchers responsible for discovering the vulnerability, at http://merlot.usc.edu/csac-f06/papers/Wang05a.pdf.

Verifying hashes of split image files

To verify the hash of the split files, the following command can be used:

```
cat split_test_usb.img.*  |  sha1sum
```

In the following screenshot, we can see that a lengthy SHA-1 hash was created using the preceding command:

```
root@kali:~# cat split_test_usb.img.*  |  sha1sum
0d5021a1abf889e4663b145f701b6e48e69e374a   -
root@kali:~#
```

Figure 5.22 – SHA1sum split-file verification output

This also matches the sha1sum output of the 2 GB flash drive itself, displayed by using the following command:

```
sha1sum /dev/sdb
```

Using this command creates the following output:

```
root@kali:~# sha1sum /dev/sdb
0d5021a1abf889e4663b145f701b6e48e69e374a   /dev/sdb
root@kali:~#
```

Figure 5.23 – SHA1sum output

With our verification processes now complete, we'll look at using dc3dd to forensically wipe drives.

Erasing a drive using dc3dd

We've seen the power of dc3dd as a very impressive forensic acquisition tool, but I'd also like to go one step further and introduce you to its capabilities as a data wiping tool.

dc3dd can wipe data and erase drives by overwriting data in three ways:

- Overwriting and filling the data and drives with zeroes. The command used is `dc3dd wipe=/dev/sdb`:

```
root@kali:~# dc3dd wipe=/dev/sdb

dc3dd 7.2.646 started at 2019-10-26 11:39:42 -0400
compiled options:
command line: dc3dd wipe=/dev/sdb
device size: 3913664 sectors (probed),    2,003,795,968 bytes
sector size: 512 bytes (probed)
  2003795968 bytes ( 1.9 G ) copied ( 100% ),   53 s, 36 M/s

input results for pattern `00':
   3913664 sectors in

output results for device `/dev/sdb':
   3913664 sectors out

dc3dd completed at 2019-10-26 11:40:34 -0400
```

Figure 5.24 – dc3dd wipe command output

- Overwriting and filling the data and drives using a hexadecimal pattern using the `pat` option. The command used is `dc3dd wipe=/dev/sdb pat=000111`:

```
root@kali:~# dc3dd wipe=/dev/sdb pat=000111

dc3dd 7.2.646 started at 2019-10-26 11:42:30 -0400
compiled options:
command line: dc3dd wipe=/dev/sdb pat=000111
device size: 3913664 sectors (probed),    2,003,795,968 bytes
sector size: 512 bytes (probed)
  2003795968 bytes ( 1.9 G ) copied ( 100% ),   165 s, 12 M/s

input results for pattern `000111':
   3913664 sectors in

output results for device `/dev/sdb':
   3913664 sectors out

dc3dd completed at 2019-10-26 11:45:16 -0400
```

Figure 5.25 – Using dc3dd to wipe a drive using a hexadecimal pattern

- Overwriting and filling the data and drives using a text pattern using the `tpat` option. The command used is `dc3dd wipe=/dev/sdb tpat=cfsi`:

```
root@kali:~# dc3dd wipe=/dev/sdb tpat=cfsi

dc3dd 7.2.646 started at 2019-10-26 11:46:20 -0400
compiled options:
command line: dc3dd wipe=/dev/sdb tpat=cfsi
device size: 3913664 sectors (probed),    2,003,795,968 bytes
sector size: 512 bytes (probed)
  2003795968 bytes ( 1.9 G ) copied ( 100% ),   238 s, 8 M/s

input results for pattern `cfsi':
   3913664 sectors in

output results for device `/dev/sdb':
   3913664 sectors out

dc3dd completed at 2019-10-26 11:50:19 -0400
```

Figure 5.26 – Using dc3dd to wipe a drive using a text pattern

All three of the preceding methods efficiently erase drives. Let's also look at using the DD command, which is pre-installed in Kali Linux, to make forensic bitstream copies of evidence.

Image acquisition using DD

Should you also wish to use the DD tool, the commands and usage are very much the same.

You may want to first ensure that you can access the DD tool by running `dd --help`. If the `dd` command cannot be found, update Kali Linux by running the `apt-get update` command and then running the `dd --help` command again:

```
root@kali:~# dd --help
Usage: dd [OPERAND]...
  or:  dd OPTION
Copy a file, converting and formatting according to the operands.

  bs=BYTES        read and write up to BYTES bytes at a time (default: 512);
                  overrides ibs and obs
  cbs=BYTES       convert BYTES bytes at a time
  conv=CONVS      convert the file as per the comma separated symbol list
  count=N         copy only N input blocks
  ibs=BYTES       read up to BYTES bytes at a time (default: 512)
  if=FILE         read from FILE instead of stdin
  iflag=FLAGS     read as per the comma separated symbol list
  obs=BYTES       write BYTES bytes at a time (default: 512)
  of=FILE         write to FILE instead of stdout
  oflag=FLAGS     write as per the comma separated symbol list
  seek=N          skip N obs-sized blocks at start of output
  skip=N          skip N ibs-sized blocks at start of input
  status=LEVEL    The LEVEL of information to print to stderr;
                  'none' suppresses everything but error messages,
                  'noxfer' suppresses the final transfer statistics,
                  'progress' shows periodic transfer statistics

N and BYTES may be followed by the following multiplicative suffixes:
c =1, w =2, b =512, kB =1000, K =1024, MB =1000*1000, M =1024*1024, xM =M,
GB =1000*1000*1000, G =1024*1024*1024, and so on for T, P, E, Z, Y.

Each CONV symbol may be:

  ascii      from EBCDIC to ASCII
  ebcdic     from ASCII to EBCDIC
  ibm        from ASCII to alternate EBCDIC
  block      pad newline-terminated records with spaces to cbs-size
  unblock    replace trailing spaces in cbs-size records with newline
  lcase      change upper case to lower case
  ucase      change lower case to upper case
  sparse     try to seek rather than write the output for NUL input blocks
  swab       swap every pair of input bytes
```

Figure 5.27 – Output of the dd help command

Attach the storage you wish to acquire. For this example, I'll be using an older 2 GB Sony Pro Duo card that I'd like to image and analyze.

Run the `fdisk -l` command in the Terminal to view the device details. In the following screenshot, we can see that the device is recognized as `/dev/sdb` and is 1.89 GB with a default sector size of 512 bytes:

```
Disk /dev/sdb: 1.89 GiB, 2011168768 bytes, 3928064 sectors
Disk model: Multi-Card
Units: sectors of 1 * 512 = 512 bytes
Sector size (logical/physical): 512 bytes / 512 bytes
I/O size (minimum/optimal): 512 bytes / 512 bytes
Disklabel type: dos
Disk identifier: 0x00000000

Device     Boot Start      End Sectors  Size Id Type
/dev/sdb1   *        1663 3923967 3922305  1.9G  6 FAT16
root@kali:~#
```

Figure 5.28 – Output of the fdisk -l command

I'll also manually create hashes to verify the integrity of the created images by comparing the hashes of the images with these.

To create the MD5 hash, run the `md5sum /dev/sbd` command:

```
root@kali:~# md5sum /dev/sdb
98b61a6bbde0237c421c84ee5dd9c453   /dev/sdb
root@kali:~#
```

Figure 5.29 – Output of the md5sum command

To create the SHA-1 hash, run the `sha1sum /dev/sbd` command:

```
root@kali:~# sha1sum /dev/sdb
f685baa1fa5f4ce306e776b1b5a874f2c8279cd9   /dev/sdb
root@kali:~#
```

Figure 5.30 – Output of the sha1sum command

To perform image acquisition, I've used this command:

```
dd if=/dev/sdb of=sdb_image.img bs=65536 conv=noerror,sync
```

The following command output shows that the input and output records match, along with the speed of the acquisition at 54.6 MB/s:

```
root@kali:~# dd if=/dev/sdb of=produo_image.dd bs=512 conv=noerror,sync
3928064+0 records in
3928064+0 records out
2011168768 bytes (2.0 GB, 1.9 GiB) copied, 36.8333 s, 54.6 MB/s
root@kali:~#
```

Figure 5.31 – Output showing a record in and record out comparison

Let's do a breakdown of the individual options in the preceding command:

- `if`: Input file (`sdb` device).
- `of`: Output file (name of the forensic image).
- `bs`: Block size (default size is 512).
- `conv=noerror, sync`: Continue the imaging even if there are errors (`noerror`) and if there are errors, null fill the blocks (`sync`).

In the preceding command, the output file extension, `.dd`, was specified. However, you can use another format, such as `.iso`, but specifying such in the output file (`of`) option:

```
root@kali:~#
root@kali:~# dd if=/dev/sdb of=produo_image.iso bs=512 conv=noerror,sync
3928064+0 records in
3928064+0 records out
2011168768 bytes (2.0 GB, 1.9 GiB) copied, 40.0282 s, 50.2 MB/s
root@kali:~#
```

Figure 5.32 – Output showing a record in and record out comparison using the .iso extension

We can view the created files in two ways. The first option is to click on **Places** and then click on **Home**. We can see two items listed as the `produo_image.dd` and `produo_image.iso` files that were created by DD:

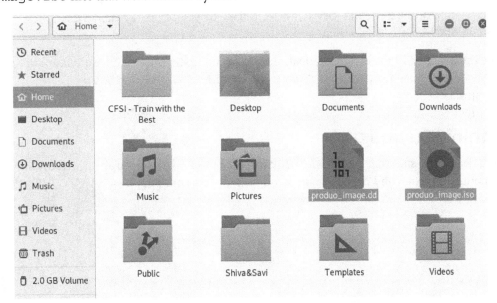

Figure 5.33 – Screenshot of the .iso file location

The second option is to simply use the `ls` command, where we can also see the two images:

```
root@kali:~# ls
'CFSI - Train with the Best'  Downloads   produo_image.dd    'Shiva&Savi'
 Desktop                      Music       produo_image.iso    Templates
 Documents                    Pictures    Public              Videos
root@kali:~# 
```

Figure 5.34 – Output of the ls command

Now that we've used dc3dd to create forensic images, used `md5sum` and `sha1sum` to verify our images, and used DD to wipe drives, let's now have a look at Guymager, which also performs image acquisition via a simple GUI.

Image acquisition using Guymager

Guymager is another standalone acquisition tool that can be used for creating forensic images and performing disk cloning. Developed by Guy Voncken, Guymager is completely open source, has many of the same features of dc3dd, and is also only available for Linux-based hosts. While some investigators may prefer CLI tools, Guymager is a GUI tool and is for beginners, so it may be preferable.

For this acquisition, I'll use the very same 2-GB flash drive used in the dc3dd examples, at the end of which we can compare results.

As previously done in the dc3dd acquisition, we should first ensure that we are familiar with the devices attached to our machine, using the `fdisk -l` or `sudo fdisk -l` command.

Running Guymager

Guymager can be started by using the menu in Kali Linux. Click on **Applications** on the side menu, then click on **Forensics** and scroll down to **Guymager**:

Figure 5.35 – Screenshot to the Forensic Tool menu in Kali Linux

Guymager can also be started using the Terminal by typing in `guymager`. You may also try the `sudo guymager` command. Once started, the default locations of the log file and configuration (`cfg`) files can be changed if required:

```
File  Edit  View  Search  Terminal  Help
root@kali:~# guymager

Using default log file name /var/log/guymager.log
Using default cfg file name /etc/guymager/guymager.cfg
```

Figure 5.36 – Starting Guymager in Kali using the CLI

The Guymager application runs and then displays the existing drives recognized in Kali Linux. As in the following screenshot, the details of the 2 GB flash drive being used are shown, including the following:

- **Linux device**: Recognized as /dev/sdb
- **Model**: USB_Flash_Memory
- **State**: Shown as **Idle** as the image acquisition has not yet begun

- **Size:** 2.0GB

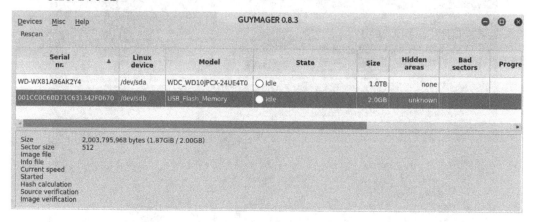

Figure 5.37 – Guymager interface displaying detected drives

Should your device not be listed in Guymager, or should you need to add an additional device, click the **Rescan** button at the top-left corner of the application.

Acquiring evidence with Guymager

To begin the acquisition process, right-click on the evidence drive (/dev/sdb in this example) and select **Acquire image**. Note that the **Clone device** option is also available should you wish to clone the evidence drive to another. Again, as previously mentioned, when cloning a device, the capacity of the destination device must be equal to or exceed that of the source (original) evidence drive:

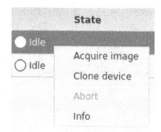

Figure 5.38 – Image acquisition shortcuts

Before the actual acquisition process starts, the investigator is prompted to enter details about themselves and the evidence under the following three sections:

File format:

- **File extensions:** .dd, .xxx, and .Exx.
- **Split size:** Allows the investigator to choose the size of multiple image parts.

- **Case management information**: Case number, evidence number, examiner name, description, and notes:

File format

- Linux dd raw image (file extension .dd or .xxx)
- ● Expert Witness Format, sub-format Guymager (file extension .Exx) | Split image files
  Split size 2047   MiB ▲▼

Case number

Evidence number

Examiner

Description

Notes   001CC0C60D71C631342F0670

Figure 5.39 – Guymager image acquisition fields

Destination:

- **Image directory**: The location of the created image file and log (info file)

- **Image filename**: The name of the image file

- **Info filename**: The name of the log file containing acquisition details:

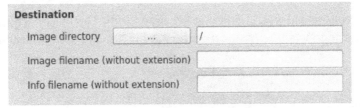

Destination

Image directory   [...]   /

Image filename (without extension)

Info filename (without extension)

Figure 5.40 – Guymager image destination fields

- **Hash calculation / verification**: Multiple hashing algorithms can be selected and calculated, allowing the investigator to choose from MD5, SHA-1, and SHA256.

- **Re-read source after acquisition for verification**: This verifies the source.

- **Verify image after acquisition**: This verifies that the image has been successfully created and does not contain any errors that may have occurred during acquisition.

> **Important note**
>
> Guymager also adds the convenience of having a **Duplicate image...** button to create duplicate copies without having to repeat the data entry process.

For new users, you may want to specify the directory where the image file will be saved. In the destination section, click on the **Image directory** button and choose your location. You should choose a drive or directory that is unique to the case as the location for both the image and the log/info file:

Figure 5.41 – Guymager image destination directory selection screen

The following screenshot shows the data that I've used for the Guymager acquisition, having chosen the desktop as the **Image directory** and MD5 and SHA-1 hashing algorithms:

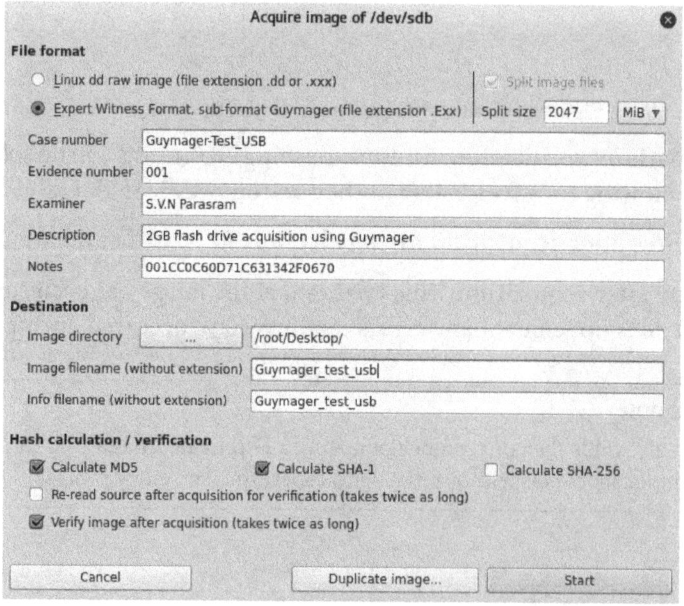

Figure 5.42 – Snippet of the completed Guymager image acquisition fields

Once the **Start** button is clicked, you will notice that the **State** changes from **Idle** to **Running**. The **Progress** field also now displays a progress bar:

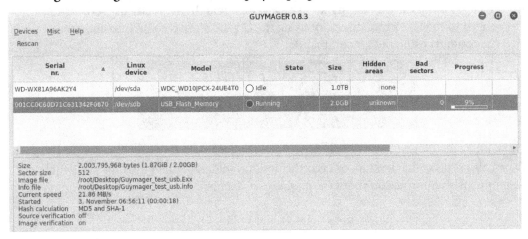

Serial nr.	▲	Linux device	Model		State	Size	Hidden areas	Bad sectors	Progress
WD-WX81A96AK2Y4		/dev/sda	WDC_WD10JPCX-24UE4T0	○	Idle	1.0TB	none		
001CC0C60D71C631342F0670		/dev/sdb	USB_Flash_Memory	◑	Running	2.0GB	unknown	0	9%

Size	2,003,795,968 bytes (1.87GiB / 2.00GB)
Sector size	512
Image file	/root/Desktop/Guymager_test_usb.Exx
Info file	/root/Desktop/Guymager_test_usb.info
Current speed	21.86 MB/s
Started	3. November 06:56:11 (00:00:18)
Hash calculation	MD5 and SHA-1
Source verification	off
Image verification	on

Figure 5.43 – Snippet of the acquisition process and status in Guymager

Taking a closer look at the details in the lower-left corner of the screen, we see the size, image, info file paths, names and extensions, current speed, and chosen hash calculations. We also see that **Image verification** is turned on:

Size	2,003,795,968 bytes (1.87GiB / 2.00GB)
Sector size	512
Image file	/root/Desktop/Guymager_test_usb.Exx
Info file	/root/Desktop/Guymager_test_usb.info
Current speed	21.94 MB/s
Started	3. November 06:56:11 (00:00:40)
Hash calculation	MD5 and SHA-1
Source verification	off
Image verification	on

Figure 5.44 – Snippet of the image acquisition details

Once the acquisition process is completed, the color of the **State** button changes from blue to green, indicating that the acquisition process is finished. It also displays **Finished - Verified & ok** if verification options were selected in the Hash verification / calculation area. The progress bar also displays **100%**:

Serial nr.	▲	Linux device	Model		State	Size	Hidden areas	Bad sectors	Progress
001CC0C60D71C631342F0670		/dev/sdb	USB_Flash_Memory	●	Finished - Verified & ok	2.0GB	unknown	0	100%
VB2aae48a1-1ad25067		/dev/sda	VBOX_HARDDISK	○	Idle	34.4GB	unknown		

Figure 5.45 – Snippet of the acquisition process and status in Guymager

Our output file and info file can be found on the desktop as this was specified in the **Acquire images** section earlier. If you have selected a different directory, change to the new directory, using the `cd` command, in a new Terminal. In the following screenshot, I've changed to the `Desktop` directory using the `cd Desktop` command and then listed the contents using the `ls` command:

```
root@kali:~#
root@kali:~# cd Desktop
root@kali:~/Desktop# ls
CFSI  Guymager_test_usb.E01  Guymager_test_usb.info
root@kali:~/Desktop#
root@kali:~/Desktop#
```

Figure 5.46 – Viewing the acquired images using the ls command

We can also browse the desktop, or even the desktop folder, to open the info file, which presents us with information about the acquisition details:

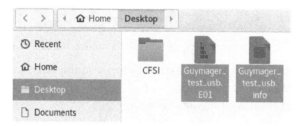

Figure 5.47 – Snippet of the location of the image file

Using Guymager may be much simpler for those that are unfamiliar with DD or dc3dd, also because Guymager comes pre-installed on Kali Linux. Let's now move on to some tools that can be used for live memory acquisition.

Windows memory acquisition

There are several tools for Windows systems that you may wish to take advantage of to be able to capture the memory and paging file on a Windows device. The forensic images can then be opened on your Kali Linux machine for analysis with Volatility, as we'll delve into in a later chapter.

FTK Imager

Forensic Toolkit (FTK) Imager from AccessData is a free tool for the live acquisition of memory, the paging file, and drive images. To download FTK Imager, visit their website at `https://accessdata.com/product-download/ftk-imager-version-4-2-1` and click on the **Download Now** button, which then carries you to their registration page.

Once all the fields are completed, a download link will be sent to the email address which you specified. The file size is approximately 53 MB and, at the time of writing, I've downloaded version 4.2.1 but any version between 4.0 and 4.2.1 will do for this exercise.

> **Important note**
> Remember that this tool is to be installed on a Windows machine and not on Kali Linux.

Once downloaded and installed, open the program:

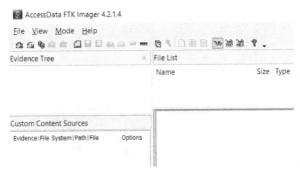

Figure 5.48 – FTK imager interface

To view the options for imaging and acquisition, click on **File**:

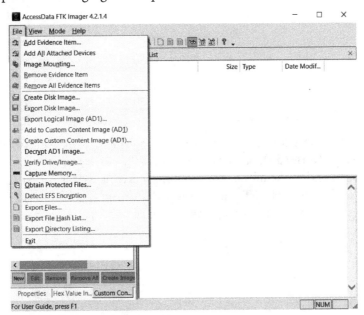

Figure 5.49 – Snippet of the File menu in FTK imager

Within the **File** menu, we are presented with all the options needed. The **Create Disk Image...** option allows you to perform a forensic acquisition of physical and logical drives, contents of a folder, and CDs and DVDs. Click on the **Create Disk Image...** option:

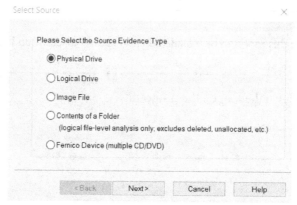

Figure 5.50 – Source evidence selection screen

Click on **Next >** to continue. I've selected a 32 GB Kingston Physical drive to acquire. You may select any drive of your choice. Once selected, click on **Finish**:

Figure 5.51 – Source drive selection screen

Next, we'll need to choose a destination to save the image file to. Click on **Add** and choose the image type (**Raw (dd)**, **SMART**, **E01**, or **AFF**). **E01** is the Expert Witness Compression Format and is one of the more common formats as it is widely recognized by many tools, including EnCase, FTK, and Autopsy. More on the file format types can be found at `https://www.loc.gov/preservation/digital/formats/fdd/generic_fdd.shtml`.

Click on **Next >** to proceed:

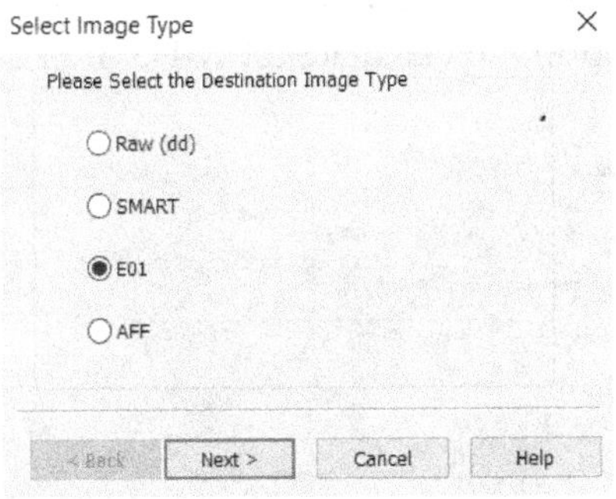

Figure 5.52 – Destination image type selection screen

Complete the forms with the **Evidence Item Information** fields and click on **Next >**:

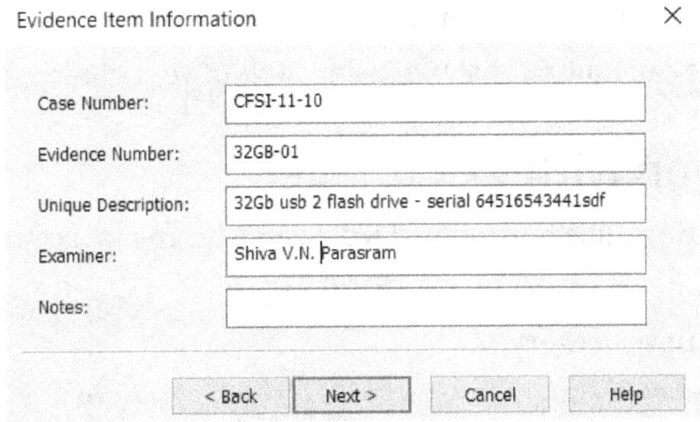

Figure 5.53 – Evidence item information details

Lastly, click on **Browse** to select the image destination folder and type in a filename with an extension:

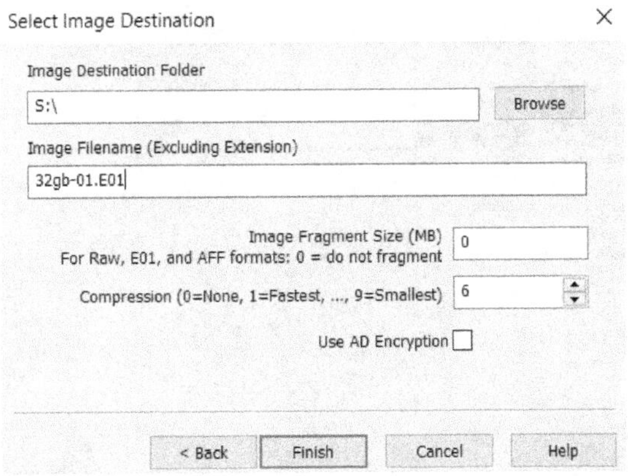

Figure 5.54 – Image destination folder and filename details

I've specified the **Image Fragment Size** to be a value of 0. This tells the software to not fragment or split the image file. Click on **Finish** and then click on **Start** to begin the process. Be sure to select the option to calculate the MD5 or SHA hash upon creation when prompted:

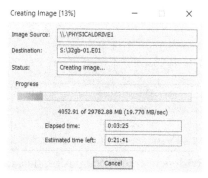

Figure 5.55 – Image creation status screen

The created disk image can now be analyzed using tools of your choice.

RAM acquisition with FTK Imager

We can also perform live acquisition with FTK Imager whereby we acquire the RAM and paging file.

Click on **File** and **Capture Memory…**:

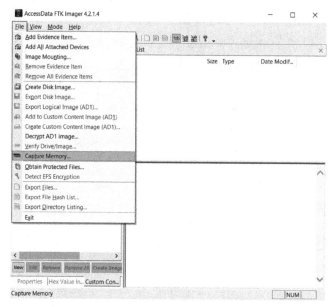

Figure 5.56 – RAM acquisition details

Next, select the destination path and specify a filename for the memory dump (.mem) file. To include the page file, select the **Include pagefile** checkbox.

Click on **Capture Memory** to begin the acquisition process:

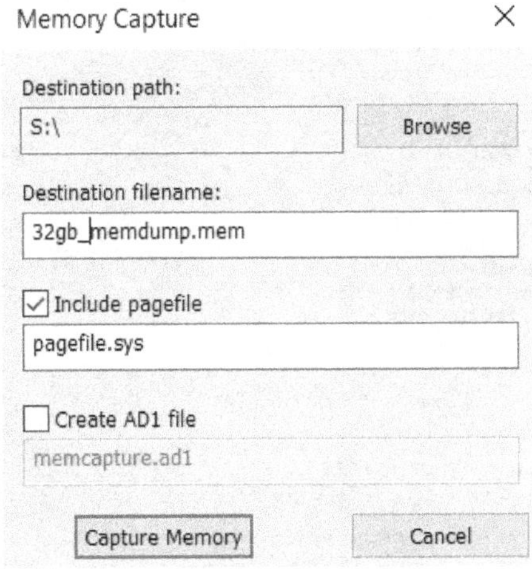

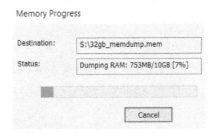

Figure 5.57 – Memory capture details screen

The status bar indicates when the process is completed. This is usually not a lengthy process compared to the static dive acquisition process:

Figure 5.58 – Memory capture progress screen

Let's look at another free tool for memory acquisition on Windows devices called Belkasoft RAM Capturer.

Belkasoft RAM Capturer

Belkasoft also has a full suite of tools available for forensic acquisition and analysis along with the free RAM capturer tool, which can be downloaded from https:// belkasoft.com/ram-capturer. Click on the **DOWNLOAD NOW** button and enter your email address, then click on **Proceed**. An email with the download link should be sent to you within an hour.

Once downloaded and extracted on your Windows machine, choose the appropriate version (x86 or x64) and launch the environment.

The GUI is as simple as it gets with Belkasoft RAM Capturer. You are prompted to specify an output folder path and from there it captures the memory and paging file after clicking on **Capture!**:

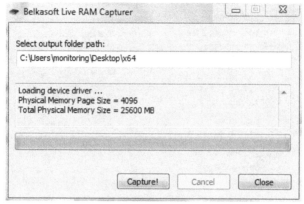

Figure 5.59 – Belkasoft Live RAM Capturer interface

The tool takes a few minutes to perform the acquisition, and from there you can hash and analyze using the tools of your choice.

Opening the output folder, I can see that the file is saved as a .mem file (20191115.mem) with the date of acquisition as the date:

20191115.mem	11/15/2019 10:06 ...	MEM File	26,214,400 ...
msvcp110.dll	10/22/2018 10:11 ...	Application extens...	646 KB
msvcr110.dll	10/22/2018 10:11 ...	Application extens...	830 KB
RamCapture64.exe	10/22/2018 10:11 ...	Application	58 KB
RamCaptureDriver64.sys	10/22/2018 10:11 ...	System file	34 KB

Figure 5.60 – Screenshot of the memory capture file within the Belkasoft folder

You'd have probably noticed that both FTK Imager and Belkasoft RAM Capturer are very fast and efficient tools for performing RAM and paging file acquisitions on Windows machines. The choice is yours when performing memory acquisitions for later analysis which we'll look at in a later chapter where we'll use Volatility to find artifacts stored in memory and even perhaps find traces of malware.

Summary

In this chapter, we've looked at two tools readily available in Kali Linux for the acquisition of digital evidence. It's very important to be able to tell your devices apart so you can accurately acquire a forensic and exact copy or image of the evidence file using the fdisk - l command. For forensic analysis, bitstream copies of the evidence are needed as these provide an exact copy of the evidence, bit by bit, which is why we used dc3dd and Guymager.

Firstly, we used **dc3dd**, the enhancement of the data dump tool, and through the Terminal performed quite a few tasks, including device imaging, hashing, splitting of files, and file verification. Our second tool, **Guymager,** has built-in case-management abilities and also has many functional similarities to dc3dd, but it comes as a GUI tool and may be easier to use.

Both tools deliver accurate and forensically sound results. For those who may not constantly work with DD and dc3dd, Guymager may be the easier tool to use seeing that all acquisition options, including cloning, are readily available through the GUI.

We also looked at FTK Imager and Belkasoft Ram Capturer. FTK Imager runs on Windows and is capable of acquiring RAM and disk images, whereas Belkasoft RAM Capturer (also for Windows) performs only RAM acquisition.

Next, we'll move on to file recovery and data carving using three very powerful tools. Exciting stuff!

6

File Recovery and Data Carving with foremost, Scalpel, and bulk_extractor

Now that we've learned how to create forensic images of evidence, let's take a look at the file recovery and data carving process using foremost, Scalpel, and bulk_extractor.

When we last covered filesystems, we saw that various operating systems use their own filesystems to store, access, and modify data. Storage media also uses filesystems to do the very same thing.

Metadata, or "data about data," helps the operating system identify data. Metadata includes technical information, such as the creation and modification dates and the file type of the data. This data makes it much easier to locate and index files.

File carving retrieves data and files from unallocated space using specific characteristics, such as the file structure and file headers, instead of traditional metadata created by or associated with filesystems.

As the name implies, unallocated space is an area of storage media that has been marked by the operating system or file table as empty or unallocated to any file or data. Although the location of, and information about, the files is not present and sometimes corrupted, there are still characteristics about them that reside in their header and footer that can identify the file, or even fragments of the file.

Even if a file extension has been changed or is missing altogether, file headers contain information that can identify the file type and attempt to carve the file by analyzing header and footer information. Data carving is quite a lengthy process and should be done using automated tools to save time. It also helps if the investigator has an idea of what file types they are looking for to have a better focus and to save time. Nevertheless, this is forensics and we know that time and patience are key.

Some common file types, as displayed in a hexadecimal format within the file headers, include the following:

- **Joint Photographic Experts Group (JPEG)**: FF D8 FF E0
- **Portable Document Format (PDF)**: 25 50 44 46

In keeping with best practices and proper case management, hashing (preferably SHA-256) of all carved data and recovered files and media should be performed. This step is important to investigators and in keeping with international best practices. The ACPO Good Practice Guide for Digital Evidence (March 2012) is available for download at `https://www.digital-detective.net/digital-forensics-documents/ ACPO_Good_Practice_Guide_for_Digital_Evidence_v5.pdf`.

In this chapter, we'll cover the following topics:

- File recovery using Foremost
- Recovering JPEG images using recoverjpeg
- File carving with Scalpel
- Data carving using bulk_extractor

Forensic test images used in Foremost and Scalpel

In this lab, we'll be using a digital forensic tool-testing image, created by Nick Mikus specifically for testing data carving tools, was used. One of the main reasons for choosing this particular image for this exercise is that Nick Mikus is listed as one of the contributing developers of **foremost**, as seen in the first line of foremost, which displays the version number alongside the authors', Jesse Kornblum and Kris Kendall, names. The image can be downloaded for free at `http://dftt.sourceforge.net/test11/index.html`.

Once you've become familiar with this exercise, you can try extracting data from other images also available on the site at `http://dftt.sourceforge.net/`.

Another file carving dataset that we'll use can be found at `https://www.cfreds. nist.gov/FileCarving/index.html`. This site contains several datasets with very small images containing archives, images, audio, and video clips, as well as documents that you may freely use for practice.

Using Foremost for file recovery and data carving

Foremost is a simple and effective **command line interface (CLI)** tool that recovers files by reading their headers and footers. We can start foremost by clicking on **Applications | 11 - Forensics | foremost:**

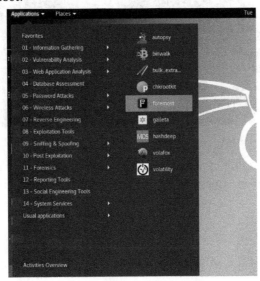

Figure 6.1 – Foremost in the Kali menu

If foremost is not listed in or installed on your version of Kali Linux, install it by typing
`sudo apt-get install`:

```
root@kali:~# sudo apt-get install foremost
Reading package lists... Done
Building dependency tree
Reading state information... Done
The following NEW packages will be installed:
  foremost
0 upgraded, 1 newly installed, 0 to remove and 1085 not upgraded.
Need to get 42.1 kB of archives.
After this operation, 103 kB of additional disk space will be used.
Get:1 http://kali.download/kali kali-rolling/main amd64 foremost amd64 1.
5.7-9+b1 [42.1 kB]
Fetched 42.1 kB in 1s (31.9 kB/s)
Selecting previously unselected package foremost.
(Reading database ... 353462 files and directories currently installed.)
Preparing to unpack .../foremost_1.5.7-9+b1_amd64.deb ...
Unpacking foremost (1.5.7-9+b1) ...
Setting up foremost (1.5.7-9+b1) ...
Processing triggers for man-db (2.8.6.1-1) ...
root@kali:~#
```

Figure 6.2 – Installing foremost in Kali

Once foremost is successfully started, a Terminal opens, displaying the program version, creators, and some of the many switches for usage:

```
root@kali:~# foremost -h
foremost version 1.5.7 by Jesse Kornblum, Kris Kendall, and Nick Mikus.
$ foremost [-v|-V|-h|-T|-Q|-q|-a|-w-d] [-t <type>] [-s <blocks>] [-k <size>]
          [-b <size>] [-c <file>] [-o <dir>] [-i <file]

-V   - display copyright information and exit
-t   - specify file type.  (-t jpeg,pdf ...)
-d   - turn on indirect block detection (for UNIX file-systems)
-i   - specify input file (default is stdin)
-a   - Write all headers, perform no error detection (corrupted files)
-w   - Only write the audit file, do not write any detected files to the disk
-o   - set output directory (defaults to output)
-c   - set configuration file to use (defaults to foremost.conf)
-q   - enables quick mode. Search are performed on 512 byte boundaries.
-Q   - enables quiet mode. Suppress output messages.
-v   - verbose mode. Logs all messages to screen
root@kali:~#
```

Figure 6.3 – Foremost help options

To have a better understanding of foremost and the switches used, try browsing the foremost system manager's manual. This can be done by entering the following command:

```
man foremost
```

The output displays the user manual for foremost along with the supported file formats:

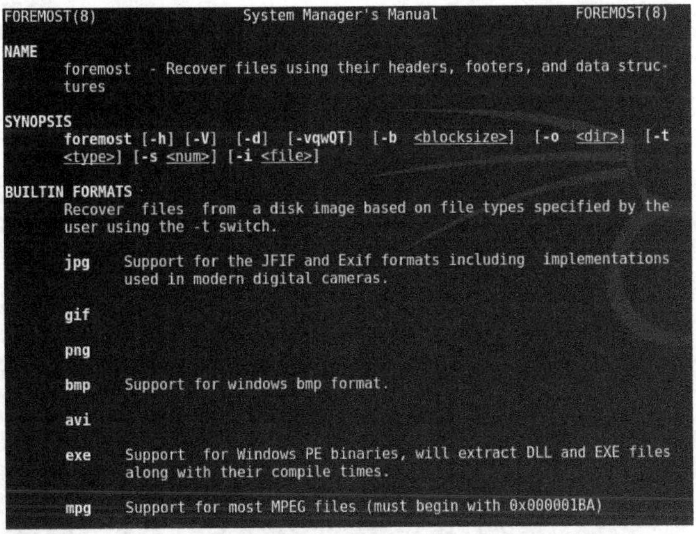

```
FOREMOST(8)                    System Manager's Manual                    FOREMOST(8)

NAME
       foremost  - Recover files using their headers, footers, and data struc-
       tures

SYNOPSIS
       foremost [-h] [-V]  [-d]  [-vqwQT]  [-b  <blocksize>]  [-o  <dir>]  [-t
       <type>] [-s <num>] [-i <file>]

BUILTIN FORMATS
       Recover  files  from  a disk image based on file types specified by the
       user using the -t switch.

       jpg     Support for the JFIF and Exif formats including  implementations
               used in modern digital cameras.

       gif

       png

       bmp     Support for windows bmp format.

       avi

       exe     Support  for Windows PE binaries, will extract DLL and EXE files
               along with their compile times.

       mpg     Support for most MPEG files (must begin with 0x000001BA)
```

Figure 6.4 – Supported file types

The syntax for using foremost is as follows:

```
foremost -i (forensic image) -o (output folder) -options
```

In this example, we have specified the 11-carve-fat.dd file located on the desktop as the input file (-i) and specified an empty folder, named Foremost_recovery, as the output file (-o). Additionally, other switches can also be specified as needed.

It should be mentioned that all the file locations of images and carved data (although specified as the desktop in these exercises) should be unique to the case and perhaps even stored on forensically sound media, in keeping with proper case management.

To begin carving the 11-carve-fat.dd image with foremost, we type the following command in the Terminal:

```
foremost -i 11-carve-fat.dd -o Foremost_recovery
```

The following image shows the command in the Terminal.

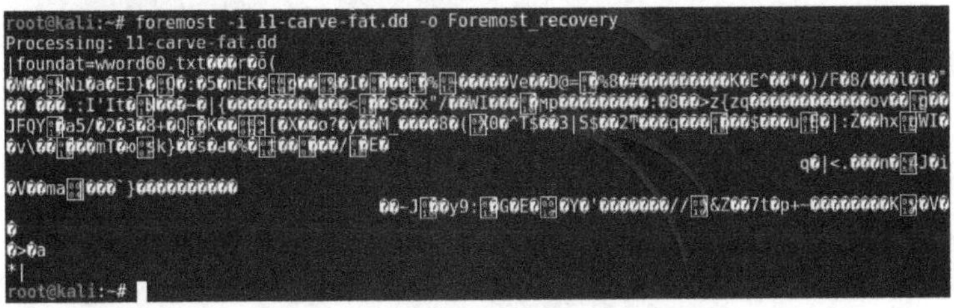

Figure 6.5 – Foremost carving process

Although the characters found look quite unclear while processing, the results will be clearly categorized and summarized in the specified output folder.

> **Tip:**
> For quick access to some of the commands in Foremost, you can use
> `foremost -h`.

It is important that the specified output folder is empty or you will encounter problems, as in the following screenshot:

```
Foremost started at Tue Oct 24 08:33:20 2017
Invocation: foremost -i/root/Desktop/Graphic.dd -o/root/Desktop/Recovered -v
Output directory: /root/Desktop/Recovered
Configuration file: /etc/foremost.conf
Processing: stdin
|------------------------------------------------------------
File: stdin
Start: Tue Oct 24 08:33:20 2019
Length: Unknown

Num      Name (bs=512)          Size      File Offset      Comment
```

Figure 6.6 – Foremost errors

Once the processes are complete, we can navigate to our output folder to view the findings.

Viewing the Foremost results

Once foremost has completed the carving process, we can proceed to the `Foremost_recovery` output folder:

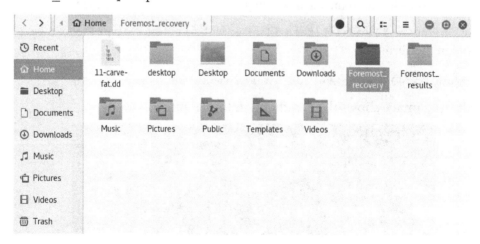

Figure 6.7 – Foremost output directory

If we open the output directory, we can see the carved items, categorized by file type, along with an audit.txt file that contains details of the findings:

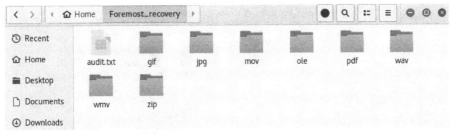

Figure 6.8 – Carved file types

Within the audit.text file, we can see a list view of the items found by foremost, along with their sizes and file offset locations:

```
                                       audit.txt
Open  ▼   🔖                         /Foremost_recovery                    Save

Foremost version 1.5.7 by Jesse Kornblum, Kris Kendall, and Nick Mikus
Audit File

Foremost started at Tue Oct 24 11:05:17 2019
Invocation: foremost -i 11-carve-fat.dd -o Foremost_recovery
Output directory: /root/Foremost_recovery
Configuration file: /etc/foremost.conf
------------------------------------------------------------------------
File: 11-carve-fat.dd
Start: Tue Oct 24 11:05:17 2019
Length: 61 MB (64979456 bytes)

Num      Name (bs=512)        Size     File Offset     Comment

0:       00019717.jpg          29 KB    10095104
1:       00019777.jpg         433 KB    10125824
2:       00020645.jpg          96 KB    10570240
3:       00020841.gif           5 KB    10670592       (88 x 31)
4:       00000321.wmv           7 MB      164352
5:       00021929.wmv        1012 KB    11227648
6:       00020853.mov         537 KB    10676736
7:       00016021.wav         311 KB     8202752
8:       00000281.ole          20 KB      143872
9:       00016693.ole          24 KB     8546816
10:      00023957.ole           6 MB    12265984
11:      00023981.zip          77 KB    12278272
12:      00016741.pdf           1 MB     8571392       (PDF is Linearized)
13:      00019477.pdf         119 KB     9972224
Finish: Tue Oct 24 11:05:18 2019
```

Figure 6.9 – Carved results as displayed by the audit.txt file

When scrolling down in the audit.txt file, you should see a summary of the files found, which is particularly useful when carving larger images:

```
14 FILES EXTRACTED

jpg:= 3
gif:= 1
wmv:= 2
mov:= 1
rif:= 1
ole:= 3
zip:= 1
pdf:= 2
----------------------
```

Figure 6.10 – Number of files carved and extracted

The first three files listed in the audit.txt file are .jpg image files, and we can see these files in the jpg sub-folder within the Foremost_recovery output folder:

Figure 6.11 – Snippet of recovered images

As we can see, foremost is quite a powerful data-recovery and file-carving tool. File carving can take a very long time, depending on the size of the drive or image used. If the type of file that needs to be recovered is already known, it may be wise to specify this type of file, using the -t option, to reduce the amount of time taken compared with searching the entire image.

> **Tip**
> Before running Foremost again, remember to choose a new or empty output folder.

We can also use foremost to specify individual file types for a faster search, using the -t option followed by the file extension. As we saw earlier when running the man foremost command, Foremost supports a variety of file types, including .jpg, .gif, .png, .bmp, .avi, .mpg, .wav, .mov, .pdf, .doc, .zip, and .mp4.

Let's try to recover only JPEG/JPG images using foremost. Firstly, download a sample image from https://www.cfreds.nist.gov/FileCarving/Images/L0_Graphic.dd.bz2.

I've saved and extracted the L0_Graphic.dd file to my desktop and will first change the directory to Desktop using the cd Desktop command and then work from there. I'll also use the ls -l command to list the files saved to the desktop:

```
root@kali:~# cd
root@kali:~# cd Desktop
root@kali:~/Desktop# ls -l
total 215528
-rw-r--r-- 1 root root 129356800 Mar 10  2005 12-carve-ext2.dd
-rw-r--r-- 1 root root  64769536 Nov 14 11:07 L0_Graphic.dd
-rw-r--r-- 1 root root  26568510 Nov 14 11:04 L0_Graphic.dd.bz2
root@kali:~/Desktop#
```

Figure 6.12 – Sample image file downloaded

To recover only JPEG images, let's run the following command:

```
foremost -t jpg -i L0_Graphic.dd -o Recovered_JPG
```

The following output shows the running process to recover JPEG images. This may take some time, depending on the number of images to be carved:

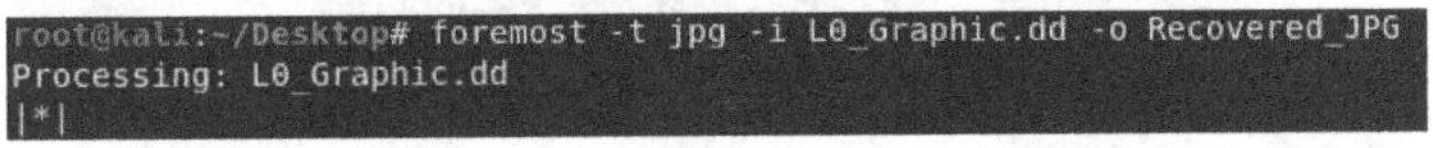

Figure 6.13 – Recovering .jpg files with Foremost

We can view the newly created folder by using the `ls` command, then changing to the `Recovered_JPG` folder using the `cd Recovered_JPG` command, and then using the `ls` command again, as in the following screenshot:

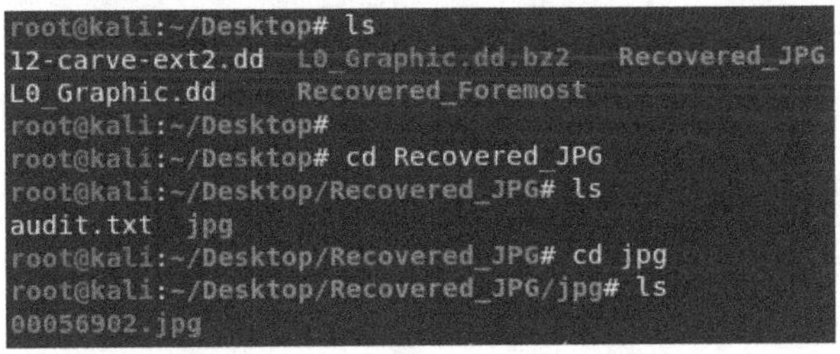

Figure 6.14 – Browsing to the recovered image via the CLI

In the preceding screenshot, we can see that the `00056902.jpg` file was recovered from the `.dd` image. You can also open the directory and view the file, and the `audit.txt` file as well.

Let's try another example to recover a video file. Download the sample file from `https://www.cfreds.nist.gov/FileCarving/Images/L2_Video.dd.bz2`. Again, I've saved and extracted this file to my desktop and changed the directory using the `cd Desktop` command, followed by the `ls` command to list the files on the desktop.

Once you're in the same directory as the extracted `L0_Graphic.dd` file, run the following command to recover videos with a `.avi` format:

```
foremost -t avi -i L2_Video.dd -o Recovered_AVI
```

The following output shows the running process to recover AVI files. Depending on the number of video files to be carved, this may take some time:

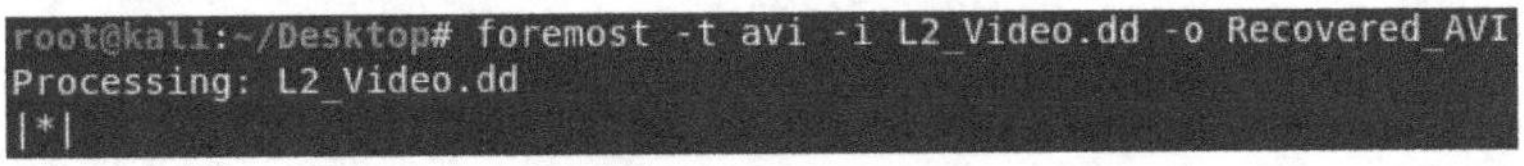

Figure 6.15 – Recovering .avi files with Foremost

From here, we can change directories to browse to the `Recovered_AVI` directory via the Terminal (or use the mouse to navigate to the recovered video):

```
root@kali:~/Desktop# cd Recovered_AVI
root@kali:~/Desktop/Recovered_AVI# ls
audit.txt  avi
root@kali:~/Desktop/Recovered_AVI# cd avi
root@kali:~/Desktop/Recovered_AVI/avi# ls
00011437.avi
```

Figure 6.16 – Browsing to the recovered file with the CLI

If we were to use the `-t all` option, this would result in foremost recovering all file types. Use the following command while in the `Desktop` directory:

```
foremost -t all -i L2_Video.dd -o Videos
```

The following output shows the running process to recover all files using the `-t` option. This process will, of course, be very lengthy as all formats will be carved from the `L2_video.dd` file:

```
root@kali:~/Desktop# foremost -t all -i L2_Video.dd -o Videos
Processing: L2_Video.dd
|*|
```

Figure 6.17 – Recovering/carving all files

If we browse to the `Videos` folder, we can see that foremost has recovered files with a `.avi`, `.mov`, and `.wmv` format for us:

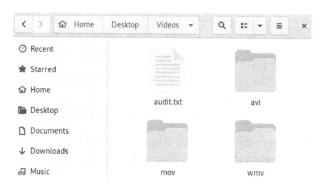

Figure 6.18 – Screenshot of the carved videos

That's all for carving files using foremost. We can see it's quite useful for data recovery and supports a variety of file formats. Let's look at image recovery and carving using **recoverjpeg** next.

Simple JPEG recovery using recoverjpeg

Another simple image recovery tool that I'll make mention of is **recoverjpeg**, which, as the name implies, recovers JPEG images. Let's first install recoverjpeg by typing the following into a Terminal:

```
sudo apt-get install recoverjpeg
```

The following output shows the installation process for recoverjpeg, which may take a couple of minutes, depending on your download speed:

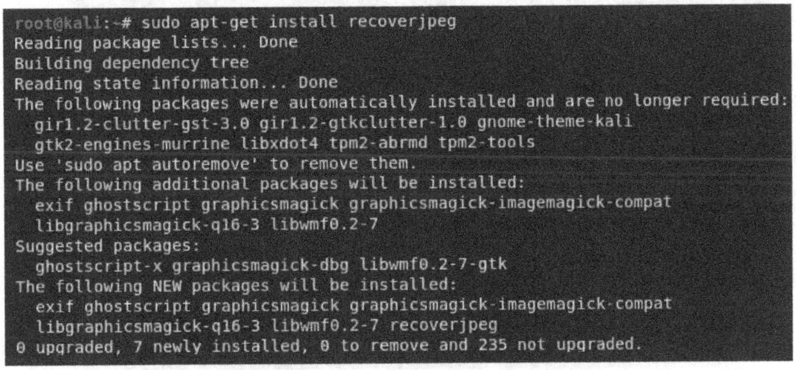

```
root@kali:~# sudo apt-get install recoverjpeg
Reading package lists... Done
Building dependency tree
Reading state information... Done
The following packages were automatically installed and are no longer required:
  gir1.2-clutter-gst-3.0 gir1.2-gtkclutter-1.0 gnome-theme-kali
  gtk2-engines-murrine libxdot4 tpm2-abrmd tpm2-tools
Use 'sudo apt autoremove' to remove them.
The following additional packages will be installed:
  exif ghostscript graphicsmagick graphicsmagick-imagemagick-compat
  libgraphicsmagick-q16-3 libwmf0.2-7
Suggested packages:
  ghostscript-x graphicsmagick-dbg libwmf0.2-7-gtk
The following NEW packages will be installed:
  exif ghostscript graphicsmagick graphicsmagick-imagemagick-compat
  libgraphicsmagick-q16-3 libwmf0.2-7 recoverjpeg
0 upgraded, 7 newly installed, 0 to remove and 235 not upgraded.
```

Figure 6.19 – Installing recoverjpeg

Once installed, view the options available by typing `recoverjpeg`:

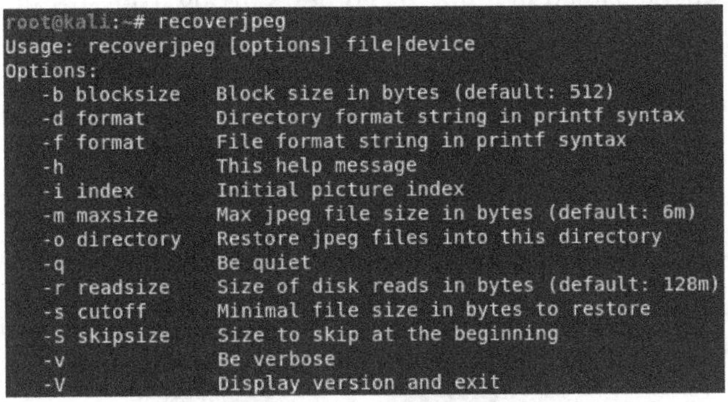

```
root@kali:~# recoverjpeg
Usage: recoverjpeg [options] file|device
Options:
  -b blocksize   Block size in bytes (default: 512)
  -d format      Directory format string in printf syntax
  -f format      File format string in printf syntax
  -h             This help message
  -i index       Initial picture index
  -m maxsize     Max jpeg file size in bytes (default: 6m)
  -o directory   Restore jpeg files into this directory
  -q             Be quiet
  -r readsize    Size of disk reads in bytes (default: 128m)
  -s cutoff      Minimal file size in bytes to restore
  -S skipsize    Size to skip at the beginning
  -v             Be verbose
  -V             Display version and exit
```

Figure 6.20 – Available help options

We can now use this tool to scan and recover images on our Kali Linux machine. For the purpose of this example, I've downloaded and deleted several images to try and recover.

Before I run `recoverjpeg`, I'll use the `fdisk -l` command to determine the drive names so that I can specify which drive I'd like to recover images from:

```
root@kali:~# fdisk -l
Disk /dev/sda: 80 GiB, 85899345920 bytes, 167772160 sectors
Disk model: VBOX HARDDISK
Units: sectors of 1 * 512 = 512 bytes
Sector size (logical/physical): 512 bytes / 512 bytes
I/O size (minimum/optimal): 512 bytes / 512 bytes
Disklabel type: dos
Disk identifier: 0x1f520778


Device     Boot     Start       End   Sectors Size Id Type
/dev/sda1  *         2048 163577855 163575808  78G 83 Linux
/dev/sda2        163579902 167770111   4190210   2G  5 Extended
/dev/sda5        163579904 167770111   4190208   2G 82 Linux swap / Solaris
root@kali:~#
```

Figure 6.21 – Viewing available storage media using fdisk

Now that I know which drive I'd like to recover images from (`sda1`), I can use the following command to start the process:

```
recoverjpeg /dev/sda1
```

This can take quite a few minutes, depending on the size of the drive or image:

```
root@kali:~# recoverjpeg /dev/sda1
Recovered files: 1406          Analyzed: 610.1 MiB
```

Figure 6.22 – recoverjpeg command and process

The recovered files will be saved in the Home folder and will not have their original names, but instead will be named in numerical order, starting from `00000.jpg`, as in the following screenshot:

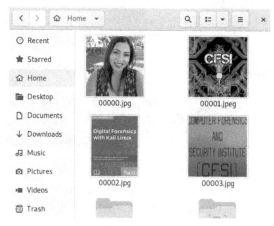

Figure 6.23 – Recovered .jpeg images

recoverjpeg is a powerful tool for image carving and recovery. The only downside is the renaming of the carved files. Let's look at another file carving tool that uses minimal resources.

Using Scalpel for data carving

Scalpel was created as an improvement of a much earlier version of foremost. Scalpel aims to address the high CPU and RAM usage issues of foremost when carving data.

Specifying file types in Scalpel

Unlike foremost, file types of interest must be specified by the investigator in the Scalpel configuration file. This file is called `scalpel.conf` and is located at `etc/scapel/`:

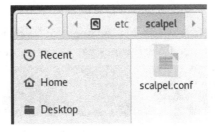

Figure 6.24 – Scalpel configuration file location

To specify the file types, the investigator must remove the comments at the start of the line containing the file type as all supported file types are commented out with a hashtag at the beginning of the file type. The following screenshot shows the default Scalpel configuration file (`scalpel.conf`) with all the file types commented out. Notice that each line begins with a hashtag:

```
#
# GIF and JPG files (very common)
#       gif     y       5000000         \x47\x49\x46\x38\x37\x61        \x00\x3b
#       gif     y       5000000         \x47\x49\x46\x38\x39\x61        \x00\x3b
#       jpg     y       200000000       \xff\xd8\xff\xe0\x00\x10        \xff\xd9
#
#
# PNG
#       png     y       20000000        \x50\x4e\x47?    \xff\xfc\xfd\xfe
#
#
# BMP     (used by MSWindows, use only if you have reason to think there are
#         BMP files worth digging for. This often kicks back a lot of false
#         positives
#
#       bmp     y       100000  BM??\x00\x00\x00
#
# TIFF
#       tif     y       200000000       \x49\x49\x2a\x00
# TIFF
#       tif     y       200000000       \x4D\x4D\x00\x2A
#
```

Figure 6.25 – All file types not selected as represented by the #

We've removed the hashtags at the beginning of some of the lines to let Scalpel know to search for these specific file types. This also reduces the time taken to otherwise search for all supported file types. The following screenshot shows that Scalpel will be searching for GIF and JPG files as the comments have been removed:

```
#
# GIF and JPG files (very common)
        gif     y     5000000         \x47\x49\x46\x38\x37\x61        \x00\x3b
        gif     y     5000000         \x47\x49\x46\x38\x39\x61        \x00\x3b
        jpg     y     200000000       \xff\xd8\xff\xe0\x00\x10        \xff\xd9
#
#
# PNG
        png     y     20000000        \x50\x4e\x47?    \xff\xfc\xfd\xfe
#
#
# BMP     (used by MSWindows, use only if you have reason to think there are
#         BMP files worth digging for. This often kicks back a lot of false
#         positives
#
|       bmp     y     100000    BM??\x00\x00\x00
#
# TIFF
#       tif     y     200000000       \x49\x49\x2a\x00
# TIFF
#       tif     y     200000000       \x4D\x4D\x00\x2A
#
```

Figure 6.26 – All files without the # will be included in the carving process

Be sure to perform this step before specifying the image to be carved. Failure to do so presents the investigator with a helpful error message as a reminder:

```
ERROR: The configuration file didn't specify any file types to carve.
(If you're using the default configuration file, you'll have to
uncomment some of the file types.)

See /etc/scalpel/scalpel.conf.
root@kali:~#
```

Figure 6.27 – File type configuration reminder

Once all the earlier configurations have been made, we can navigate to Scalpel in the GUI menu and begin carving.

Using Scalpel for file carving

Once we have made our changes to include file types and saved the `scalpel.conf` file, we can then start Scalpel by clicking on the **Show Applications** button on the sidebar and enter `scalpel` into the search box, which then appears at the top of the screen, as in the following screenshot. Click on the `scalpel` box to begin:

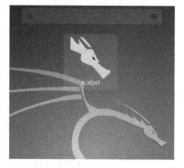

Figure 6.28 – Scalpel icon

Once started, a Terminal opens up showing the version number (1.60) and the author (Golden G. Richard III), and, as mentioned, it states that it is based on foremost 0.69. As with foremost, Scalpel's usage syntax and additional options are also displayed:

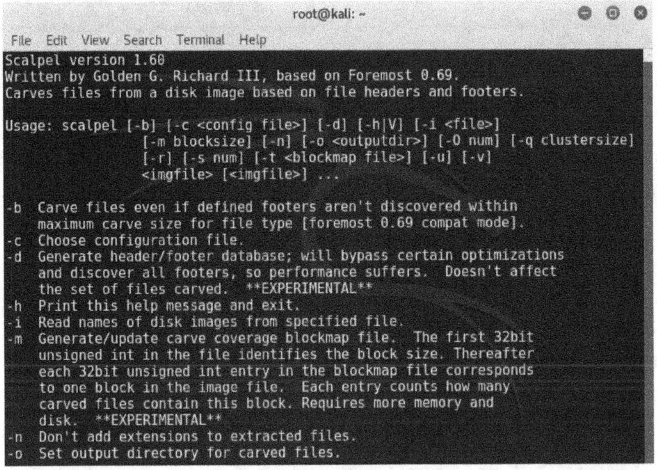

Figure 6.29 – Scalpel options

For this example, the same image used for carving with foremost (11-carve-fat.dd) was used. As with foremost, the input file and output folder must be specified. To list the available options and switches in Scalpel, use scalpel -h.

The following syntax was used in Scalpel:

```
scalpel -o scalpelOutput/ 11-carve-fat.dd
```

In the following screenshot, we can see that Scalpel builds a carve list showing the file type with header and footer information, as well as the number of files carved:

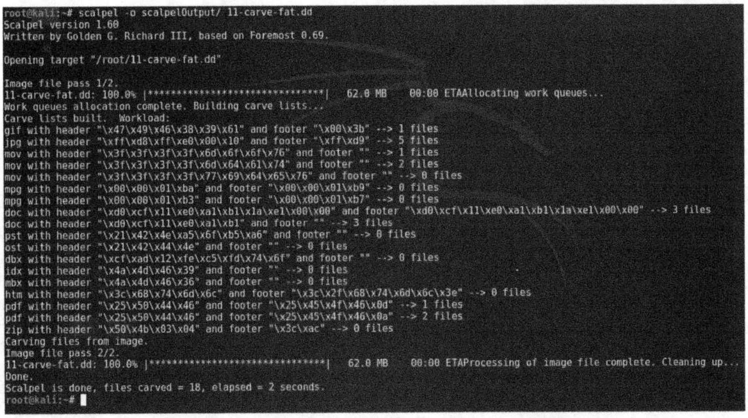

Figure 6.30 – Scalpel carving process

Taking a closer look at the last few lines produced by the Scalpel output, we can see that the carving process is 100% complete with 18 files being carved:

Figure 6.31 – Scalpel results

As shown in the preceding screenshot, Scalpel has now completed all carving processes. Let's now have a look at the findings.

Viewing the results of Scalpel

Now we can head over to the output folder, named scalpelOutput, to have a look at the carved files:

Figure 6.32 – Scalpel output folder

The results of the Scalpel output are similar to those of foremost, with both output folders containing various subfolders with carved files, along with an audit.txt file with details of the findings:

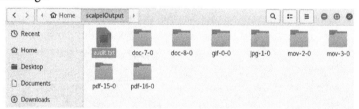

Figure 6.33 – Sub-directories of the Scalpel output folder containing carved images

Within the jpg-1-0 folder, we can see five .jpg files, three with actual images:

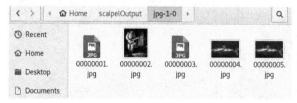

Figure 6.34 – Carved .jpg files

Even though Scalpel's results showed that five files with .jpg headers and footers were identified in the carve list when the tool was run, some of these may not open. These files are most likely false positives:

```
Carve lists built.  Workload:
gif with header "\x47\x49\x46\x38\x39\x61" and footer "\x00\x3b" --> 1 files
jpg with header "\xff\xd8\xff\xe0\x00\x10" and footer "\xff\xd9" --> 5 files
mov with header "\x3f\x3f\x3f\x3f\x6d\x6f\x6f\x76" and footer "" --> 1 files
mov with header "\x3f\x3f\x3f\x3f\x6d\x64\x61\x74" and footer "" --> 2 files
```

Figure 6.35 – False positives

The following screenshot shows a snippet of the audit.txt file, displaying information about the carved files:

```
Open ▾   ⌂                          audit.txt                          Save   ≡
                                  ~/scalpelOutput

|
Scalpel version 1.60 audit file
Started at Wed Oct 25 12:03:15 2017
Command line:
scalpel -o scalpelOutput/ 11-carve-fat.dd

Output directory: /root/scalpelOutput
Configuration file: /etc/scalpel/scalpel.conf

Opening target "/root/11-carve-fat.dd"

The following files were carved:
File            Start       Chop        Length      Extracted From
00000009.doc    143872      NO          8402944     11-carve-fat.dd
00000002.jpg    10095104    NO          29885       11-carve-fat.dd
00000001.jpg    8522240     NO          24367       11-carve-fat.dd
00000012.doc    143872      YES         10000000    11-carve-fat.dd
00000015.pdf    8571392     NO          1399508     11-carve-fat.dd
00000016.pdf    8571392     NO          1523266     11-carve-fat.dd
00000017.pdf    9972224     NO          122434      11-carve-fat.dd
00000010.doc    8546816     NO          3719168     11-carve-fat.dd
00000013.doc    8546816     YES         10000000    11-carve-fat.dd
00000008.mov    10678017    YES         10000000    11-carve-fat.dd
00000007.mov    10678001    YES         10000000    11-carve-fat.dd
00000006.mov    10676736    YES         10000000    11-carve-fat.dd
00000005.jpg    10574693    NO          2655        11-carve-fat.dd
00000004.jpg    10570636    NO          2655        11-carve-fat.dd
00000003.jpg    10570240    NO          3051        11-carve-fat.dd
00000000.gif    10670592    NO          5498        11-carve-fat.dd
00000014.doc    12265984    YES         10000000    11-carve-fat.dd
00000011.doc    12265984    NO          10000000    11-carve-fat.dd
```

Figure 6.36 – Scalpel output results listed within the audit.txt file

Scalpel gave us a numerical listing of all the files that were carved in the audit.txt file and also saved each file type in separate folders within the ScalpelOutput folder. For file carving purposes, you may use either foremost or Scalpel.

Comparing Foremost and Scalpel

Although Scalpel returned more files than foremost, carry out your own exercise in comparing the carved files found by both foremost and Scalpel. Unfortunately, the filenames returned by both tools are not the original filenames and, in some instances, there may be duplicates of carved files, as many files may be fragmented and appear to be separate files. Try manually going through the files found in the output folders of both foremost and Scalpel and do your own comparative research to see which tool was more successful.

The image file (`11-carve-fat.dd`) used in both foremost and Scalpel contains 15 files of various types, as listed on the download page (`http://dftt.sourceforge.net/test11/`) and in the following screenshot:

Num	Name	MD5	Size	Note	Sectors
1	2003_document.doc	e72f388b36f9370f19696b164c308482	19968	A Valid DOC file	(0-38) 281 -320
2	enterprise.wav	7629b59adade055f6783dc1773274215	318895	A valid WAV file	(0-622) 16021 -16644
3	haxor2.jpg	84e1dceac2eb127fef5bfdcb0eae324b	24367	An invalid JPEG with only 1 header byte corrupted. This byte is located at offset 19 within the file.	(0-47)16645 -16692
4	holly.xls	7917baf0219645afef8b381570c41211	23040	A valid XLS file	(0-44) 16693-16738
5	lin_1.2.pdf	e026ec863410725ba1f5765a1874800d	1399508	A linearized PDF	(0-2733) 16741 -19475
6	nlin_14.pdf	5b3e806e8c9c06a475cd45bf821af709	122434	A non-linearized PDF	(0-239) 19477 -19716
7	paul.jpg	37a49f97ed279832cd4f7bd002c826a2	29885	A valid jpeg	(0-58) 19717 -19776
8	pumpkin.jpg	6c9859e5121ff54d5d6298f65f0bf3b3	444314	A valid EXIF jpeg	(0-867) 19777-20644
9	shark.jpg	d83428b8742a075b57b0dc424cd297c4	99298	A valid JPEG	(0-193) 20645-20839
10	sml.gif	d25fb845e6a41395adaed8bd14db7bf2	5498	A valid GIF	(0-10) 20841-20852
11	surf.mov	5328d2b066f428ea95b2793849ab97fa	550653	A valid MOV	(0-1075) 20853-21928
12	surf.wmv	ff085d0c4d0e0fdc8f3427db68e26266	1036994	A valid WMV	(0-2025) 21929-23955
13	test.ppt	7b74c2c608d92f4bb76c1d3b6bd1decc	11264	A deleted PPT	(0-21) 23957 -23978
14	wword60t.zip	c0be59d49b7ee0fdc492d2df32f2c6c6	78899	A valid ZIP	(0-154) 23981 -24135
15	domopers.wmv	63c0c6986cf0a446cb54b0ac65a921a5	8037267	A deleted wmv	(0-15697) 321-16018

Figure 6.37 – Sample file contents

You should always use multiple tools when performing forensics to ensure that the results are accurate by comparing the results of the tools used. I would also encourage investigators to test their tools before handling and acquiring *evidence*. You should also keep a log of tool testing as this is usually requested by organizations/individuals who are verifying the findings of the digital forensic processes. Let's move on to our final carving tool, `bulk_extractor`.

bulk_extractor

bulk_extractor is the third and final tool that we'll cover in this chapter. foremost and Scalpel, as we've seen so far, are quite impressive at file recovery and carving, but are limited to specific file types. For further extraction of data, we can use bulk_extractor.

While foremost and Scalpel can recover images, audio, video, and compressed files, bulk_extractor extracts several additional types of information that can be very useful in investigations.

Although bulk_extractor is quite capable of recovering and carving image, video, and document type files, other data that can be carved and extracted by bulk_extractor includes the following:

- Credit card numbers
- Email addresses
- URLs
- Online searches
- Website information
- Social media profiles and information

Forensic test image used in bulk_extractor

For this example, we will work with a freely available evidence file named `terry-work-usb-2009-12-11.E01`.

This file can be downloaded directly from the Digital Corpora website, which allows the use of forensic evidence images for forensic research purposes. The file used in this exercise can be downloaded directly from `http://downloads.digitalcorpora.org/corpora/scenarios/2009-m57-patents/drives-redacted/`.

The required file is the last file on the download page and is only 32 MB in size:

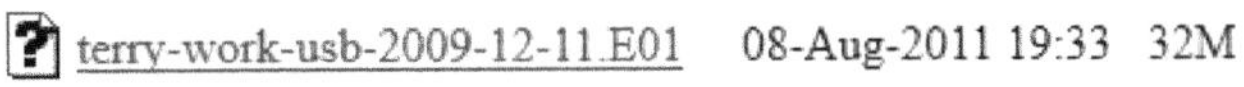

[?] terry-work-usb-2009-12-11.E01   08-Aug-2011 19:33   32M

Figure 6.38 – Sample file to be used

There are several other datasets and image files that you can download from the Digital Corpora site, which you can use once you become familiar with the tool's usage.

Using bulk_extractor

Start bulk_extractor by first typing `bulk_extractor -h` to display some commonly used parameters and options:

```
root@kali:~# bulk_extractor -h
bulk_extractor version 1.6.0-dev
Usage: bulk_extractor [options] imagefile
  runs bulk_extractor and outputs to stdout a summary of what was found where

Required parameters:
   imagefile      - the file to extract
or  -R filedir   - recurse through a directory of files
                   HAS SUPPORT FOR E01 FILES
                   HAS SUPPORT FOR AFF FILES
   -o outdir     - specifies output directory. Must not exist.
                   bulk_extractor creates this directory.
Options:
   -i            - INFO mode. Do a quick random sample and print a report.
   -b banner.txt- Add banner.txt contents to the top of every output file.
   -r alert_list.txt  - a file containing the alert list of features to alert
                   (can be a feature file or a list of globs)
                   (can be repeated.)
   -w stop_list.txt   - a file containing the stop list of features (white list
                   (can be a feature file or a list of globs)s
                   (can be repeated.)
   -F <rfile>    - Read a list of regular expressions from <rfile> to find
   -f <regex>    - find occurrences of <regex>; may be repeated.
                   results go into find.txt
   -q nn         - Quiet Rate; only print every nn status reports. Default 0; -1
for no status at all
   -s frac[:passes] - Set random sampling parameters
```

Figure 6.39 – Available options

As with foremost and Scalpel, the syntax for using `bulk_extractor` is quite simple and requires an output folder (-o) and the forensic image to be specified. For this exercise, as previously mentioned, we will be extracting data from the `terry-work-usb-2009-12-11.E01` image and saving the output to a folder named `bulk-output`.

The syntax used is as follows:

```
bulk_extractor -o bulk_output terry-work-usb-2009-12-11.E01
```

Carving data from large files can be time-consuming. However, once the preceding command has been run, a status update is displayed, as in the following screenshot:

```
root@kali:~# bulk_extractor -o bulk_output terry-work-usb-2009-12-11.E01
bulk_extractor version: 1.6.0-dev
Hostname: kali
Input file: terry-work-usb-2009-12-11.E01
Output directory: bulk_output
Disk Size: 2097152000
Threads: 4
 8:13:52 Offset 67MB (3.20%) Done in  0:02:35 at 08:16:27
 8:13:53 Offset 150MB (7.20%) Done in  0:01:21 at 08:15:14
 8:13:54 Offset 234MB (11.20%) Done in  0:00:58 at 08:14:52
 8:13:55 Offset 318MB (15.20%) Done in  0:00:46 at 08:14:41
 8:13:56 Offset 402MB (19.20%) Done in  0:00:39 at 08:14:35
 8:13:57 Offset 486MB (23.20%) Done in  0:00:34 at 08:14:31
 8:13:58 Offset 570MB (27.20%) Done in  0:00:29 at 08:14:27
 8:13:59 Offset 654MB (31.20%) Done in  0:00:26 at 08:14:25
 8:13:59 Offset 738MB (35.20%) Done in  0:00:22 at 08:14:21
 8:14:00 Offset 822MB (39.20%) Done in  0:00:20 at 08:14:20
 8:14:01 Offset 905MB (43.20%) Done in  0:00:18 at 08:14:19
 8:14:01 Offset 989MB (47.20%) Done in  0:00:16 at 08:14:17
 8:14:02 Offset 1073MB (51.20%) Done in  0:00:14 at 08:14:16
 8:14:02 Offset 1157MB (55.20%) Done in  0:00:12 at 08:14:14
 8:14:03 Offset 1241MB (59.20%) Done in  0:00:11 at 08:14:14
 8:14:04 Offset 1325MB (63.20%) Done in  0:00:09 at 08:14:13
 8:14:04 Offset 1409MB (67.20%) Done in  0:00:08 at 08:14:12
 8:14:05 Offset 1493MB (71.20%) Done in  0:00:07 at 08:14:12
 8:14:05 Offset 1577MB (75.20%) Done in  0:00:06 at 08:14:11
 8:14:06 Offset 1660MB (79.20%) Done in  0:00:05 at 08:14:11
 8:14:06 Offset 1744MB (83.20%) Done in  0:00:03 at 08:14:09
 8:14:07 Offset 1828MB (87.20%) Done in  0:00:02 at 08:14:09
 8:14:08 Offset 1912MB (91.20%) Done in  0:00:02 at 08:14:10
 8:14:08 Offset 1996MB (95.20%) Done in  0:00:01 at 08:14:09
 8:14:09 Offset 2080MB (99.20%) Done in  0:00:00 at 08:14:09
All data are read; waiting for threads to finish...
Time elapsed waiting for 3 threads to finish:
     (timeout in 60 min.)
```

Figure 6.40 – bulk_extractor process

Once completed, `bulk_extractor` indicates that all threads have finished and provides a summary of the process and even some findings:

```
All Threads Finished!
Producer time spent waiting: 5.42133 sec.
Average consumer time spent waiting: 4.0313 sec.
MD5 of Disk Image: e07f26954b23db1a44dfd28ecd717da9
Phase 2. Shutting down scanners
Phase 3. Creating Histograms
Elapsed time: 23.3436 sec.
Total MB processed: 2097
Overall performance: 89.8384 MBytes/sec (22.4596 MBytes/sec/thread)
Total email features found: 3
root@kali:~#
```

Figure 6.41 – bulk_extractor status

As in the previous screenshot, `bulk_extractor` displays the MD5 hash, the total amount of MB processed, and even reports that three email features have been found. Let's have a detailed look at the findings in the next section.

Viewing the results of bulk_extractor

When we view the output and findings of `bulk_extractor`, we can also display a list of directories within the Terminal by typing `ls -l`. We can see that the `bulk_output` folder has been created by `bulk_extractor`:

```
root@kali:~# ls -l
total 32768
drwxr-xr-x  3 root root     4096 Oct 26 08:14 bulk_output
drwxr-xr--  34 root root    4096 Oct 24 10:58 desktop
drwxr-xr-x  4 root root     4096 Oct 26 08:07 Desktop
drwxr-xr-x  2 root root     4096 Sep 25 13:04 Documents
drwxr-xr-x  3 root root     4096 Oct 26 08:02 Downloads
drwxr-xr--  11 root root    4096 Oct 25 12:01 Foremost_recovery
drwxr-xr-x  2 root root     4096 Oct 26 08:07 Images
drwxr-xr-x  2 root root     4096 Sep 25 13:04 Music
drwxr-xr-x  3 root root     4096 Oct 26 08:24 Pictures
drwxr-xr-x  2 root root     4096 Sep 25 13:04 Public
drwxr-xr-x  10 root root    4096 Oct 25 12:03 scalpelOutput
drwxr-xr-x  2 root root     4096 Sep 25 13:04 Templates
-rw-r--r--  1 root root 33499203 Oct 26 08:02 terry-work-usb-2009-12-11.E01
drwxr-xr-x  2 root root     4096 Sep 25 13:04 Videos
root@kali:~#
root@kali:~#
```

Figure 6.42 – bulk_extractor output directory

We can now list the contents of our output folder (`bulk_output`) by typing `ls -l bulk_output`:

```
root@kali:~# ls -l bulk_output
total 30600
-rw-r--r-- 1 root root       0 Oct 26 08:13 aes_keys.txt
-rw-r--r-- 1 root root       0 Oct 26 08:13 alerts.txt
-rw-r--r-- 1 root root       0 Oct 26 08:14 ccn_histogram.txt
-rw-r--r-- 1 root root       0 Oct 26 08:14 ccn_track2_histogram.txt
-rw-r--r-- 1 root root       0 Oct 26 08:13 ccn_track2.txt
-rw-r--r-- 1 root root       0 Oct 26 08:13 ccn.txt
-rw-r--r-- 1 root root   68140 Oct 26 08:14 domain_histogram.txt
-rw-r--r-- 1 root root 7603392 Oct 26 08:13 domain.txt
-rw-r--r-- 1 root root       0 Oct 26 08:13 elf.txt
-rw-r--r-- 1 root root       0 Oct 26 08:14 email_domain_histogram.txt
-rw-r--r-- 1 root root     260 Oct 26 08:14 email_histogram.txt
-rw-r--r-- 1 root root    1116 Oct 26 08:13 email.txt
-rw-r--r-- 1 root root       0 Oct 26 08:14 ether_histogram.txt
-rw-r--r-- 1 root root       0 Oct 26 08:13 ether.txt
-rw-r--r-- 1 root root     517 Oct 26 08:13 exif.txt
-rw-r--r-- 1 root root       0 Oct 26 08:14 find_histogram.txt
-rw-r--r-- 1 root root       0 Oct 26 08:13 find.txt
-rw-r--r-- 1 root root       0 Oct 26 08:13 gps.txt
-rw-r--r-- 1 root root       0 Oct 26 08:13 httplogs.txt
-rw-r--r-- 1 root root       0 Oct 26 08:14 ip_histogram.txt
-rw-r--r-- 1 root root       0 Oct 26 08:13 ip.txt
-rw-r--r-- 1 root root       0 Oct 26 08:13 jpeg_carved.txt
-rw-r--r-- 1 root root       0 Oct 26 08:13 json.txt
-rw-r--r-- 1 root root       0 Oct 26 08:13 kml.txt
-rw-r--r-- 1 root root       0 Oct 26 08:14 pii_teamviewer.txt
-rw-r--r-- 1 root root       0 Oct 26 08:13 pii.txt
-rw-r--r-- 1 root root       0 Oct 26 08:13 rar.txt
-rw-r--r-- 1 root root   31229 Oct 26 08:14 report.xml
-rw-r--r-- 1 root root       0 Oct 26 08:13 rfc822.txt
-rw-r--r-- 1 root root       0 Oct 26 08:13 sqlite_carved.txt
-rw-r--r-- 1 root root     238 Oct 26 08:14 telephone_histogram.txt
-rw-r--r-- 1 root root     740 Oct 26 08:13 telephone.txt
-rw-r--r-- 1 root root       0 Oct 26 08:13 unrar_carved.txt
-rw-r--r-- 1 root root       0 Oct 26 08:13 unzip_carved.txt
-rw-r--r-- 1 root root       0 Oct 26 08:14 url_facebook-address.txt
```

Figure 6.43 – Carved files

The list has been split in two to show some of the artifacts found by `bulk_extractor`:

```
-rw-r--r-- 1 root root        0 Oct 26 08:13 ether.txt
-rw-r--r-- 1 root root      517 Oct 26 08:13 exif.txt
-rw-r--r-- 1 root root        0 Oct 26 08:14 find_histogram.txt
-rw-r--r-- 1 root root        0 Oct 26 08:13 find.txt
-rw-r--r-- 1 root root        0 Oct 26 08:13 gps.txt
-rw-r--r-- 1 root root        0 Oct 26 08:13 httplogs.txt
-rw-r--r-- 1 root root        0 Oct 26 08:14 ip_histogram.txt
-rw-r--r-- 1 root root        0 Oct 26 08:13 ip.txt
-rw-r--r-- 1 root root        0 Oct 26 08:13 jpeg_carved.txt
-rw-r--r-- 1 root root        0 Oct 26 08:13 json.txt
-rw-r--r-- 1 root root        0 Oct 26 08:13 kml.txt
-rw-r--r-- 1 root root        0 Oct 26 08:14 pii_teamviewer.txt
-rw-r--r-- 1 root root        0 Oct 26 08:13 pii.txt
-rw-r--r-- 1 root root        0 Oct 26 08:13 rar.txt
-rw-r--r-- 1 root root    31229 Oct 26 08:14 report.xml
-rw-r--r-- 1 root root        0 Oct 26 08:13 rfc822.txt
-rw-r--r-- 1 root root        0 Oct 26 08:13 sqlite_carved.txt
-rw-r--r-- 1 root root      238 Oct 26 08:14 telephone_histogram.txt
-rw-r--r-- 1 root root      740 Oct 26 08:13 telephone.txt
-rw-r--r-- 1 root root        0 Oct 26 08:13 unrar_carved.txt
-rw-r--r-- 1 root root        0 Oct 26 08:13 unzip_carved.txt
-rw-r--r-- 1 root root        0 Oct 26 08:14 url_facebook-address.txt
-rw-r--r-- 1 root root        0 Oct 26 08:14 url_facebook-id.txt
-rw-r--r-- 1 root root  3118516 Oct 26 08:14 url_histogram.txt
-rw-r--r-- 1 root root        0 Oct 26 08:14 url_microsoft-live.txt
-rw-r--r-- 1 root root        0 Oct 26 08:14 url_searches.txt
-rw-r--r-- 1 root root    68107 Oct 26 08:14 url_services.txt
-rw-r--r-- 1 root root 18809144 Oct 26 08:13 url.txt
-rw-r--r-- 1 root root        0 Oct 26 08:13 vcard.txt
-rw-r--r-- 1 root root  1483960 Oct 26 08:13 windirs.txt
-rw-r--r-- 1 root root        0 Oct 26 08:13 winlnk.txt
drwxr-xr-x 3 root root     4096 Oct 26 08:13 winpe_carved
-rw-r--r-- 1 root root     6192 Oct 26 08:13 winpe_carved.txt
-rw-r--r-- 1 root root    76280 Oct 26 08:13 winpe.txt
-rw-r--r-- 1 root root        0 Oct 26 08:13 winprefetch.txt
-rw-r--r-- 1 root root    24457 Oct 26 08:13 zip.txt
root@kali:~#
```

Figure 6.44 – Carved files (continued)

It should be noted that not all the listed text files will contain data. Only the ones with numbers larger than 0 to the left of the text filenames will actually contain data.

Important note

The `ccn.txt` text file is an abbreviation for credit card numbers and will contain credit card information that may have been stolen, illegally used, or stored with the possible intention to commit credit card fraud.

If we browse to the output folder, we can view all the extracted data within the individual text files. Viewing the `telephone_histogram.txt` file reveals telephone numbers:

```
Open  ▼   ⌂              telephone_histogram.txt
                             ~/bulk_output
# BANNER FILE NOT PROVIDED (-b option)
# BULK_EXTRACTOR-Version: 1.6.0-dev ($Rev: 10844 $)
# Feature-Recorder: telephone
# Filename: terry-work-usb-2009-12-11.E01
# Histogram-File-Version: 1.1
n=6     1771881984
n=1     1181501746
n=1     6003707924
```

Figure 6.45 – Carved and extracted telephone numbers

The `url.txt` file reveals many of the websites and links visited:

```
Open  ▼   ⌂                      url.txt                    Save   ≡  ⊖ ⊡ ⊗
                               ~/bulk_output
# BANNER FILE NOT PROVIDED (-b option)
# BULK_EXTRACTOR-Version: 1.6.0-dev ($Rev: 10844 $)
# Feature-Recorder: url
# Filename: terry-work-usb-2009-12-11.E01
# Feature-File-Version: 1.1
4174429 http://www.apple.com/DTDs/PropertyList-1.0.dtd  PLIST 1.0//EN" "http://www.apple.com/DTDs/
PropertyList-1.0.dtd">\x0A<plist versio
4227766 https://domex.nps.edu/domex/svn/src/m57patents/s_time_machine.txt      s\x00bplist00\xA2
\x01\x02_\x10Ahttps://domex.nps.edu/domex/svn/src/m57patents/s_time_machine.txt_\x10/https://domex.
4227834 https://domex.nps.edu/domex/svn/src/m57patents/_e_machine.txt_\x10/https://domex.nps.edu/
domex/svn/src/m57patents/\x08\x0B0\x00\x00\x00\x00\x00\x00\x01\x01\x00\x00\x00\x00\x00\x00
4289206 https://domex.nps.edu/domex/svn/src/m57patents/s_patent.txt      s\x00bplist00\xA2\x01\x02_
\x10;https://domex.nps.edu/domex/svn/src/m57patents/s_patent.txt_\x10/https://domex.
4289268 https://domex.nps.edu/domex/svn/src/m57patents/_/s_patent.txt_\x10/https://domex.nps.edu/
domex/svn/src/m57patents/\x08\x0BI\x00\x00\x00\x00\x00\x00\x01\x01\x00\x00\x00\x00\x00\x00
4600502 https://domex.nps.edu/domex/svn/src/m57patents/s_cryptography.txt_       s\x00bplist00\xA2
\x01\x02_\x10Ahttps://domex.nps.edu/domex/svn/src/m57patents/s_cryptography.txt_\x10/https://domex.
4600570 https://domex.nps.edu/domex/svn/src/m57patents/_ptography.txt_\x10/https://domex.nps.edu/
domex/svn/src/m57patents/\x08\x0B0\x00\x00\x00\x00\x00\x00\x01\x01\x00\x00\x00\x00\x00\x00
4620982 https://domex.nps.edu/domex/svn/src/m57patents/s_copyright.txt  s\x00bplist00\xA2\x01\x02_
\x10>https://domex.nps.edu/domex/svn/src/m57patents/s_copyright.txt_\x10/https://domex.
4621047 https://domex.nps.edu/domex/svn/src/m57patents/_copyright.txt_\x10/https://domex.nps.edu/
domex/svn/src/m57patents/\x08\x0BL\x00\x00\x00\x00\x00\x00\x01\x01\x00\x00\x00\x00\x00\x00
4633315 http://wiki.github.com/bard/mozrepl     gin at:\x0A#       http://wiki.github.com/bard/
mozrepl\x0A#     Once in
4641280 http://www.espn.com     \x00\x00\x00\x00\x00\x00\x00\x00\x00\x00\x00\x00\x00\x00
\x00http://www.espn.com\x0Ahttp://espn.go.
4641300 http://espn.go.com/      ://www.espn.com\x0Ahttp://espn.go.com/\x0Ahttp://sports-a
4641320 http://sports-ak.espn.go.com/nfl/index  ://espn.go.com/\x0Ahttp://sports-ak.espn.go.com/
nfl/index\x0Ahttp://espn.go.
4641359 http://espn.go.com/nfl/clubhouse?team=pit         o.com/nfl/index\x0Ahttp://espn.go.com/nfl/
clubhouse?team=pit\x0Ahttp://espn.go.
4641401 http://espn.go.com/nfl/injuries/_/team/pit/pittsburgh-steelers  bhouse?team=pit\x0Ahttp://
espn.go.com/nfl/injuries/_/team/pit/pittsburgh-steelers\x0Ahttp://www.slas
4641464 http://www.slashdot.org sburgh-steelers\x0Ahttp://www.slashdot.org\x0Ahttp://hardware
4641488 http://hardware.slashdot.org/   ww.slashdot.org\x0Ahttp://hardware.slashdot.org/\x0Ahttp://
hardware
```

Figure 6.46 – Extracted URLs

While this was a simple exercise carried out with a small evidence file, be sure to have a look at the many others available at `http://digitalcorpora.org/` and see what `bulk_extractor` reveals.

Summary

In this chapter, we learned about file recovery and data extraction using popular open source tools in Kali Linux. We first performed file carving using the very impressive foremost, which searched an entire image for supported file types within the file's headers and footers. We then did the same using recoverjpg and the newer Scalpel, but had to make a slight modification by selecting the file types we wished to carve. Both foremost and Scalpel presented us with an `audit.txt` file summarizing the carve list and its details, along with subfolders containing the actual evidence.

bulk_extractor is a wonderful tool that carves data and also finds useful information, such as email addresses, visited URLs, Facebook URLs, credit card numbers, and a variety of other information. bulk_extractor is great for investigations requiring file recovery and carving, together with either foremost or Scalpel, or even both.

Now that we've covered file carving and recovery, let's move on to something more analytical. In the next chapter, we'll take a look at exploring RAM and the paging file as part of memory forensics using the very powerful Volatility. See you there!

7

Memory Forensics with Volatility

In the previous chapters, we looked at the various types of memory. This included RAM and the swap (or paging) file, which is an area of the hard disk drive which, although slower, functions as RAM. We also discussed the issue of RAM being volatile, meaning the data in RAM is easily lost when there is no longer an electrical charge or current to RAM. With the data on RAM being the most volatile, it ranks high in the order of volatility and must be forensically acquired and preserved as a matter of high priority.

Many types of data and forensic artifacts reside in RAM and the paging file. As discussed earlier, login passwords, user information, running and hidden processes, and even encrypted passwords are just some of the many types of interesting data that can be found when performing RAM analysis, further compounding the need for memory forensics.

In this chapter, we will look at the very powerful Volatility Framework and its many uses in memory forensics.

In this chapter, we'll cover the following topics:

- Downloading sample test files for analysis within Volatility
- Installing the Volatility Framework in Kali Linux
- Using various plugins to analyze memory dumps
- Installing and using Evolve (a Volatility GUI)

Introducing the Volatility Framework

The **Volatility Framework** is an open source, cross-platform, incident response framework that comes with many useful plugins that provide the investigator with a wealth of information from a snapshot of memory, also known as a **memory dump**. The concept of volatility has been around for a decade, and apart from analyzing running and hidden processes, it is also a very popular choice for malware analysis.

To create a memory dump, several tools, such as Belkasoft Ram Capturer, **FTK Imager**, **DD, DC3DD, Computer Aided INvestigative Environment (CAINE), Helix**, and **Linux Memory Extractor (LiME)**, can be used to acquire the memory image or memory dump, and then be investigated and analyzed by the tools within the Volatility Framework.

The Volatility Framework can be run on any operating system (32- and 64-bit) that supports Python, including the following:

- Windows XP, 7, 8, 8.1, and Windows 10 (14393.447)
- Windows Server 2003, 2008, 2012/R2, and 2016
- Linux 2.6.11–4.2.3 (including Kali, Debian, Ubuntu, CentOS, and more)
- macOS Leopard (10.5.x) and Sierra (10.12.x)

Volatility supports several memory dump formats (both 32- and 64-bit), including the following:

- Windows crash and hibernation dumps (Windows 7 and earlier)
- VirtualBox core dumps
- VMware `.vmem` dumps
- VMware saved state and snapshots: `.vmss`/`.vmsn`
- Raw physical memory: `.dd`
- Direct physical memory dump over IEEE 1394 FireWire
- **Expert Witness Format (EWF)**: `.E01`
- **QEMU (Quick Emulator)**
- Firewire
- HPAK

Volatility even allows for conversion between these formats and boasts of being able to accomplish everything similar tools can.

Downloading test images for use with Volatility

For this chapter, we'll be using a Windows XP image named Ozapftis.vmem, which can be downloaded directly from https://github.com/volatilityfoundation/volatility/wiki/Memory-Samples.

The reason for using this specific Windows XP sample memory dump is that it is one of the very few dumps publicly available that contains isolated malware that will *not* affect the user's machines.

Select the link within the **Description** column, **Malware – R2D2 (pw: infected)**, to download the Ozapftis.vmem image. When prompted to extract, the password is infected:

Description	OS
Art of Memory Forensics Images	Assorted Windows, Linux, and Mac
Mac OSX 10.8.3 x64	Mac Mountain Lion 10.8.3 x64
Jackcr's forensic challenge	Windows XP x86 and Windows 2003 SP0 x86 (4 images)
GrrCon forensic challenge ISO (also see PDF questions)	Windows XP x86
Malware Cookbook DVD	Black Energy, CoreFlood, Laqma, Prolaco, Sality, Silent Banker, Tigger, Zeus, and so on
Malware - Cridex	Windows XP SP2 x86
Malware - Shylock	Windows XP SP3 x86
Malware - R2D2 (pw: infected)	Windows XP SP2 x86
Windows 7 x64	Windows 7 SP1 x64
NIST (5 samples)	Windows XP SP2, 2003 SP0, and Vista

Figure 7.1 – Volatility sample file download list

It can also be downloaded directly from http://www.mediafire.com/file/yxqodp1p2aca91x/Ozapftis.rar.

> **Important note**
> There are many other images on this page that are also publicly available for analysis. To practice working with the Volatility Framework and further enhance your analytical skills, you may wish to download as many as you like and use the various plugins available in Volatility.

Image location

As we'll soon see, all the plugins in the Volatility Framework are used through the terminal. To make access to the image file easier by not having to specify a lengthy path to the image, I've saved the `0zapftis.rar` file to my desktop and I'll need to extract the file using `unrar`. UnRAR is already installed in Kali Linux, but you can install it by typing `apt install unrar` into the terminal.

You can also list the contents of the `0zapftis.rar` file by first changing directories to the folder in which you downloaded the file and then typing in `unrar l 0zapftis.rar`. Remember that the password to view or extract the contents is `infected`:

```
root@kali:~/Desktop# unrar l 0zapftis.rar

UNRAR 5.61 beta 1 freeware      Copyright (c) 1993-2018 Alexander Roshal

Enter password (will not be echoed) for 0zapftis.rar:

Archive: 0zapftis.rar
Details: RAR 4, encrypted headers

 Attributes      Size     Date    Time   Name
---------- ----------- ---------- -----  ----
*  ..A....   268435456  2011-10-10 12:42  0zapftis.vmem
---------- ----------- ---------- -----  ----
             268435456                    1
```

Figure 7.2 – Using the unrar command to extract the sample file

Now, we can extract the `0zaoftis.vmem` file by typing in `unrar e -r 0zapftis.rar`:

```
root@kali:~/Desktop# unrar e -r 0zapftis.rar

UNRAR 5.61 beta 1 freeware      Copyright (c) 1993-2018 Alexander Roshal

Enter password (will not be echoed) for 0zapftis.rar:


Extracting from 0zapftis.rar

Extracting  0zapftis.vmem                                         OK
All OK
root@kali:~/Desktop# ls
0zapftis.rar  0zapftis.vmem  CFSI
```

Figure 7.3 – Extraction of the compressed sample file

Once the memory file (`0zapftis.vmem`) has been extracted to the desktop (or the location of your preference), we can now use the Volatility Framework to analyze the dump.

Using Volatility in Kali Linux

While still within the desktop directory, we can now install a stable version of Volatility and begin our forensic investigation and analysis of the memory dump (the `vmem` file) and search for various artifacts.

To view the options within Volatility, type in `volatility -h`. If Volatility does not start, or a `command not found` error is returned, install the Volatility Framework by typing `apt-get install volatility`. During the installation, you will be prompted to press Y (yes) to download the files required for the installation:

```
root@kali:~/Desktop# apt-get install volatility
Reading package lists... Done
Building dependency tree
Reading state information... Done
The following packages were automatically installed and are no longer requi
red:
  gir1.2-clutter-gst-3.0 gir1.2-gtkclutter-1.0 gnome-theme-kali
  gtk2-engines-murrine libxdot4 tpm2-abrmd tpm2-tools
Use 'apt autoremove' to remove them.
The following additional packages will be installed:
  dwarfdump libdistorm3-3 libdwarf1 python-atomicwrites
  python-contextlib2 python-distorm3 python-et-xmlfile python-funcsigs
  python-importlib-metadata python-jdcal python-more-itertools
  python-openpyxl python-pathlib2 python-pluggy python-py python-pytest
  python-scandir python-yara python-zipp volatility-tools
Suggested packages:
  python-funcsigs-doc python-pytest-xdist python-mock lime-forensics-dkms
  linux-headers
```

Figure 7.4 – Installing Volatility in Kali Linux

Once the installation is complete, type `volatility -h` to view the options within the Volatility Framework:

```
root@kali:~/Desktop# volatility -h
Volatility Foundation Volatility Framework 2.6
Usage: Volatility - A memory forensics analysis platform.

Options:
  -h, --help              list all available options and their default values.
                          Default values may be set in the configuration file
                          (/etc/volatilityrc)
  --conf-file=/root/.volatilityrc
                          User based configuration file
  -d, --debug             Debug volatility
  --plugins=PLUGINS       Additional plugin directories to use (colon separated)
  --info                  Print information about all registered objects
  --cache-directory=/root/.cache/volatility
                          Directory where cache files are stored
  --cache                 Use caching
  --tz=TZ                 Sets the (Olson) timezone for displaying timestamps
                          using pytz (if installed) or tzset
```

Figure 7.5 – Using the help command in Volatility

Important note

For easy reference and a complete list of all the plugins at your fingertips, open a separate terminal and run the `volatility -h` command. This is far easier than having to scroll to the top of the terminal to **Volatility** plugin commands.

The following screenshot shows a snippet of some of the many plugins within the Volatility Framework:

```
cmdline          Display process command-line arguments
cmdscan          Extract command history by scanning for _COMMAND_HISTORY
connections      Print list of open connections [Windows XP and 2003 Only]
connscan         Pool scanner for tcp connections
consoles         Extract command history by scanning for _CONSOLE_INFORMATION
crashinfo        Dump crash-dump information
deskscan         Poolscaner for tagDESKTOP (desktops)
devicetree       Show device tree
dlldump          Dump DLLs from a process address space
dlllist          Print list of loaded dlls for each process
driverirp        Driver IRP hook detection
drivermodule     Associate driver objects to kernel modules
driverscan       Pool scanner for driver objects
dumpcerts        Dump RSA private and public SSL keys
dumpfiles        Extract memory mapped and cached files
dumpregistry     Dumps registry files out to disk
editbox          Displays information about Edit controls. (Listbox experimental.)
envars           Display process environment variables
eventhooks       Print details on windows event hooks
evtlogs          Extract Windows Event Logs (XP/2003 only)
filescan         Pool scanner for file objects
gahti            Dump the USER handle type information
gditimers        Print installed GDI timers and callbacks
gdt              Display Global Descriptor Table
getservicesids   Get the names of services in the Registry and return Calculated SID
getsids          Print the SIDs owning each process
handles          Print list of open handles for each process
hashdump         Dumps passwords hashes (LM/NTLM) from memory
hibinfo          Dump hibernation file information
hivedump         Prints out a hive
hivelist         Print list of registry hives.
hivescan         Pool scanner for registry hives
hpakextract      Extract physical memory from an HPAK file
hpakinfo         Info on an HPAK file
idt              Display Interrupt Descriptor Table
iehistory        Reconstruct Internet Explorer cache / history
imagecopy        Copies a physical address space out as a raw DD image
imageinfo        Identify information for the image
impscan          Scan for calls to imported functions
```

Figure 7.6 – Plugins available in Volatility

This list comes in handy when performing analysis as each plugin comes with its own short description. The following screenshot shows a snippet of the help command, which gives a description of the imageinfo plugin:

```
imageinfo        Identify information for the image
```

Figure 7.7 – The imageinfo plugin

The format for using plugins in Volatility is as follows:

```
volatility -f [filename] [plugin] [options]
```

For example, to use the imageinfo plugin against the .vmem file we downloaded, we would type the following:

```
volatility -f 0zapftis.vmem imageinfo
```

It's good practice to have the Volatility help commands open in a second terminal for easy access to the commands without having to constantly scroll up and down. We now need to choose a profile (operating system version) to work with in Volatility.

Choosing a profile in Volatility

All operating systems store information in RAM. However, they may be situated in different locations within the memory according to the operating system used. In Volatility, we must choose a profile that best identifies the type of operating system and service pack that helps Volatility in identifying locations that store artifacts and useful information.

Choosing a profile is relatively simple as Volatility does all the work for us using the `imageinfo` plugin.

The imageinfo plugin

This plugin gives information about the images used, including the suggested operating system and Image Type (Service Pack, the Number of Processors used, and the date and time of the image).

The following command is used to provide the image information:

```
volatility -f 0zapftis.vmem imageinfo
```

The output from this command displays the suggested profiles we should consider using when analyzing the memory file using various plugins:

```
root@kali:~/Desktop#
root@kali:~/Desktop# volatility -f 0zapftis.vmem imageinfo
Volatility Foundation Volatility Framework 2.6
INFO     : volatility.debug    : Determining profile based on KDBG search...
         Suggested Profile(s) : WinXPSP2x86, WinXPSP3x86 (Instantiated with WinXPSP2
x86)
                    AS Layer1 : IA32PagedMemoryPae (Kernel AS)
                    AS Layer2 : FileAddressSpace (/root/Desktop/0zapftis.vmem)
                    PAE type : PAE
                         DTB : 0x319000L
                        KDBG : 0x80544ce0L
         Number of Processors : 1
    Image Type (Service Pack) : 2
           KPCR for CPU 0 : 0xffdff000L
        KUSER_SHARED_DATA : 0xffdf0000L
         Image date and time : 2011-10-10 17:06:54 UTC+0000
    Image local date and time : 2011-10-10 13:06:54 -0400
```

Figure 7.8 – Using the imageinfo plugin

The `imageinfo` output shows the suggested profiles as `WinXPSP2x86`:

- **WinXP**: Windows XP
- **SP2/SP3**: Service Pack 2/Service Pack 3
- **x86**: 32-bit architecture

The image type, or service pack, is displayed as 2, suggesting that this is a Windows XP Service Pack 2 32-bit (x86) operating system, which will be used as the profile for the case along with the plugins:

```
Image Type (Service Pack) : 2
          KPCR for CPU 0 : 0xffdff000L
       KUSER_SHARED_DATA : 0xffdf0000L
     Image date and time : 2011-10-10 17:06:54 UTC+0000
Image local date and time : 2011-10-10 13:06:54 -0400
```

Figure 7.9 – Results of the imageinfo plugin

Once the profile has been chosen, we can proceed with using Volatility plugins for the analysis of the `0zapftis.vmem` image.

Process identification and analysis

To identify and link connected processes, their IDs, times started, and offset locations within the memory image, we will be using the following four plugins to get us started:

- `pslist`
- `pstree`
- `psscan`
- `psxview`

The pslist plugin

This tool not only displays a list of all running processes, but also gives useful information, such as the **Process ID (PID)** and the **Parent Process ID (PPID)**, and also shows the time the processes were started.

The command to run the `pslist` plugin is as follows:

```
volatility --profile=WinXPSP2x86 -f 0zapftis.vmem pslist
```

The output of the `pslist` plugin is as follows:

```
root@kali:~/Desktop# volatility --profile=WinXPSP2x86 -f 0zapftis.vmem pslist
Volatility Foundation Volatility Framework 2.6
Offset(V)   Name                    PID   PPID   Thds    Hnds   Sess  Wow64 Start
it

--------------------------------- ------ ------ ------- ------- ------ ----- ----------
0x819cc830 System                    4      0     55      162  ------        0
0x81945020 smss.exe                536      4      3       21  ------        0 2011-10-10
0x816c6020 csrss.exe               608    536     11      355       0        0 2011-10-10
0x813a9020 winlogon.exe            632    536     24      533       0        0 2011-10-10
0x816da020 services.exe            676    632     16      261       0        0 2011-10-10
0x813c4020 lsass.exe               688    632     23      336       0        0 2011-10-10
0x81772ca8 vmacthlp.exe            832    676      1       24       0        0 2011-10-10
0x8167e9d0 svchost.exe             848    676     20      194       0        0 2011-10-10
0x817757f0 svchost.exe             916    676      9      217       0        0 2011-10-10
0x816c6da0 svchost.exe             964    676     63     1058       0        0 2011-10-10
0x815daca8 svchost.exe            1020    676      5       58       0        0 2011-10-10
0x813aeda0 svchost.exe            1148    676     12      187       0        0 2011-10-10
0x817937e0 spoolsv.exe            1260    676     13      140       0        0 2011-10-10
0x81754990 VMwareService.e        1444    676      3      145       0        0 2011-10-10
0x8136c5a0 alg.exe                1616    676      7       99       0        0 2011-10-10
0x815c4da0 wscntfy.exe            1920    964      1       27       0        0 2011-10-10
0x813bcda0 explorer.exe           1956   1884     18      322       0        0 2011-10-10
0x816d63d0 VMwareTray.exe          184   1956      1       28       0        0 2011-10-10
0x8180b478 VMwareUser.exe          192   1956      6       83       0        0 2011-10-10
```

Figure 7.10 – Results of the pslist plugin

In the preceding screenshot, we can see the that `System`, `winlogon.exe`, `services. exe`, `svchost.exe`, and `explorer.exe` services were all started first, followed by `reader_sl.exe`, `alg.exe`, and finally `VMWareUser.exe`.

The PID identifies the process and the PPID identifies the parent of the process. Looking at the `pslist` output, we can see that the `winlogon.exe` process has a PID of 632 and a PPID of 536. The PPIDs of the `services.exe` and `lsass.exe` processes (directly after the `winlogon.exe` process) are both 632, indicating that `winlogon.exe` is, in fact, the PPID for both `services.exe` and `lsass.exe`.

For those new to PIDs and processes themselves, a quick Google search can assist with identification and description information. It is also useful to become familiar with many of the start up processes in order to readily point out processes that may be unusual or suspect.

The timing and order of the processes should also be noted as these may assist in investigations. Although not seen in the previous output due to limited screen space on our monitors, if we scroll down a bit, we can also see that `explorer.exe`, with a PID of `1956`, is the PPID of `reader_sl.exe`.

Adding to this analysis, we can see that there are two instances of `wuauclt.exe` with `svchost.exe` as the PPID.

The pstree plugin

Another process identification command that can be used to list processes is the `pstree` command. This command shows the same list of processes as the `pslist` plugin, but indentation is also used to identify child and parent processes.

Run the `pstree` plugin by typing the following command:

```
volatility --profile=WinXPSP2x86 -f 0zapftis.vmem pstree
```

The output of the `pstree` plugin is as follows:

```
root@kali:~/Desktop# volatility --profile=WinXPSP2x86 -f 0zapftis.vmem pstree
Volatility Foundation Volatility Framework 2.6
Name                                    Pid    PPid   Thds   Hnds  Time
-------------------------------------- ------ ------ ------ ------ ----
0x819cc830:System                         4      0     55    162 1970-01-01
. 0x81945020:smss.exe                    536      4      3     21 2011-10-10
.. 0x816c6020:csrss.exe                  608    536     11    355 2011-10-10
.. 0x813a9020:winlogon.exe               632    536     24    533 2011-10-10
... 0x816da020:services.exe              676    632     16    261 2011-10-10
.... 0x817757f0:svchost.exe              916    676      9    217 2011-10-10
.... 0x81772ca8:vmacthlp.exe             832    676      1     24 2011-10-10
.... 0x816c6da0:svchost.exe              964    676     63   1058 2011-10-10
..... 0x815c4da0:wscntfy.exe            1920    964      1     27 2011-10-10
..... 0x815e7be0:wuauclt.exe             400    964      8    173 2011-10-10
.... 0x8167e9d0:svchost.exe             848    676     20    194 2011-10-10
.... 0x81754990:VMwareService.e         1444    676      3    145 2011-10-10
.... 0x8136c5a0:alg.exe                 1616    676      7     99 2011-10-10
.... 0x813aeda0:svchost.exe            1148    676     12    187 2011-10-10
.... 0x817937e0:spoolsv.exe            1260    676     13    140 2011-10-10
.... 0x815daca8:svchost.exe            1020    676      5     58 2011-10-10
... 0x813c4020:lsass.exe                688    632     23    336 2011-10-10
0x813bcda0:explorer.exe                1956   1884     18    322 2011-10-10
. 0x8180b478:VMwareUser.exe             192   1956      6     83 2011-10-10
. 0x817a34b0:cmd.exe                    544   1956      1     30 2011-10-10
. 0x816d63d0:VMwareTray.exe             184   1956      1     28 2011-10-10
. 0x818233c8:reader_sl.exe              228   1956      2     26 2011-10-10
root@kali:~/Desktop#
```

Figure 7.11 – Results of the pstree plugin

In the preceding screenshot, the last five processes listed are `explorer.exe`, `VMWareUser.exe`, `cmd.exe`, `VMWareTray.exe`, and `reader_sl.exe`. `explorer.exe` is not indented, while all the others are, indicating that they are all child processes of `explorer.exe` (which is the parent process).

The psscan plugin

The psscan command displays inactive and even hidden processes that can be used by malware, such as rootkits, and are well known for doing just that to evade discovery by users and antivirus programs.

Let's run the psscan plugin by typing the following:

```
volatility --profile=WinXPSP2x86 -f 0zapftis.vmem psscan
```

The output of the psscan plugin is as follows:

```
root@kali:~/Desktop# volatility --profile=WinXPSP2x86 -f 0zapftis.vmem psscan
Volatility Foundation Volatility Framework 2.6
Offset(P)              Name            PID   PPID PDB        Time created
------------------     --------------- ----- ---- ---------- --------------------
0x000000000156c5a0 alg.exe            1616    676 0x05e001e0 2011-10-10 17:04:01

0x00000000015a9020 winlogon.exe        632    536 0x05e00060 2011-10-10 17:03:58

0x00000000015aeda0 svchost.exe        1148    676 0x05e00180 2011-10-10 17:04:00

0x00000000015bcda0 explorer.exe       1956   1884 0x05e00220 2011-10-10 17:04:39

0x00000000015c4020 lsass.exe           688    632 0x05e000a0 2011-10-10 17:03:58

0x00000000017c4da0 wscntfy.exe        1920    964 0x05e00240 2011-10-10 17:04:39

0x00000000017daca8 svchost.exe        1020    676 0x05e00140 2011-10-10 17:03:59

0x00000000017e7be0 wuauclt.exe         400    964 0x05e002c0 2011-10-10 17:04:46

0x000000000187e9d0 svchost.exe         848    676 0x05e000e0 2011-10-10 17:03:59

0x00000000018c6020 csrss.exe           608    536 0x05e00040 2011-10-10 17:03:58

0x00000000018c6da0 svchost.exe         964    676 0x05e00120 2011-10-10 17:03:59

0x00000000018d63d0 VMwareTray.exe      184   1956 0x05e00160 2011-10-10 17:04:41

0x00000000018da020 services.exe        676    632 0x05e00080 2011-10-10 17:03:58

0x0000000001954990 VMwareService.e    1444    676 0x05e001c0 2011-10-10 17:04:00

0x0000000001972ca8 vmacthlp.exe        832    676 0x05e000c0 2011-10-10 17:03:59

0x00000000019757f0 svchost.exe         916    676 0x05e00100 2011-10-10 17:03:59

0x00000000019937e0 spoolsv.exe        1260    676 0x05e001a0 2011-10-10 17:04:00

0x0000000001 9a34b0 cmd.exe            544   1956 0x05e00200 2011-10-10 17:06:42
```

Figure 7.12 – Results of the psscan plugin

The output of both the pslist and psscan commands should be compared to observe any anomalies.

The psxview plugin

As with the psscan plugin, the psxview plugin is used to find and list hidden processes. With psxview, however, a variety of scans are run, including pslist and psscan.

The command to run the `psxview` plugin is as follows:

```
volatility --profile=WinXPSP2x86 -f 0zapftis.vmem psxview
```

The output of the `psxview` plugin is as follows:

```
root@kali:~/Desktop# volatility --profile=WinXPSP2x86 -f 0zapftis.vmem psxview
Volatility Foundation Volatility Framework 2.6
Offset(P)    Name              PID pslist psscan thrdproc pspcid csrss session deskthrd
----------   -------           --- ------ ------ -------- ------ ----- ------- --------
0x015a9020   winlogon.exe      632 True   True   True     True   True  True    True
0x018da020   services.exe      676 True   True   True     True   True  True    True
0x0156c5a0   alg.exe          1616 True   True   True     True   True  True    True
0x018d63d0   VMwareTray.exe    184 True   True   True     True   True  True    True
0x019757f0   svchost.exe       916 True   True   True     True   True  True    True
0x015c4020   lsass.exe         688 True   True   True     True   True  True    True
0x01972ca8   vmacthlp.exe      832 True   True   True     True   True  True    True
0x019a34b0   cmd.exe           544 True   True   True     True   True  True    True
0x0187e9d0   svchost.exe       848 True   True   True     True   True  True    True
0x017daca8   svchost.exe      1020 True   True   True     True   True  True    True
0x01954990   VMwareService.e  1444 True   True   True     True   True  True    True
0x018c6da0   svchost.exe       964 True   True   True     True   True  True    True
0x01a233c8   reader_sl.exe     228 True   True   True     True   True  True    True
0x017e7be0   wuauclt.exe       400 True   True   True     True   True  True    True
0x019937e0   spoolsv.exe      1260 True   True   True     True   True  True    True
0x015bcda0   explorer.exe     1956 True   True   True     True   True  True    True
0x017c4da0   wscntfy.exe      1920 True   True   True     True   True  True    True
0x01a0b478   VMwareUser.exe    192 True   True   True     True   True  True    True
0x015aeda0   svchost.exe      1148 True   True   True     True   True  True    True
0x01bcc830   System              4 True   True   True     True   False False   False
0x01b45020   smss.exe          536 True   True   True     True   False False   False
0x018c6020   csrss.exe         608 True   True   True     True   False True    True
root@kali:~/Desktop#
```

Figure 7.13 – Results of the psxview plugin

The `psxview` plugin lists the processes and compares the outputs listed as `True` or `False`. A `False` output means that the process is hidden, as in the `csrss`, `session`, and `deskthrd` columns, with `False` outputs for `System`, `sms.exe`, and `csrss.exe`, which tells us that the processes are not found in these areas and should be inspected further.

Now that we have viewed and documented the services that were running at the time the memory dump was taken, let's try to find network services and connections that may also have been established at that time.

Analyzing network services and connections

Volatility can be used to identify and analyze active, terminated, and hidden connections, along with ports and processes. All protocols are supported and Volatility also reveals details of ports used by processes, including the times they were started.

For these purposes, we use the following two commands:

- `connscan`
- `sockets`

The connscan plugin

To display a list of connections that have been terminated, the `connscan` command is used. The `connscan` command is also only used for Windows XP and 2003 servers (both 32- and 64-bit) systems:

```
volatility --profile=WinXPSP2x86 -f 0zapftis.vmem connscan
```

The output of the `connscan` plugin is as follows:

```
root@kali:~/Desktop# volatility --profile=WinXPSP2x86 -f 0zapftis.vmem connscan
Volatility Foundation Volatility Framework 2.6
Offset(P)   Local Address               Remote Address              Pid
----------  --------------------------  --------------------------  ---
0x01a25a50  0.0.0.0:1026                172.16.98.1:6666            1956
root@kali:~/Desktop#
```

Figure 7.14 – Results of the connscan plugin

Looking at the preceding screenshot, we see that a connection was made to 172.16.98.1 on port 6666.

For those knowledgeable about port numbers, port 6666 is usually an indication of malware. According to https://www.speedguide.net/port.php?port=6666, port 6666 is usually used by Trojans to maintain backdoor connections to hosts and possibly steal information.

We will also look into finding and analyzing traces of malware using the Volatility Framework in *Chapter 8, Artifact Analysis,* where we'll revisit Volatility and have a look at ransomware analysis.

If using the connections plugin on other examples and cases, you can obtain more information on remote IP addresses using IP lookup tools, such as whois, and websites, such as http://whatismyipaddress.com/ip-lookup.

The sockets plugin

The `sockets` plugin can be used to give additional information on listening sockets. Although **User Datagram Protocol (UDP)** and **Transmission Control Protocol (TCP)** are the only protocols listed in the output in the following screenshot, the `sockets` command supports all protocols.

To use the `sockets` plugin, type the following command:

```
volatility --profile=WinXPSP2x86 -f 0zapftis.vmem sockets
```

The output of the sockets plugin is as follows:

```
root@kali:~/Desktop# volatility --profile=WinXPSP2x86 -f 0zapftis.vmem sockets
Volatility Foundation Volatility Framework 2.6
Offset(V)      PID   Port  Proto Protocol     Address          Create Time
---------- -------- ------ ------ --------     ---------------  -----------
0x8177e3c0    1956   1026      6 TCP          0.0.0.0          2011-10-10 17:04:39
0x81596a78     688    500     17 UDP          0.0.0.0          2011-10-10 17:04:00
0x8166a008     964   1029     17 UDP          127.0.0.1        2011-10-10 17:04:42
0x818ddc08       4    445      6 TCP          0.0.0.0          2011-10-10 17:03:55
0x818328d8     916    135      6 TCP          0.0.0.0          2011-10-10 17:03:59
0x81687e98    1616   1025      6 TCP          127.0.0.1        2011-10-10 17:04:01
0x817517e8     964    123     17 UDP          127.0.0.1        2011-10-10 17:04:00
0x81753b20     688      0    255 Reserved     0.0.0.0          2011-10-10 17:04:00
0x8174fe98    1148   1900     17 UDP          127.0.0.1        2011-10-10 17:04:41
0x81753008     688   4500     17 UDP          0.0.0.0          2011-10-10 17:04:00
0x816118d8       4    445     17 UDP          0.0.0.0          2011-10-10 17:03:55
root@kali:~/Desktop#
```

Figure 7.15 – Results of the sockets plugin

We were able to view network and socket information in this section. Let's now delve a bit deeper into memory analysis using other plugins to reveal programs and users that may have been running and active at the time of the memory acquisition.

DLL analysis

Dynamic Link Libraries (DLLs) are specific to Microsoft and contain code that can be used by multiple programs simultaneously. Inspection of a process's running DLLs and the version information of files and products may assist in correlating processes. Processes and DLL information should also be analyzed as they relate to user accounts.

For these tasks, we can use the following plugins:

- `verinfo`
- `dlllist`
- `getsids`

The verinfo plugin

This command lists version information (`verinfo`) about **portable executable** (**PE**) files. The output of this file is usually quite lengthy and so can be run in a separate terminal, should the investigator not wish to continuously scroll through the current terminal to review past plugin command lists and output.

The `verinfo` command is used as follows:

```
volatility --profile=WinXPSP2x86 -f 0zapftis.vmem verinfo
```

The output of the `verinfo` plugin is as follows:

```
root@kali:~/Desktop# volatility --profile=WinXPSP2x86 -f 0zapftis.vmem verinfo
Volatility Foundation Volatility Framework 2.6
\SystemRoot\System32\smss.exe
C:\WINDOWS\system32\ntdll.dll
\??\C:\WINDOWS\system32\csrss.exe
C:\WINDOWS\system32\ntdll.dll
C:\WINDOWS\system32\CSRSRV.dll
C:\WINDOWS\system32\basesrv.dll
C:\WINDOWS\system32\winsrv.dll
  File version    : 5.1.2600.2180
  Product version : 5.1.2600.2180
  Flags           :
  OS              : Windows NT
  File Type       : Dynamic Link Library
  File Date       :
  CompanyName : Microsoft Corporation
  FileDescription : Windows Server DLL
  FileVersion : 5.1.2600.2180 (xpsp_sp2_rtm.040803-2158)
  InternalName : winsrv
  LegalCopyright : \xa9 Microsoft Corporation. All rights reserved.
  OriginalFilename : winsrv.dll
  ProductName : Microsoft\xae Windows\xae Operating System
  ProductVersion : 5.1.2600.2180
C:\WINDOWS\system32\USER32.dll
  File version    : 5.1.2600.2180
  Product version : 5.1.2600.2180
```

Figure 7.16 – Results of the verinfo plugin

Let's now have a look at any DLL information that may be relevant.

The dlllist plugin

The `dlllist` plugin lists all the running DLLs at that time in memory. DLLs are composed of code that can be used by multiple programs simultaneously.

The `dlllist` plugin is used as follows:

```
volatility --profile=WinXPSP2x86 -f 0zapftis.vmem dlllist
```

The output of the `dllist` plugin is as follows:

```
root@kali:~/Desktop# volatility --profile=WinXPSP2x86 -f 0zapftis.vmem dlllist
Volatility Foundation Volatility Framework 2.6
************************************************************************
System pid:      4
Unable to read PEB for task.
************************************************************************
smss.exe pid:    536
Command line : \SystemRoot\System32\smss.exe


Base              Size  LoadCount LoadTime                       Path
---------- ---------- ---------- ------------------------------ ----
0x48580000     0xf000     0xffff                                \SystemRoot\System32\smss.exe
0x7c900000    0xb0000     0xffff                                C:\WINDOWS\system32\ntdll.dll
************************************************************************
csrss.exe pid:    608
Command line : C:\WINDOWS\system32\csrss.exe ObjectDirectory=\Windows SharedSection=1024,3072,512
SubSystemType=Windows ServerDll=basesrv,1 ServerDll=winsrv:UserServerDllInitialization,3 ServerDl
ServerDllInitialization,2 ProfileControl=Off MaxRequestThreads=16
Service Pack 2

Base              Size  LoadCount LoadTime                       Path
---------- ---------- ---------- ------------------------------ ----
0x4a680000     0x5000     0xffff                                \??\C:\WINDOWS\system32\csrss.exe
0x7c900000    0xb0000     0xffff                                C:\WINDOWS\system32\ntdll.dll
0x75b40000     0xb000     0xffff                                C:\WINDOWS\system32\CSRSRV.dll
0x75b50000    0x10000        0x3                                C:\WINDOWS\system32\basesrv.dll
0x75b60000    0x4a000        0x2                                C:\WINDOWS\system32\winsrv.dll
```

Figure 7.17 – Results of the dlllist plugin

The getsids plugin

All users can also be uniquely identified by a **Security Identifier** (**SID**). The `getsids` command has four very useful items in the order in which the processes were started (refer to the `pslist` and `pstree` command screenshots in Figure 7.10 and Figure 7.11).

The format for the `getsids` command output is as follows:

```
[Process] (PID) [SID] (User)
```

The first result in the list, for example, lists the following:

```
System (4) : S - 1 - 5- 18 (User)
```

- `System`: Process
- `(4)`: PID
- `S - 1 - 5- 18`: SID
- `User`: Local system

> **Important note**
>
> If the last number in the SID is in the range of 500, this indicates a user with administrator privileges. For example, S – 1 – 5 – 32 – 544 (administrators).

The `getsids` plugin is used as follows:

```
volatility --profile=WinXPSP2x86 -f 0zapftis.vmem getsids
```

The output of the `getsids` plugin is as follows:

```
root@kali:~/Desktop# volatility --profile=WinXPSP2x86 -f 0zapftis.vmem getsids
Volatility Foundation Volatility Framework 2.6
System (4): S-1-5-18 (Local System)
System (4): S-1-5-32-544 (Administrators)
System (4): S-1-1-0 (Everyone)
System (4): S-1-5-11 (Authenticated Users)
smss.exe (536): S-1-5-18 (Local System)
smss.exe (536): S-1-5-32-544 (Administrators)
smss.exe (536): S-1-1-0 (Everyone)
smss.exe (536): S-1-5-11 (Authenticated Users)
csrss.exe (608): S-1-5-18 (Local System)
csrss.exe (608): S-1-5-32-544 (Administrators)
csrss.exe (608): S-1-1-0 (Everyone)
csrss.exe (608): S-1-5-11 (Authenticated Users)
winlogon.exe (632): S-1-5-18 (Local System)
winlogon.exe (632): S-1-5-32-544 (Administrators)
winlogon.exe (632): S-1-1-0 (Everyone)
winlogon.exe (632): S-1-5-11 (Authenticated Users)
services.exe (676): S-1-5-18 (Local System)
services.exe (676): S-1-5-32-544 (Administrators)
services.exe (676): S-1-1-0 (Everyone)
services.exe (676): S-1-5-11 (Authenticated Users)
lsass.exe (688): S-1-5-18 (Local System)
lsass.exe (688): S-1-5-32-544 (Administrators)
lsass.exe (688): S-1-1-0 (Everyone)
lsass.exe (688): S-1-5-11 (Authenticated Users)
vmacthlp.exe (832): S-1-5-18 (Local System)
vmacthlp.exe (832): S-1-5-32-544 (Administrators)
```

Figure 7.18 – Results of the getsids plugin

So far, we've found some very interesting artifacts, including programs that were running and users who were logged on to the machine. Let's perform registry analysis now.

Registry analysis

Information about every user, setting, program, and the Windows operating system itself can be found within the registry. Even hashed passwords can be found in the registry. In the Windows registry analysis, we will be using the following two plugins:

- `hivescan`
- `hivelist`

The hivescan plugin

The `hivescan` plugin displays the physical locations of available registry hives. The command to run `hivescan` is as follows:

```
volatility --profile=WinXPSP2x86 -f 0zapftis.vmem hivescan
```

The output of the `hivescan` plugin is as follows:

```
root@kali:~/Desktop# volatility --profile=WinXPSP2x86 -f 0zapftis.vmem hivescan
Volatility Foundation Volatility Framework 2.6
Offset(P)
----------
0x020bf388
0x020c3b60
0x02463a40
0x05c63008
0x05c63b60
0x05c6f008
0x05c6fb60
0x076b8008
0x07741458
0x07d9ab60
0x08b7cb60
0x0accab60
0x0af3cb60
root@kali:~/Desktop#
```

Figure 7.19 – Results of the hivescan plugin

In the preceding output, the numbers represent the physical location of the hives on the hard disk. More on the registry can be found at `https://en.wikipedia.org/wiki/Windows_Registry`.

The hivelist plugin

For more detailed (and helpful) information on registry hives and locations within RAM, the `hivelist` plugin can be used. The `hivelist` command shows the details of virtual and physical addresses along with the more easily readable plaintext names and locations.

The command used to run `hivelist` is as follows:

```
volatility --profile=WinXPSP2x86 -f 0zapftis.vmem hivelist
```

The output of the `hivelist` plugin is as follows:

```
root@kali:~/Desktop# volatility --profile=WinXPSP2x86 -f 0zapftis.vmem hivelist
Volatility Foundation Volatility Framework 2.6
Virtual    Physical   Name
---------- ---------- ----
0xe1bf6b60 0x0af3cb60 \Device\HarddiskVolume1\Documents and Settings\Administrator\Local Settings\Application
 Data\Microsoft\Windows\UsrClass.dat
0xe1bb2b60 0x0accab60 \Device\HarddiskVolume1\Documents and Settings\Administrator\NTUSER.DAT
0xe1a4db60 0x08b7cb60 \Device\HarddiskVolume1\Documents and Settings\LocalService\Local Settings\Application
Data\Microsoft\Windows\UsrClass.dat
0xe1991b60 0x07d9ab60 \Device\HarddiskVolume1\Documents and Settings\LocalService\NTUSER.DAT
0xe1844458 0x07741458 \Device\HarddiskVolume1\Documents and Settings\NetworkService\Local Settings\Applicatio
n Data\Microsoft\Windows\UsrClass.dat
0xe183e008 0x076b8008 \Device\HarddiskVolume1\Documents and Settings\NetworkService\NTUSER.DAT
0xe1544b60 0x05c63b60 \Device\HarddiskVolume1\WINDOWS\system32\config\software
0xe154db60 0x05c6fb60 \Device\HarddiskVolume1\WINDOWS\system32\config\SAM
0xe154d008 0x05c6f008 \Device\HarddiskVolume1\WINDOWS\system32\config\default
0xe1544008 0x05c63008 \Device\HarddiskVolume1\WINDOWS\system32\config\SECURITY
0xe13b5a40 0x02463a40 [no name]
0xe1018388 0x020bf388 \Device\HarddiskVolume1\WINDOWS\system32\config\system
0xe1008b60 0x020c3b60 [no name]
root@kali:~/Desktop#
```

Figure 7.20 – Results of the hivelist plugin

More information on registry hives and their supporting files can be found at `https://docs.microsoft.com/en-us/windows/win32/sysinfo/registry-hives`.

Password dumping

The location of the **Security Accounts Manager (SAM)** file is also listed using the `hivelist` plugin, shown in the following screenshot. The SAM file contains hashed passwords for usernames in Windows machines. The path to the SAM file is seen in the following screenshot as `Windows\system32\config\SAM`:

```
0xe154db60 0x05c6fb60 \Device\HarddiskVolume1\WINDOWS\system32\config\SAM
```

Figure 7.21 – Snippet to the hivelist plugin displaying the SAM file location

This file cannot be accessed by users within Windows while the system is on. It can be further used to acquire the hashed passwords in the SAM file to crack passwords using a `wordlist`, along with password-cracking tools such as **John the Ripper**, also available in Kali Linux.

Timeline of events

Volatility can produce a list of timestamped events, which is essential to any investigation. To produce this list, we will use the `timeliner` plugin.

The timeliner plugin

The `timeliner` plugin helps investigators by providing a timeline of all the events that took place when the image was acquired. Although we have an idea of what took place within this scenario, many other dumps may be quite large and far more detailed and complex.

The `timeliner` plugin groups details by time and includes process, PID, process offset, DDLs used, registry details, and other useful information.

To run the `timeliner` command, type the following:

```
volatility --profile=WinXPSP2x86 -f 0zapftis.vmem timeliner
```

The output of the `timeliner` plugin is as follows:

Figure 7.22 – Output of the timeliner plugin

The following is a snippet of the `timeliner` command when scrolling further through its output:

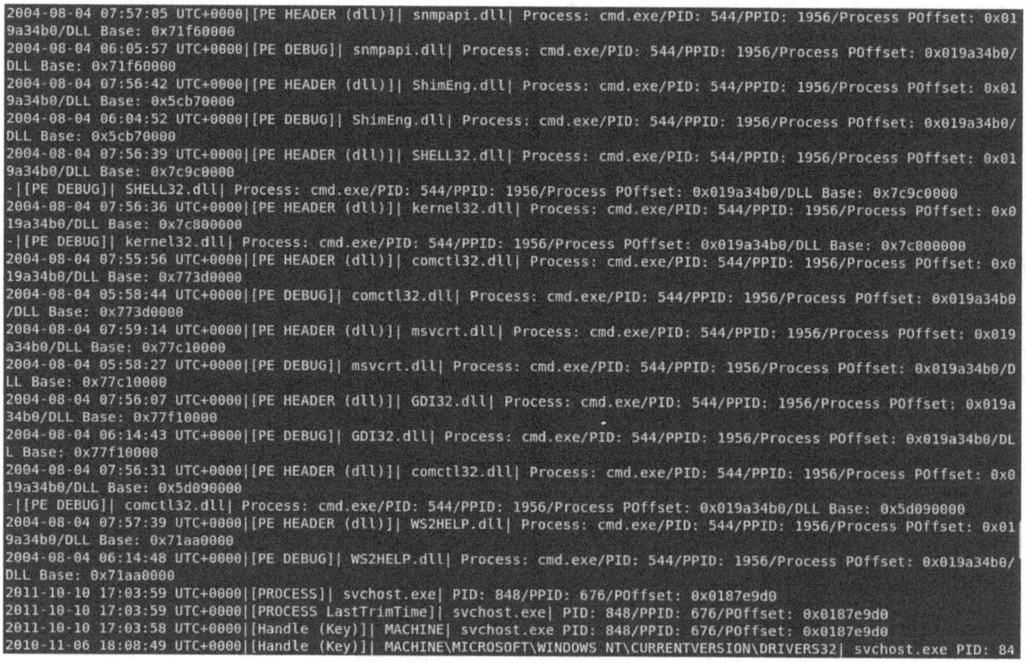

Figure 7.23 – Output of the timeliner plugin (continued)

The output of the `timeliner` plugin can be very lengthy, but we can find useful timeline information as it relates to processes, users, programs, and other artifacts if we take the time to sift through the output. Let's now move on to the Volatility **Graphical User Interface** (**GUI**): Evolve.

Memory analysis using Evolve (a Volatility GUI)

In this section, we'll be looking at the GUI for Volatility called Evolve.

For this example, I'll install **Volatility** and **Evolve** on my desktop. Change to the desktop directory by typing cd Desktop in a new terminal and then download Volatility by typing the following: git clone https://github.com/volatilityfoundation/volatility.git:

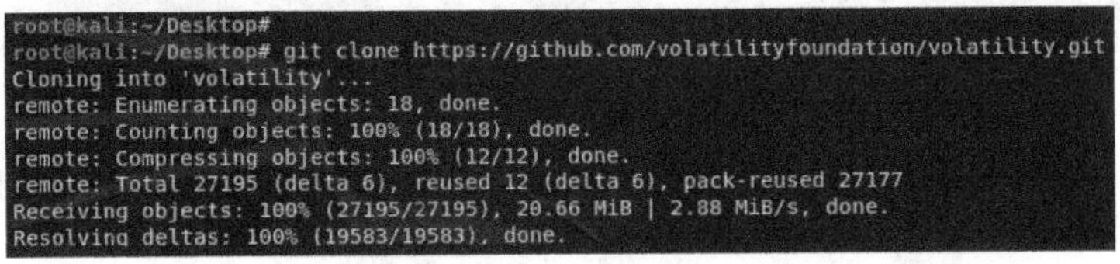

Figure 7.24 – Cloning the Evolve GUI tool to the desktop in Kali

Change to the Volatility directory by typing cd volatility and then show the contents of the folder by typing ls:

Figure 7.25 – Changing to the Volatility directory

You should see setup.py in the list. Type python setup.py install:

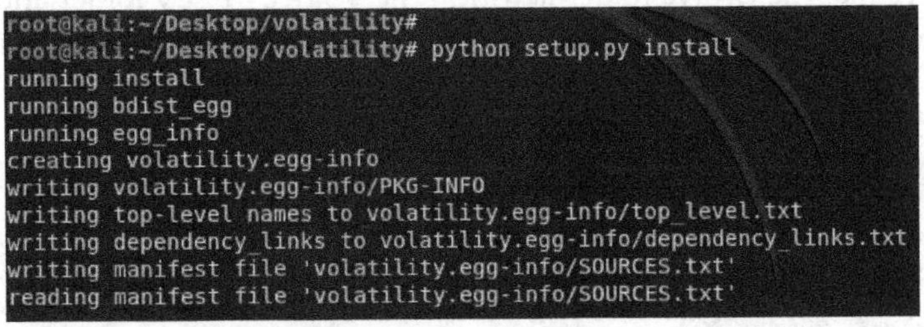

Figure 7.26 – Installing Python within the Volatility directory

Once completed, we'll also need to install the dependencies required for the tool to work. To install the dependencies, type each line from the following list and press **Enter**:

- pip install bottle
- pip install yara
- pip install distorm3

- `pip install maxminddb`

```
Finished processing dependencies for volatility==2.6.1
root@kali:~/Desktop/volatility# pip install bottle
Requirement already satisfied: bottle in /usr/local/lib/python2.7/dist-packages (0.12.1
7)
root@kali:~/Desktop/volatility# pip install yara
Requirement already satisfied: yara in /usr/local/lib/python2.7/dist-packages (1.7.7)
root@kali:~/Desktop/volatility# pip install distorm3
Requirement already satisfied: distorm3 in /usr/lib/python2.7/dist-packages (3.3.4)
root@kali:~/Desktop/volatility# pip install maxminddb
Requirement already satisfied: maxminddb in /usr/local/lib/python2.7/dist-packages (1.4
```

Figure 7.27 – Installing Volatility dependencies

While still in the Volatility directory, we can also now clone and install the **Evolve WebGUI**. Type the following command:

```
git clone https://github.com/JamesHabben/evolve.git
```

The following output displays the Evolve installation cloning process:

```
root@kali:~/Desktop/volatility#
root@kali:~/Desktop/volatility# git clone https://github.com/JamesHabben/evolve.git
Cloning into 'evolve'...
remote: Enumerating objects: 529, done.
remote: Total 529 (delta 0), reused 0 (delta 0), pack-reused 529
Receiving objects: 100% (529/529), 1.78 MiB | 2.18 MiB/s, done.
Resolving deltas: 100% (116/116), done.
```

Figure 7.28 – Cloning Evolve to the Volatility directory

Type `ls` to ensure that the Evolve folder is within the `volatility` folder and then change to the `evolve` directory by typing in `cd evolve`. Then, type `ls` to view the contents within the `evolve` folder:

```
root@kali:~/Desktop/volatility# ls
AUTHORS.txt    CREDITS.txt  LICENSE.txt   pyinstaller       setup.py              vol.py
build          dist         Makefile      pyinstaller.spec  tools
CHANGELOG.txt  evolve       MANIFEST.in   README.txt        volatility
contrib        LEGAL.txt    PKG-INFO      resources         volatility.egg-info
root@kali:~/Desktop/volatility#
root@kali:~/Desktop/volatility#
root@kali:~/Desktop/volatility# cd evolve
root@kali:~/Desktop/volatility/evolve#
root@kali:~/Desktop/volatility/evolve# ls
 Docker     images   'Plugins with SQLite output'   README.md   web
 evolve.py  morphs   'query list.txt'               setup.py
root@kali:~/Desktop/volatility/evolve#
root@kali:~/Desktop/volatility/evolve# python evolve.py --help
Python Version: 2.7.16+ (default, Sep  4 2019, 08:19:57)
[GCC 9.2.1 20190827]
Evolve Version: 1.6
usage: evolve.py [-h] [--version] [-d DBFOLDER] [-f FILE] [-l LOCAL]
                 [-w WEBPORT] [-r RUN] [-p PROFILE] [--kdbg KDBG] [--dtb DTB]
                 [--plugins PLUGINS]
```

Figure 7.29 – Viewing the content of the Volatility and Evolve directories

To view all the available options for use within the Evolve web interface, type `python.py --help` while still in the `evolve` directory:

```
root@kali:~/Desktop/volatility/evolve# python evolve.py --help
Python Version: 2.7.16+ (default, Sep  4 2019, 08:19:57)
[GCC 9.2.1 20190827]
Evolve Version: 1.6
usage: evolve.py [-h] [--version] [-d DBFOLDER] [-f FILE] [-l LOCAL]
                 [-w WEBPORT] [-r RUN] [-p PROFILE] [--kdbg KDBG] [--dtb DTB]
                 [--plugins PLUGINS]

Web interface for Volatility Framework.

optional arguments:
  -h, --help            show this help message and exit
  --version             show program's version number and exit
  -d DBFOLDER, --dbfolder DBFOLDER
                        Optional database location
  -f FILE, --file FILE  RAM dump to analyze
  -l LOCAL, --local LOCAL
                        Restrict webserver to serving 'localhost' only
  -w WEBPORT, --webport WEBPORT
                        Port to bind Web Server on
  -r RUN, --run RUN     Give a comma separated list of plugins to run on
                        startup
  -p PROFILE, --profile PROFILE
                        VOL: Memory profile to use with Volatility
  --kdbg KDBG           VOL: Offset of KDBG for faster searching
  --dtb DTB             VOL: Offset of DTB for faster searching
  --plugins PLUGINS     VOL: Path to additional Volatility plugins to use
root@kali:~/Desktop/volatility/evolve#
```

Figure 7.30 – Using the Volatility help command

You can now copy the `cridex.vmem` file, or any other memory dump file you'd like to analyze, into the `evolve` folder. The `cridex.vmem` file can be downloaded directly at `https://github.com/volatilityfoundation/volatility/wiki/Memory-Samples` under the name `Malware - Cridex`.

To open the `cridex.vmem` file within Evolve, type the following (while still in the Evolve directory): `python evolve.py -f cridex.vmem`.

Note: The `-f` option specifies the file we'd like to open and analyze:

```
root@kali:~/Desktop/volatility/evolve#
root@kali:~/Desktop/volatility/evolve# python evolve.py -f cridex.vmem
Python Version: 2.7.16+ (default, Sep  4 2019, 08:19:57)
[GCC 9.2.1 20190827]
Evolve Version: 1.6
Volatility Version: 2.6.1
```

Figure 7.31 – Opening the sample file in Evolve

A web page should now open with the name of the `cridex` file listed in a tab:

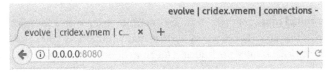

Figure 7.32 – Snippet of the Evolve tab in the Browser

Within the Evolve web interface, the plugins are listed in the left pane, which you can click on to run. In the following screenshot, I've run the `pslist` plugin, which is exactly the same as we did using Volatility in the terminal earlier in this chapter:

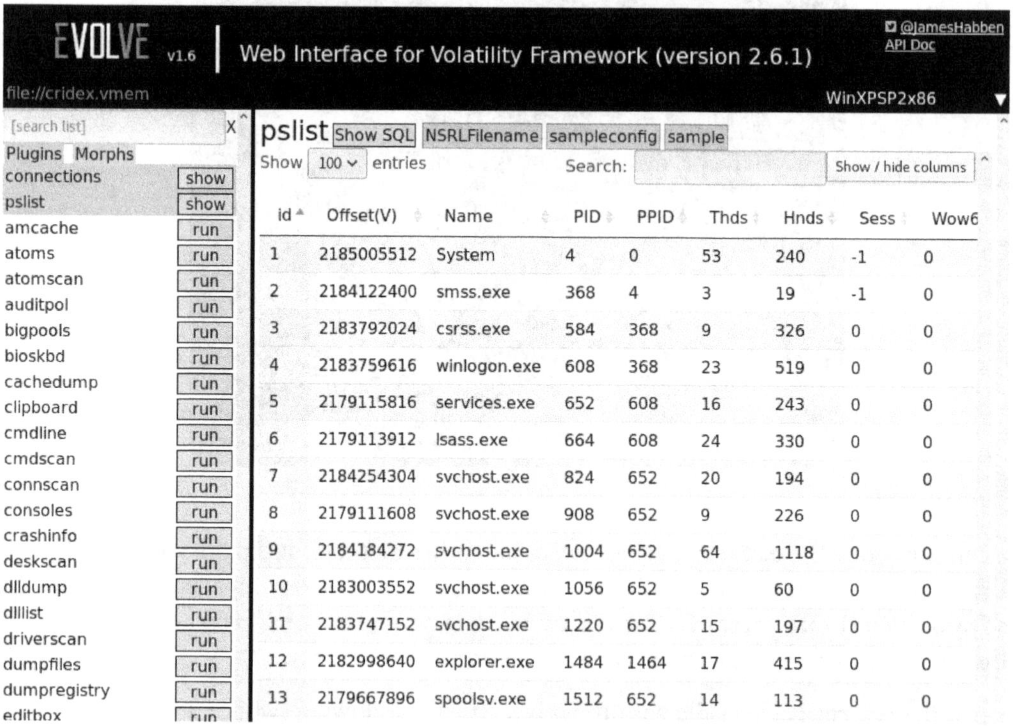

Figure 7.33 – The Evolve Web Interface for Volatility with automated pslist output

Try opening and analyzing some of the other memory samples available for download at `https://github.com/volatilityfoundation/volatility/wiki/Memory-Samples`. You may also want to have a look at Volatility Workbench v3.0-beta, which runs on Windows machines, for user testing with memory dumps. Volatility Workbench 3.0-beta and sample memory dumps can be downloaded at `https://www.osforensics.com/tools/volatility-workbench.html`.

> **Tip**
>
> Be sure to download more publicly available memory images and samples to test your skills in this area. Experiment with as many plugins as you can and, of course, be sure to document your findings and consider sharing them online.

Summary

In this chapter, we looked at memory forensics and analysis using some of the many plugins available within the Volatility Framework. One of the first and most important steps in working with Volatility is choosing the profile that Volatility will use throughout the analysis. This profile tells Volatility what type of operating system is being used. Once the profile was chosen, we were able to successfully perform process, network, registry, DLL, and even malware analysis using this versatile tool. As we've seen, Volatility can perform several important functions in digital forensics and should be used together with the other tools we've used previously to perform in-depth and detailed forensic analysis and investigations. We also went a bit further in this edition by installing the web interface for the Volatility Framework for those who may prefer a GUI approach to memory analysis.

In our next chapter, we'll move on to another powerful tool that does everything from acquisition to reporting. Let's get started with Autopsy—the Sleuth Kit®.

8

Artifact Analysis

In this chapter, we'll cover several different tools to uncover various artifacts that may be very useful to our forensic investigations. Most of the tools used in this chapter focus specifically on memory and swap analysis, while **Network Mapper** (**Nmap**) and p0f focus more on the network and device.

In this chapter, we'll cover the following topics:

- Identifying and fingerprinting devices, operating systems, and running services with p0f and Nmap
- Analyzing memory dumps to discover traces of ransomware
- Performing swap analysis
- Using `swap_digger` and `mimipenguin` for password dumping
- Examining the Firefox browser and Gmail artifacts using `pdgmail`

Identifying devices and operating systems with p0f

If you're using the VirtualBox version of Kali 2019.3 (`kali-linux-2019.3a-vbox-amd64.ova`), you may have to install p0f by typing in `apt-install get p0f`. If you're using the `Kali 2019.3 Large.iso` image, it should come preinstalled.

You may also use the help option within p0f to verify that it is installed on your system by typing p0f -h. This displays the network interface options, operating mode, output settings, and performance-related options:

```
root@kali:~# p0f -h
--- p0f 3.09b by Michal Zalewski <lcamtuf@coredump.cx> ---

p0f: invalid option -- 'h'
Usage: p0f [ ...options... ] [ 'filter rule' ]

Network interface options:

  -i iface  - listen on the specified network interface
  -r file   - read offline pcap data from a given file
  -p        - put the listening interface in promiscuous mode
  -L        - list all available interfaces

Operating mode and output settings:

  -f file   - read fingerprint database from 'file' (/etc/p0f/p0f.fp)
  -o file   - write information to the specified log file
  -s name   - answer to API queries at a named unix socket
  -u user   - switch to the specified unprivileged account and chroot
  -d        - fork into background (requires -o or -s)
```

Figure 8.1 – p0f help options

Once verified, we can run the p0f command without additional switches or options by typing in p0f, which runs the tool against our machine. In this scenario, my IP address is 172.16.77.159:

1. Typing in the p0f command starts the fingerprint process. It may look like the tool has stopped but give it a couple of minutes to perform the scan and display the output:

```
root@kali:~# p0f
--- p0f 3.09b by Michal Zalewski <lcamtuf@coredump.cx> ---

[+] Closed 1 file descriptor.
[+] Loaded 322 signatures from '/etc/p0f/p0f.fp'.
[+] Intercepting traffic on default interface 'eth0'.
[+] Default packet filtering configured [+VLAN].
[+] Entered main event loop.
```

Figure 8.2 – Starting p0f in Kali

2. We can also specify the interface on which we'd like to run p0f in the event where we have multiple network interface cards. Let's first view our interfaces by typing ifconfig -a into the Terminal:

```
root@kali:~# ifconfig -a
eth0: flags=4163<UP,BROADCAST,RUNNING,MULTICAST>  mtu 1500
        inet 172.16.77.159  netmask 255.255.0.0  broadcast 172.16.255.255
        inet6 fe80::a00:27ff:fe42:e90  prefixlen 64  scopeid 0x20<link>
        ether 08:00:27:42:0e:90  txqueuelen 1000  (Ethernet)
        RX packets 228  bytes 18623 (18.1 KiB)
        RX errors 0  dropped 4  overruns 0  frame 0
        TX packets 269  bytes 44562 (43.5 KiB)
        TX errors 0  dropped 0 overruns 0  carrier 0  collisions 0

lo: flags=73<UP,LOOPBACK,RUNNING>  mtu 65536
        inet 127.0.0.1  netmask 255.0.0.0
        inet6 ::1  prefixlen 128  scopeid 0x10<host>
        loop  txqueuelen 1000  (Local Loopback)
        RX packets 1572  bytes 130588 (127.5 KiB)
        RX errors 0  dropped 0  overruns 0  frame 0
        TX packets 1572  bytes 130588 (127.5 KiB)
        TX errors 0  dropped 0 overruns 0  carrier 0  collisions 0
```

Figure 8.3 – Network adapter settings

The output shows that I have two interfaces, with eth0 being my Ethernet/LAN interface, with an IP of 172.16.77.159 and a loopback address of the default 127.0.0.1. I'll be using the eth0 interface with p0f.

3. We can also use the p0f -L command to list all the interfaces:

```
root@kali:~# p0f -L
--- p0f 3.09b by Michal Zalewski <lcamtuf@coredump.cx> ---

-- Available interfaces --

  0: Name          : eth0
     Description : -
     IP address  : 172.16.77.159

  1: Name          : lo
     Description : -
     IP address  : 127.0.0.1

  2: Name          : any
     Description : Pseudo-device that captures on all interfaces
     IP address  : (none)

  3: Name          : nflog
     Description : Linux netfilter log (NFLOG) interface
     IP address  : (none)

  4: Name          : nfqueue
     Description : Linux netfilter queue (NFQUEUE) interface
     IP address  : (none)
```

Figure 8.4 – Interfaces detected by p0f

4. To specify the interface when using p0f, I'll type p0f -i eth0 into the Terminal:

```
root@kali:~# p0f -i eth0
--- p0f 3.09b by Michal Zalewski <lcamtuf@coredump.cx> ---

[+] Closed 1 file descriptor.
[+] Loaded 322 signatures from '/etc/p0f/p0f.fp'.
[+] Intercepting traffic on interface 'eth0'.
[+] Default packet filtering configured [+VLAN].
[+] Entered main event loop.

.-[ 172.16.77.161/33364 -> 172.16.77.159/7 (syn) ]-
|
| client    = 172.16.77.161/33364
| os        = Linux 2.2.x-3.x
| dist      = 0
| params    = generic
| raw_sig   = 4:64+0:0:1460:65535,7:mss,sok,ts,nop,ws:df,id+:0
|
`---- '

.-[ 172.16.77.161/33364 -> 172.16.77.159/7 (mtu) ]-
|
| client    = 172.16.77.161/33364
| link      = Ethernet or modem
| raw_mtu   = 1500
|
`----
```

Figure 8.5 – Specifying the Ethernet interface in p0f

5. Open the web browser in Kali and you'll see the Terminal being populated with more IP information. By default, the Firefox web browser's home page carries us to the offensive security site and so p0f shows information about the connections and hops (the process of packets passing from one point to another) to the server and information about the server.

6. Try browsing to a site. I've opened www.cfsi.co in the browser. p0f updates the information in the Terminal in real time and the first entry displayed shows an SYN request from 172.16.77.159 (my Kali machine) to 185.230.60.211 via port 80. We can also see information about my Kali machine, such as the OS (Linux 2.2-3.x), as fingerprinted by p0f:

```
.-[ 172.16.77.159/53382 -> 185.230.60.211/80 (syn) ]-
|
| client    = 172.16.77.159/53382
| os        = Linux 2.2.x-3.x
| dist      = 0
| params    = generic
| raw_sig   = 4:64+0:0:1460:mss*44,7:mss,sok,ts,nop,ws:df,id+:0
|
`----

.-[ 172.16.77.159/53382 -> 185.230.60.211/80 (mtu) ]-
|
| client    = 172.16.77.159/53382
| link      = Ethernet or modem
| raw_mtu   = 1500
|
```

Figure 8.6 – IP and OS information displayed on the p0f output

7. Let's get more information about the IP address `185.230.60.211`. In the Terminal window, click on **File | New Tab**. In the new tab, type `whois 185.230.60.211`.

The output of the `whois` command can be seen in the following screenshot:

```
root@kali:~# whois 185.230.60.211
% This is the RIPE Database query service.
% The objects are in RPSL format.
%
% The RIPE Database is subject to Terms and Conditions.
% See http://www.ripe.net/db/support/db-terms-conditions.pdf

% Note: this output has been filtered.
%       To receive output for a database update, use the "-B" flag.

% Information related to '185.230.60.0 - 185.230.60.255'

% Abuse contact for '185.230.60.0 - 185.230.60.255' is 'abuse@wix.com'

inetnum:        185.230.60.0 - 185.230.60.255
netname:        wix_com_inc
country:        US
admin-c:        SP17239-RIPE
tech-c:         SP17239-RIPE
status:         LIR-PARTITIONED PA
mnt-by:         il-wixcom-sys-mnt
mnt-by:         il-wixcom-1-mnt
created:        2018-05-21T15:00:58Z
last-modified:  2019-10-10T07:20:09Z
source:         RIPE

person:         Stanislav Panich
address:        Namal Tel Aviv 40
phone:          +972 3 5454900
nic-hdl:        SP17239-RIPE
mnt-by:         il-wixcom-sys-mnt
created:        2018-05-09T15:30:17Z
last-modified:  2018-05-09T15:30:17Z
source:         RIPE
```

Figure 8.7 – The whois command

In this `whois` output, we can see that the IP points to `wix.com`, which is the host for the `www.cfsi.co` website.

Scrolling through the `p0f` output, we can see several other pieces of information, including the uptime of the server and other IP addresses and hops along the way:

```
.-[ 172.16.77.159/47460 -> 185.230.60.211/443 (uptime) ]-
|
| server   = 185.230.60.211/443
| uptime   = 33 days 15 hrs 14 min (modulo 49 days)
| raw_freq = 1003.42 Hz
|
`----

.-[ 172.16.77.159/52308 -> 35.241.16.116/443 (syn) ]-
|
| client   = 172.16.77.159/52308
| os       = Linux 2.2.x-3.x
| dist     = 0
| params   = generic
| raw_sig  = 4:64+0:0:1460:mss*44,7:mss,sok,ts,nop,ws:df,id+:0
```

Figure 8.8 – p0f output displaying server uptime details

Now that we've found some very useful information on our target network IPs, let's have a look at another tool, Nmap, which can also be used to fingerprint and discover devices, services, and more.

Information gathering and fingerprinting with Nmap

Let's now use the Nmap tool to gather information about resources and devices on the network and discover any open, filtered (monitored or firewalled), or closed ports and also fingerprint their operating systems:

1. To view the usage options for Nmap, type in `nmap  -h`:

```
root@kali:~# nmap -h
Nmap 7.80 ( https://nmap.org )
Usage: nmap [Scan Type(s)] [Options] {target specification}
TARGET SPECIFICATION:
  Can pass hostnames, IP addresses, networks, etc.
  Ex: scanme.nmap.org, microsoft.com/24, 192.168.0.1; 10.0.0-255.1-254
  -iL <inputfilename>: Input from list of hosts/networks
  -iR <num hosts>: Choose random targets
  --exclude <host1[,host2][,host3],...>: Exclude hosts/networks
  --excludefile <exclude_file>: Exclude list from file
HOST DISCOVERY:
  -sL: List Scan - simply list targets to scan
  -sn: Ping Scan - disable port scan
  -Pn: Treat all hosts as online -- skip host discovery
  -PS/PA/PU/PY[portlist]: TCP SYN/ACK, UDP or SCTP discovery to given ports
  -PE/PP/PM: ICMP echo, timestamp, and netmask request discovery probes
  -PO[protocol list]: IP Protocol Ping
```

Figure 8.9 – Nmap help options

2. I'll scan the devices on my network by typing the following command into a new Terminal:

```
nmap -v -O -sV 172.16.0.0/24 -Pn
```

The following list details the options used in the previous command:

- `-v` : Verbose output

- `-O` : Enable operating system detection

- `-sV` : Probe open ports to determine service and version information

- `-Pn` : Treat all hosts as online (skip discovery)

The following screenshot shows some of the output of the Nmap version scan:

```
root@kali:~# nmap -v -O -sV 172.16.0.0/24 -Pn
Starting Nmap 7.80 ( https://nmap.org ) at 2019-11-27 10:51 AST
NSE: Loaded 45 scripts for scanning.
Initiating ARP Ping Scan at 10:51
Scanning 256 hosts [1 port/host]
Completed ARP Ping Scan at 10:51, 1.94s elapsed (256 total hosts)
Initiating Parallel DNS resolution of 256 hosts. at 10:51
Completed Parallel DNS resolution of 256 hosts. at 10:51, 0.11s elapsed
```

Figure 8.10 – Nmap service scan output

This scan can take some time to run due to the service version scanning in particular. Here's the output of one host (`172.16.0.1`):

```
Nmap scan report for 172.16.0.1
Host is up (0.0033s latency).
Not shown: 994 closed ports
PORT     STATE SERVICE    VERSION
22/tcp   open  ssh        Cisco SSH 1.25 (protocol 2.0)
80/tcp   open  http       Cisco IOS http config
443/tcp  open  ssl/https?
1720/tcp open  h323q931?
5060/tcp open  sip-proxy  Cisco SIP Gateway (IOS 15.2.4.M5)
5061/tcp open  tcpwrapped
MAC Address: 3C:08:F6:25:35:52 (Cisco Systems)
OS details: Cisco 836, 890, 1751, 1841, 2800, or 2900 router (IOS 12.4 - 15.1),
, Cisco Aironet 2600-series WAP (IOS 15.2(2))
Network Distance: 1 hop
TCP Sequence Prediction: Difficulty=257 (Good luck!)
IP ID Sequence Generation: Randomized
Service Info: OS: IOS; Device: router; CPE: cpe:/o:cisco:ios
```

Figure 8.11 – Nmap scan output

In this Nmap result, we can see that six ports are open and running various services, such as SSH 1.25, SIP Proxy, and SSL, inclusive of service version information as specified when using the -sV option. We can also see that Nmap has fingerprinted the OS to be a Cisco router.

We've discovered some very interesting information using Nmap and p0f. Let's move on to our next topic, which covers Linux forensics.

Live Linux forensics with Linux Explorer

When performing live forensics on Linux machines, Linux Explorer can be used to gather information and artifacts.

Linux Explorer can be used to find the following artifacts:

- Processes and process IDs
- Usernames and logins
- Ports and service information
- Suspicious files
- Rootkit detection

Ransomware analysis

The **WannaCry cryptoworm** became well-known around May 2017, when several large organizations started reporting ransomware infections that spread via EternalBlue exploits on vulnerable Windows systems. A splash screen appeared on users' machines, which then instructed users to pay $300.00 in Bitcoin to have their infected/encrypted file decrypted.

More on the WannaCry ransomware can be found at `https://en.wikipedia.org/wiki/WannaCry_ransomware_attack`.

Further reading on the WannaCry ransomware can be found by visiting the following links:

- Automated Behavioral Analysis of Malware. A Case Study of WannaCry Ransomware (Chen and Bridges): `https://www.osti.gov/servlets/purl/1423027`

- A Study of WannaCry Ransomware Attack (Dr. Supreet Kaur Sahi): `https://www.technoarete.org/common_abstract/pdf/IJERCSE/v4/i9/Ext_89621.pdf`

- WannaCry Ransomware: Analysis of Infection, Persistence, Recovery, Prevention and Propagation Mechanisms (Akbanov, Vassilakis, Logothetis): `https://www.il-pib.pl/czasopisma/JTIT/2019/1/113.pdf`

For this lab, we'll be using Volatility to analyze the ransomware and attempt to trace and view the originating sources of infection by analyzing a memory dump taken from an infected machine.

> **Important note**
> We will not be downloading the actual ransomware but merely a memory dump file of an infected machine.

For additional safety, you may switch your network adapter settings to NAT (if on bridged mode) in VirtualBox or your platform of choice, before downloading the file and then disable your network adapter after downloading the file to ensure that you are working in an isolated VM.

Downloading and extracting a sample ransomware file

The memory dump of the machine infected with the WannaCry ransomware can be downloaded from here: `https://mega.nz/#!Au5xlCAS!KX5ZJKYzQgDHSa721PFwqKL6CsZS7oQGbyyQrMTH9XY`.

Thanks to Donny at `https://www.null0x4d5a.com/` for providing the mega link and password to the file in his blog.

I've saved the downloaded file to my `Downloads` folder. In the Terminal, I'll switch to the `Downloads` folder and view the contents by typing in `cd Downloads` and then issuing the `ls` command. There I can see the `wannacry.7z` file, as in the following screenshot:

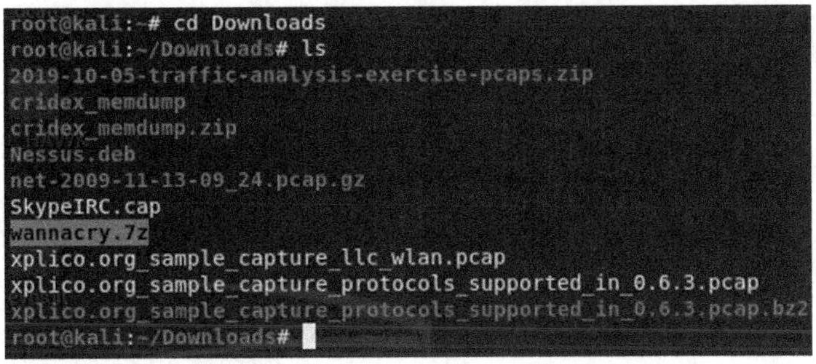

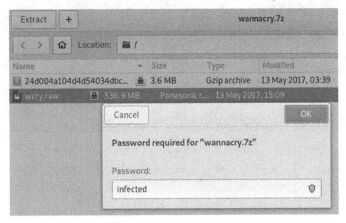

Figure 8.12 – Viewing the downloaded sample file using the ls command

For integrity purposes, I've run the **sha1sum** and **sha256sum** tools against the downloaded file. To extract the file, I've opened my `Downloads` folder, double-clicked on the file, right-clicked on `wcry.raw`, and then clicked on the **Extract** option. The password for the file is the word `infected`, as in the following screenshot:

Figure 8.13 – Screenshot of the password to extract the sample file

Click on **OK** to start the extraction and then click on **Show the Files** when completed:

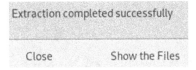

Figure 8.14 – Extraction completion options

The extracted memory dump file is named `wcry.raw` and shows a file size of 536.9 MB:

Figure 8.15 – Extracted wcry.raw file

Once the file has been downloaded and extracted, let's begin analyzing the ransomware.

WannaCry analysis using Volatility

Open a new Terminal and navigate to the `Downloads` folder. Let's start by running the `image info` plugin to determine the profile to use, just as we did in the earlier Volatility exercise in the previous chapter:

1. In the Terminal, type `volatility -f wcry.raw imageinfo`:

```
root@kali:~/Downloads# volatility -f wcry.raw imageinfo
Volatility Foundation Volatility Framework 2.6
INFO    : volatility.debug    : Determining profile based on KDBG search...
          Suggested Profile(s) : WinXPSP2x86, WinXPSP3x86 (Instantiated with WinXPSP2x86)
                     AS Layer1 : IA32PagedMemory (Kernel AS)
                     AS Layer2 : FileAddressSpace (/root/Downloads/wcry.raw)
                      PAE type : No PAE
                           DTB : 0x39000L
                          KDBG : 0x8054cf60L
          Number of Processors : 1
     Image Type (Service Pack) : 3
                KPCR for CPU 0 : 0xffdff000L
             KUSER_SHARED_DATA : 0xffdf0000L
           Image date and time : 2019-05-12 21:26:32 UTC+0000
     Image local date and time : 2019-05-13 02:56:32 +0530
root@kali:~/Downloads# 
```

Figure 8.16 – Output of the imageinfo plugin in Volatility

The suggested profiles for our `wcry.raw` image are `WinXPSP2x86` and `WinXPSP3x86`, but we'll use `WinXPSP2x86` from here on.

2. Let's first analyze the `wcry.raw` file by looking at the running processes at the time the dump was acquired.

We'll start with the `pslist` plugin. Type the following command into the Terminal:

```
volatility –profile=WinXPSP2x86 -f wcry.raw pslist
```

The following screenshot displays the output of the `pslist` command:

```
root@kali:~/Downloads# volatility --profile=WinXPSP2x86 -f wcry.raw pslist
Volatility Foundation Volatility Framework 2.6
Offset(V)   Name                    PID   PPID   Thds    Hnds   Sess  Wow64 Start
---------- -------------------- ------ ------ ------ ------- ------ ------ ------------------------------
0x823c8830 System                    4      0     51     244  ------      0 0
0x82169020 smss.exe                348      4      3      19  ------      0 2019-05-12 21:21:55 UTC+0000
0x82161da0 csrss.exe               596    348     12     352       0      0 2019-05-12 21:22:00 UTC+0000
0x8216e020 winlogon.exe            620    348     23     536       0      0 2019-05-12 21:22:01 UTC+0000
0x821937f0 services.exe            664    620     15     265       0      0 2019-05-12 21:22:01 UTC+0000
0x82191658 lsass.exe               676    620     23     353       0      0 2019-05-12 21:22:01 UTC+0000
0x8221a2c0 svchost.exe             836    664     19     211       0      0 2019-05-12 21:22:02 UTC+0000
0x821b5230 svchost.exe             904    664      9     227       0      0 2019-05-12 21:22:03 UTC+0000
0x821af7e8 svchost.exe            1024    664     79    1366       0      0 2019-05-12 21:22:03 UTC+0000
0x8203b7a8 svchost.exe            1084    664      6      72       0      0 2019-05-12 21:22:03 UTC+0000
0x821bea78 svchost.exe            1152    664     10     173       0      0 2019-05-12 21:22:06 UTC+0000
0x821e2da0 spoolsv.exe            1484    664     14     124       0      0 2019-05-12 21:22:09 UTC+0000
0x821d9da0 explorer.exe           1636   1608     11     331       0      0 2019-05-12 21:22:10 UTC+0000
0x82218da0 tasksche.exe           1940   1636      7      51       0      0 2019-05-12 21:22:14 UTC+0000
0x82231da0 ctfmon.exe             1956   1636      1      86       0      0 2019-05-12 21:22:14 UTC+0000
0x81fb95d8 svchost.exe             260    664      5     105       0      0 2019-05-12 21:22:18 UTC+0000
0x81fde308 @WanaDecryptor@        740   1940      2      70       0      0 2019-05-12 21:22:22 UTC+0000
0x81f747c0 wuauclt.exe            1768   1024      7     132       0      0 2019-05-12 21:22:52 UTC+0000
0x82010020 alg.exe                 544    664      6     101       0      0 2019-05-12 21:22:55 UTC+0000
```

Figure 8.17 – Output of the pslist plugin in Volatility

In the preceding screenshot, we can see that there is an entry (third from last) for a process named @WanaDecryptor@ with a PID of 740 and a PPID of 1940. This is a good indicator that an instance of the WannaCry ramsomware may exist within an infected process or file.

3. Let's take a more detailed look by using the `pstree` plugin, which produces the same output but in a format that's easier to follow when identifying the parent processes. Type the following command into the Terminal:

```
volatility -profile=WinXPSP2x86 -f wcry.raw pstree
```

The following screenshot displays the output of the `pstree` command:

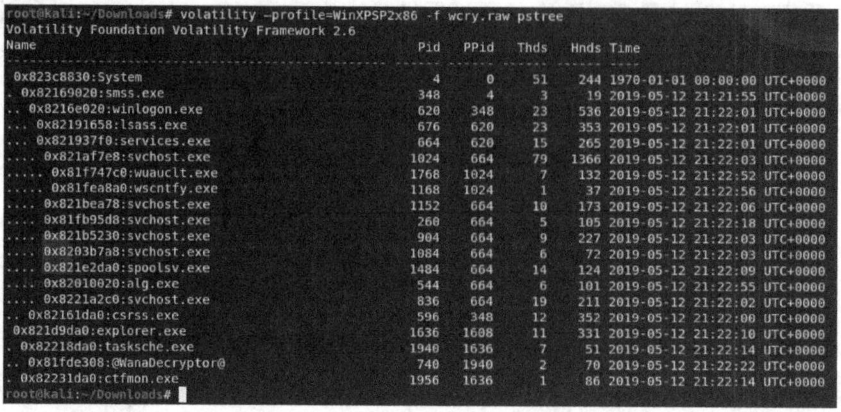

Figure 8.18 – Output of the pstree plugin in Volatility

Using the `pslist`, `psscan`, and `pstree` plugins, we saw the @
WanaDecryptor@ process (with a PID of `740` and a PPID of `1940`) spawned
by the Windows task scheduler (`tasksch.exe`, PID: `1940`) under Windows
Explorer (`explorer.exe`).

4. We can also view this information by issuing the `psscan` plugin by typing the
    following command into the Terminal:

```
volatility –profile=WinXPSP2x86 -f wcry.raw psscan
```

The following screenshot displays the output of the `psscan` command:

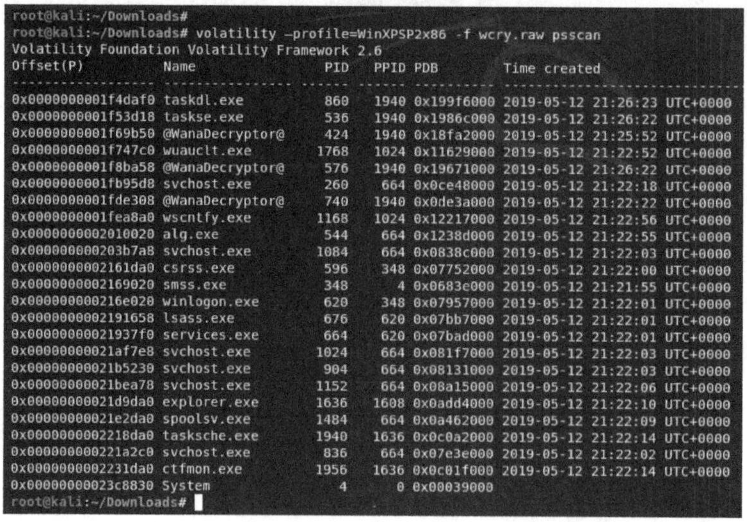

Figure 8.19 – Output of the psscan plugin in Volatility

In this output, we can see four instances of processes that have a PPID of `1940`:

`Taskdl.exe`: PID of `860`

`Taskse.exe`: PID of `536`

`@WanaDecryptor@`: PID of `424`

`@WanaDecryptor@`: PID of `576`

5. Let's narrow down the output by adding `| grep 1940` to `pslist` and `psscans`, which will search for any processes associated with the `1940` process.

   Let's first run `pslist` again with the `grep` option by running the following command:

```
volatility –profile=WinXPSP2x86 -f wcry.raw pslist | grep 1940
```

The following screenshot displays the output of the `pslist` command:

```
root@kali:~/Downloads# volatility –profile=WinXPSP2x86 -f wcry.raw pslist | grep 1940
Volatility Foundation Volatility Framework 2.6
0x82218da0 tasksche.exe          1940   1636    7     51      0        0 2019-05-12 21:22:14 UTC+0000

0x81fde308 @WanaDecryptor@        740   1940    2     70      0        0 2019-05-12 21:22:22 UTC+0000

root@kali:~/Downloads#
```

Figure 8.20 – Output of the pslist plugin using the grep option in Volatility

Let's also run the `psscan` plugin with the `grep` option to view the processes by running the following command:

```
volatility –profile=WinXPSP2x86 -f wcry.raw psscan | grep 1940
```

The following screenshot displays the output of the `psscan` command:

```
root@kali:~/Downloads#
root@kali:~/Downloads# volatility –profile=WinXPSP2x86 -f wcry.raw psscan | grep 1940
Volatility Foundation Volatility Framework 2.6
0x0000000001f4daf0 taskdl.exe       860   1940 0x199f6000 2019-05-12 21:26:23 UTC+0000   2019-05-12 21:26:23
0x0000000001f53d18 taskse.exe       536   1940 0x1986c000 2019-05-12 21:26:22 UTC+0000   2019-05-12 21:26:23
0x0000000001f69b50 @WanaDecryptor@  424   1940 0x18fa2000 2019-05-12 21:25:52 UTC+0000   2019-05-12 21:25:53
0x0000000001f8ba58 @WanaDecryptor@  576   1940 0x19671000 2019-05-12 21:26:22 UTC+0000   2019-05-12 21:26:23
0x0000000001fde308 @WanaDecryptor@  740   1940 0x0de3a000 2019-05-12 21:22:22 UTC+0000
0x0000000002218da0 tasksche.exe    1940   1636 0x0c0a2000 2019-05-12 21:22:14 UTC+0000
root@kali:~/Downloads#
```

Figure 8.21 – Output of the psscan plugin using the grep option in Volatility

6. To obtain more information on the processes, we can run the `dlllist` plugin and also specify the process ID to determine the DLL libraries used. You may want to run this command in a new tab in the Terminal as the output is quite lengthy. In the output for this command, we'll be looking for processes with the PIDs listed in the previous screenshots (`860`, `536`, `424`, `576`, `740`, `1940`).

Run the `dlllist` plugin by typing the following into the new tab Terminal:

```
volatility –profile=WinXPSP2x86 -f wcry.raw dlllist –p 1940
```

The following screenshot displays the output of the `dlllist` command. The `dlllist` plugin, when specified with the `-p 1940` process number, displays the directories and libraries used by the process:

```
root@kali:~/Downloads# volatility –profile=WinXPSP2x86 -f wcry.raw dlllist –p 1940
Volatility Foundation Volatility Framework 2.6
************************************************************************
System pid:       4
Unable to read PEB for task.
************************************************************************
smss.exe pid:    348
Command line : \SystemRoot\System32\smss.exe


Base          Size      LoadCount LoadTime                        Path
----------    --------- --------- -----------------------------  ----
0x48580000    0xf000    0xffff                                   \SystemRoot\System32\smss.exe
0x7c900000    0xb2000   0xffff                                   C:\WINDOWS\system32\ntdll.dll
************************************************************************
```

Figure 8.22 – Output of the dlllist plugin

Scrolling down through the output, we can see the output for `tasksche.exe`, with a PID of `1940` and all the associated DLLs:

```
tasksche.exe pid:    1940
Command line : "C:\Intel\ivecuqmanpnirkt615\tasksche.exe"
Service Pack 3

Base          Size      LoadCount LoadTime                       Path
----------    --------- --------- -----------------------------  ----
0x00400000    0x35a000  0xffff                                   C:\Intel\ivecuqmanpnirkt615\tasksche.exe
0x7c900000    0xb2000   0xffff                                   C:\WINDOWS\system32\ntdll.dll
0x7c800000    0xf6000   0xffff                                   C:\WINDOWS\system32\kernel32.dll
0x7e410000    0x91000   0xffff                                   C:\WINDOWS\system32\USER32.dll
0x77f10000    0x49000   0xffff                                   C:\WINDOWS\system32\GDI32.dll
0x77dd0000    0x9b000   0xffff                                   C:\WINDOWS\system32\ADVAPI32.dll
0x77e70000    0x93000   0xffff                                   C:\WINDOWS\system32\RPCRT4.dll
0x77fe0000    0x11000   0xffff                                   C:\WINDOWS\system32\Secur32.dll
0x77c10000    0x58000   0xffff                                   C:\WINDOWS\system32\MSVCRT.dll
0x76390000    0x1d000   0x1                                      C:\WINDOWS\system32\IMM32.DLL
0x629c0000    0x9000    0x1                                      C:\WINDOWS\system32\LPK.DLL
0x74d90000    0x6b000   0x1                                      C:\WINDOWS\system32\USP10.dll
0x77b40000    0x22000   0x1                                      C:\WINDOWS\system32\Apphelp.dll
0x77c00000    0x8000    0x1                                      C:\WINDOWS\system32\VERSION.dll
0x68000000    0x36000   0x1                                      C:\WINDOWS\system32\rsaenh.dll
0x7c9c0000    0x818000  0x1                                      C:\WINDOWS\system32\SHELL32.dll
0x77f60000    0x76000   0x3                                      C:\WINDOWS\system32\SHLWAPI.dll
0x773d0000    0x103000  0x2                                      C:\WINDOWS\WinSxS\x86_Microsoft.Windows.C
f1df_6.0.2600.6028_x-ww_61e65202\comctl32.dll
0x76080000    0x65000   0x1                                      C:\WINDOWS\system32\MSVCP60.dll
0x77690000    0x21000   0x1                                      C:\WINDOWS\system32\NTMARTA.DLL
0x774e0000    0x13e000  0x1                                      C:\WINDOWS\system32\ole32.dll
0x71bf0000    0x13000   0x1                                      C:\WINDOWS\system32\SAMLIB.dll
0x76f60000    0x2c000   0x1                                      C:\WINDOWS\system32\WLDAP32.dll
0x769c0000    0xb4000   0x1                                      C:\WINDOWS\system32\USERENV.dll
0x5ad70000    0x38000   0x2                                      C:\WINDOWS\system32\uxtheme.dll
************************************************************************
```

Figure 8.23 – Snippet of the dlllist plugin displaying PID 1940 details

A closeup of the output shows us the command line entry for `taksche.exe` as `C:\Intel\ivecuqmanpnirkt615\tasksche.exe`:

```
****************************************************************
tasksche.exe pid:    1940
Command line : "C:\Intel\ivecuqmanpnirkt615\tasksche.exe"
Service Pack 3
```

Figure 8.24 – Snippet of tasksche.exe

The path, specifically the `ivecuqmanpnirkt615` folder, is a bit suspicious here but let's have a look at some more `dlllist` outputs before we go further. Here's the output for `@WanaDecryptor@`, with a PID of `740`:

```
@WanaDecryptor@ pid:    740
Command line : @WanaDecryptor@.exe
Service Pack 3

Base        Size     LoadCount LoadTime                          Path
----------  -------- --------- ------------------------------    ----
0x00400000  0x3d000  0xffff                                      C:\Intel\ivecuqmanpnirkt615\@WanaDecryptor@.exe
0x7c900000  0xb2000  0xffff                                      C:\WINDOWS\system32\ntdll.dll
0x7c800000  0xf6000  0xffff                                      C:\WINDOWS\system32\kernel32.dll
0x73dd0000  0xf2000  0xffff                                      C:\WINDOWS\system32\MFC42.DLL
0x77c10000  0x58000  0xffff                                      C:\WINDOWS\system32\msvcrt.dll
0x77f10000  0x49000  0xffff                                      C:\WINDOWS\system32\GDI32.dll
0x7e410000  0x91000  0xffff                                      C:\WINDOWS\system32\USER32.dll
0x77dd0000  0x9b000  0xffff                                      C:\WINDOWS\system32\ADVAPI32.dll
0x77e70000  0x93000  0xffff                                      C:\WINDOWS\system32\RPCRT4.dll
0x77fe0000  0x11000  0xffff                                      C:\WINDOWS\system32\Secur32.dll
0x7c9c0000  0x818000 0xffff                                      C:\WINDOWS\system32\SHELL32.dll
0x77f60000  0x76000  0xffff                                      C:\WINDOWS\system32\SHLWAPI.dll
0x773d0000  0x103000 0xffff                                      C:\WINDOWS\WinSxS\X86_Microsoft.Windows.Common-C
ontrols_6595b64144ccf1df_6.0.2600.6028_x-ww_61e65202\COMCTL32.dll
0x77120000  0x8b000  0xffff                                      C:\WINDOWS\system32\OLEAUT32.dll
0x774e0000  0x13e000 0xffff                                      C:\WINDOWS\system32\ole32.dll
0x78130000  0x134000 0xffff                                      C:\WINDOWS\system32\urlmon.dll
0x3dfd0000  0x1ec000 0xffff                                      C:\WINDOWS\system32\iertutil.dll
0x76080000  0x65000  0xffff                                      C:\WINDOWS\system32\MSVCP60.dll
0x71ab0000  0x17000  0xffff                                      C:\WINDOWS\system32\WS2_32.dll
0x71aa0000  0x8000   0xffff                                      C:\WINDOWS\system32\WS2HELP.dll
0x3d930000  0xe7000  0xffff                                      C:\WINDOWS\system32\WININET.dll
0x00340000  0x9000   0xffff                                      C:\WINDOWS\system32\Normaliz.dll
```

Figure 8.25 – Snippet of PID 740 details in the dlllist output

A closer look at the output shows that the path for `@WanaDecryptor@.exe` is also the same as `tasksche.exe`, listed as `C:\Intel\ivecuqmanpnirkt615\@WanaDecryptor@.exe`.

The path for `@WanaDecryptor@.exe` can be seen in the following screenshot:

```
@WanaDecryptor@ pid:    740
Command line : @WanaDecryptor@.exe
Service Pack 3

Base        Size     LoadCount LoadTime                          Path
----------  -------- --------- ------------------------------    ----
0x00400000  0x3d000  0xffff                                      C:\Intel\ivecuqmanpnirkt615\@WanaDecryptor@.exe
```

Figure 8.26 – Snippet of PID 740 details

7. We can now assume that based on the output so far, the processes responsible for the execution of the ransomware have originated from the path `C:\Intel\ivecuqmanpnirkt615\@WanaDecryptor@.exe`.

    To confirm this, we can use the `dlllist` plugin with `| grep ivecuqmanpnirkt615` to search for the folder path and the associated .exe files:

```
root@kali:~/Downloads# volatility –profile=WinXPSP2x86 -f wcry.raw dlllist –p 1940 | grep ivecuqmanpnirkt615
Volatility Foundation Volatility Framework 2.6
Command line : "C:\Intel\ivecuqmanpnirkt615\tasksche.exe"
0x00400000    0x35a000    0xffff                              C:\Intel\ivecuqmanpnirkt615\tasksche.exe
0x00400000    0x3d000     0xffff                              C:\Intel\ivecuqmanpnirkt615\@WanaDecryptor@.exe
root@kali:~/Downloads#
```

Figure 8.27 – Snippet of associated exe's

8. Let's now use the `handles` plugin, which is used to display the handles for a process to view the access and type. For this ransomware, we'll be looking for a mutex, which prevents the malware from running in multiple instances by specifying the mutant type option.

    Type in the following command to run this plugin:

```
volatility –profile=WinXPSP2x86 -f wcry.raw handles -p 1940 -t
mutant
```

The following screenshot displays the output of the `handles` plugin used with the mutant option:

```
root@kali:~/Downloads# volatility –profile=WinXPSP2x86 -f wcry.raw handles -p 1940 -t mutant
Volatility Foundation Volatility Framework 2.6
Offset(V)     Pid      Handle     Access  Type         Details
----------    -----    -------    ------- ----         -------
0x821883e8    1940     0x40       0x120001 Mutant       ShimCacheMutex
0x8224f180    1940     0x54       0x1f0001 Mutant       MsWinZonesCacheCounterMutexA
0x822e3b08    1940     0x58       0x1f0001 Mutant       MsWinZonesCacheCounterMutexA0
root@kali:~/Downloads#
```

Figure 8.28 – Output of the handles plugin

9. Let's do a quick search for the items listed in the details section at www.virustotal.com. As you can see in the following screenshot, **VirusTotal** detection reveals that antivirus programs detect **MsWinZonesCacheCounterMutexA** as the WannaCryptor ransomware:

SUMMARY | DETECTION | DETAILS | RELATIONS | BEHAVIOR | COMMUNITY 10+

Acronis	Suspicious
Ad-Aware	Trojan.Ransom.WannaCryptor.A
AegisLab	Trojan.Win32.Wanna.toNn
AhnLab-V3	Trojan/Win32.WannaCryptor.R200571
Alibaba	Ransom:Win32/Wanna.7c953283
ALYac	Trojan.Ransom.WannaCryptor
SecureAge APEX	Malicious
Arcabit	Trojan.Ransom.WannaCryptor.A
Avast	Win32:WanaCry-A [Trj]
AVG	Win32:WanaCry-A [Trj]
Avira (no cloud)	TR/Ransom.JB
Baidu	Win32.Trojan.WannaCry.c
BitDefender	Trojan.Ransom.WannaCryptor.A
BitDefenderTheta	Gen:NN.ZexaF.32515.wt0@aGEmS3di
Bkav	W32.RansomwareTBE.Trojan

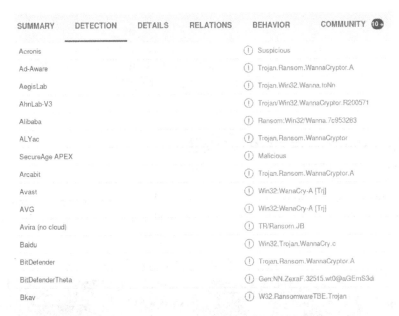

Figure 8.29 – Snippet of the file results from VirusTotal.com

10. Clicking on the **DETAILS** section in the VirusTotal results page, we can see that there are many names for the WannaCryptor ransomware, including `tasksche.exe`:

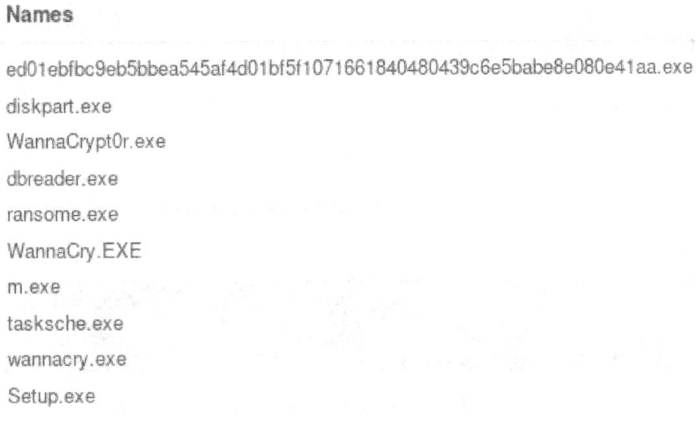

Names

ed01ebfbc9eb5bbea545af4d01bf5f1071661840480439c6e5babe8e080e41aa.exe
diskpart.exe
WannaCrypt0r.exe
dbreader.exe
ransome.exe
WannaCry.EXE
m.exe
tasksche.exe
wannacry.exe
Setup.exe

Figure 8.30 – Snippet of the Wanna Decryptor alias results from VirusTotal.com

This was a lengthy exercise but I hope you've enjoyed finding artifacts, including the processes, IDs, and paths that have all helped us to identify the ransomware, along with verification from VirusTotal. We'll now move on to Linux swap file analysis using `swap_digger`.

swap_digger

`swap_digger` performs an automated analysis of the Linux swap file and can retrieve artifacts such as system passwords, usernames, form credentials, and even Wi-Fi information, such as the SSID and perhaps even passwords if they are stored in the swap file.

Installing and using swap_digger

Let's now clone and install `swap_digger` in Kali Linux:

1. Change directories to the desktop in the Terminal and clone `swap_digger` to the desktop by typing in: `git clone https://github.com/sevagas/swap_digger.git`.

   The preceding `git clone` command clones and installs `swap_digger`:

```
root@kali:~# cd Desktop
root@kali:~/Desktop# git clone https://github.com/sevagas/swap_digger.git
Cloning into 'swap_digger'...
remote: Enumerating objects: 117, done.
remote: Total 117 (delta 0), reused 0 (delta 0), pack-reused 117
Receiving objects: 100% (117/117), 342.53 KiB | 283.00 KiB/s, done.
Resolving deltas: 100% (54/54), done.
```

Figure 8.31 – Installing swap_digger in Kali Linux

2. Change to the `swap_digger` directory by typing in `cd swap_digger`. Type in the following two commands to start `swap_digger`:

```
chmod +x swap_digger.sh
sudo ./swap_digger.sh -vx
```

`swap_digger` will run after typing in the preceding commands, as in the following output:

```
root@kali:~/Desktop# cd swap_digger
root@kali:~/Desktop/swap_digger# chmod +x swap_digger.sh
root@kali:~/Desktop/swap_digger# sudo ./swap_digger.sh -vx
```

Figure 8.32 – Configuring permissions of swap_digger

3. `swap_digger` runs and starts by looking for the swap partition (located at `/dev/sda5` on my machine) and begins dumping the swap strings. It also digs for user credentials in the `etc/shadow` file and prompts you to perform a dictionary attack against the file. Press *Y* and *Enter* to confirm and continue digging for the hash:

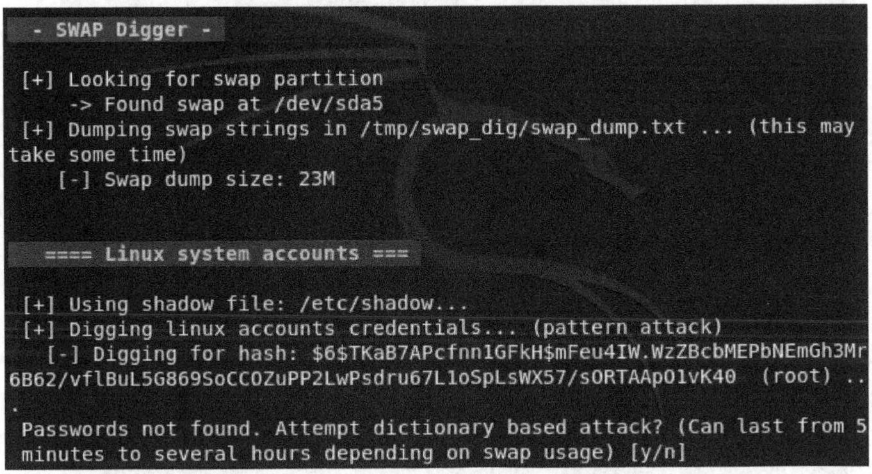

```
- SWAP Digger -

[+] Looking for swap partition
    -> Found swap at /dev/sda5
[+] Dumping swap strings in /tmp/swap_dig/swap_dump.txt ... (this may
take some time)
    [-] Swap dump size: 23M


 ==== Linux system accounts ===

[+] Using shadow file: /etc/shadow...
[+] Digging linux accounts credentials... (pattern attack)
    [-] Digging for hash: $6$TKaB7APcfnn1GFkH$mFeu4IW.WzZBcbMEPbNEmGh3Mr
6B62/vflBuL5G869SoCCOZuPP2LwPsdru67L1oSpLsWX57/sORTAApOlvK40  (root) ..
.

Passwords not found. Attempt dictionary based attack? (Can last from 5
minutes to several hours depending on swap usage) [y/n]
```

Figure 8.33 – Swap_digger CLI interface

As mentioned in the last line of the preceding screenshot, the dictionary attack can take anywhere from five minutes to several hours:

```
[+] Digging linux accounts credentials method 2 ... (dictionary attack
)
    [-] Generating wordlist file...
    [-] Digging passwords in wordlist... (This may take 5min to few hour
s!)
    [-] Digging for hash: $6$TKaB7APcfnn1GFkH$mFeu4IW.WzZBcbMEPbNEmGh3Mr
6B62/vflBuL5G869SoCCOZuPP2LwPsdru67L1oSpLsWX57/sORTAApOlvK40 ...
```

Figure 8.34 – Swap_digger password cracking process

This may take a while but it will at least show your default password once complete.

If left to run, `swap_digger` will also search for web and email passwords, XML data, and Wi-Fi passwords. I haven't entered any of those on my Kali machine but here's a screenshot of the process:

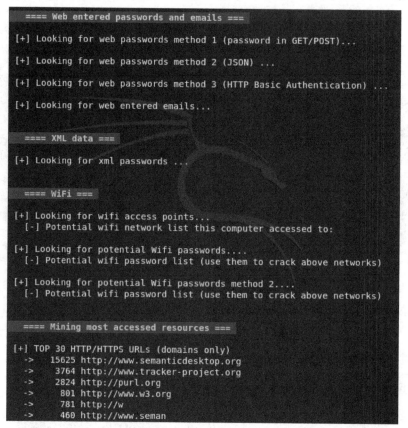

Figure 8.35 – Swap_digger scanning process

As the preceding screenshot shows, `swap_digger` is a very useful tool for live analysis on Linux machines, which can be used to discover artifacts running in the swap file, including passwords. Let's now move on to another password-dumping file in the next section.

Password dumping with mimipenguin

Mimipenguin is based on the very popular password-cracking tool **mimikatz**. Much like swap_digger, mimipenguin can also retrieve artifacts running in memory by dumping memory processes that may contain unencrypted passwords in plaintext:

1. Let's start by changing to the Desktop folder and then cloning mimipenguin to desktop by typing git clone into a new Terminal:

```
root@kali:~/Desktop# git clone https://github.com/huntergregal/mimipenguin
Cloning into 'mimipenguin'...
remote: Enumerating objects: 460, done.
remote: Total 460 (delta 0), reused 0 (delta 0), pack-reused 460
Receiving objects: 100% (460/460), 157.60 KiB | 187.00 KiB/s, done.
Resolving deltas: 100% (207/207), done.
root@kali:~/Desktop#
```

Figure 8.36 – Cloning mimipenguin onto the Kali Desktop

2. Change to the mimipenguin directory by typing in cd mimipenguin, then show the files within by typing in ls:

```
root@kali:~/Desktop#
root@kali:~/Desktop# cd mimipenguin
root@kali:~/Desktop/mimipenguin#
root@kali:~/Desktop/mimipenguin# ls
LICENSE  Makefile  mimipenguin  mimipenguin_x32  README.md  src
root@kali:~/Desktop/mimipenguin#
root@kali:~/Desktop/mimipenguin#
```

Figure 8.37 – Viewing the contents of the mimipenguin folder

3. Run mimipenguin by typing in ./mimipenguin:

```
root@kali:~/Desktop/mimipenguin# ./mimipenguin
[+] GNOME KEYRING (823)
    [-] root:toor
root@kali:~/Desktop/mimipenguin#
```

Figure 8.38 – Password discovery using mimipenguin in Kali Linux

In the previous screenshot, we can see that the username and password for the Kali machine was discovered (root : toor).

Examining Firefox artifacts with pdgmail

In this section, we'll use pdgmail, which also performs memory analysis but specifically looks for web artifacts, such as emails, contacts, IP addresses, and even inbox or sent items, by analyzing the memory dump process.

For this lab, I'll be using the Kali Linux Large ISO, which I have installed as a virtual machine in VirtualBox:

1. Let's first view some available options in `pdgmail` by opening a new Terminal and typing in `pdgmail -h`:

```
root@kali:~# pdgmail -h
Usage: /usr/bin/pdgmail [OPTIONS]

Options:
  -f, --file        the file to use (stdin if no file given)
  -b, --bodies      don't look for message bodies (helpful if you're getting too many
false positives on the mb regex)
  -h, --help        prints this
  -v,--verbose      be verbose (prints filename, other junk)
  -V,--version      prints just the version info and exits.

This expects to be unleashed on the result of running strings -el on a pd dump from w
indows process memory. Anything other than that, your mileage will certainly vary.
```

Figure 8.39 – Viewing the help options of pdgmail

I've also opened a Firefox browser and logged into a Gmail account, then clicked on my inbox and sent items box so that this process can be run in memory. I've also visited some other sites, such as www.20minutemail.com, where I signed up for a temporary email address, and www.netcraft.com, where I looked up certifiedhacker.com.

2. To find the Firefox process ID (just as we saw in *Chapter 7*, *Memory Forensics with Volatility*, using the `pslist` module) we can run the following command:

```
ps -ef | grep fire
```

The following screenshot displays the output of the previous command:

```
root@kali:~# ps -ef | grep fire
root       324 32600  0 15:28 pts/0    00:00:00 grep fire
root     19622  1381  2 14:46 tty2     00:00:55 /usr/lib/firefox-esr/firefox-esr
root     19908 19622  8 14:47 tty2     00:03:25 /usr/lib/firefox-esr/plugin-container
-greomni /usr/lib/firefox-esr/omni.ja -appomni /usr/lib/firefox-esr/browser/omni.ja
-appdir /usr/lib/firefox-esr/browser 19622 true tab
root@kali:~#
```

Figure 8.40 – Finding Firefox processes

3. In the previous screenshot, we can see that the second entry with a `19622` process is the process ID for Firefox (note that your process ID may be a different number). Let's dump this process to be analyzed by running the following command:

```
gcore -o firegmail.dmp 19622
```

The following screenshot displays the output of the previous command:

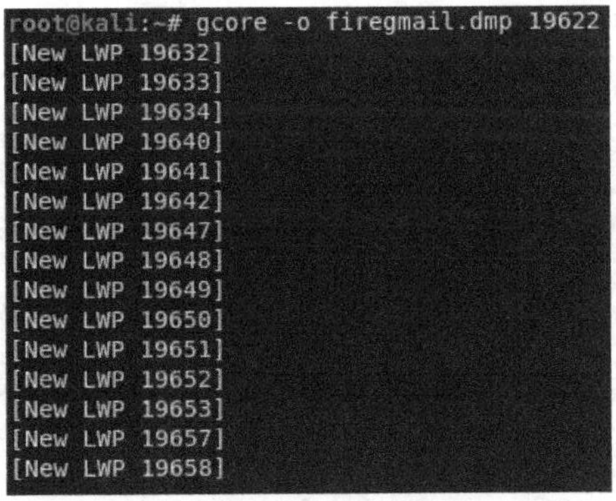

```
root@kali:~# gcore -o firegmail.dmp 19622
[New LWP 19632]
[New LWP 19633]
[New LWP 19634]
[New LWP 19640]
[New LWP 19641]
[New LWP 19642]
[New LWP 19647]
[New LWP 19648]
[New LWP 19649]
[New LWP 19650]
[New LWP 19651]
[New LWP 19652]
[New LWP 19653]
[New LWP 19657]
[New LWP 19658]
```

Figure 8.41 – Firefox process dump output

Once the process dump is completed, the last line should read as `Saved corefile firegmail 19622`.

We can see the last line of the output of the `gcore` command in the following screenshot:

```
[New LWP 26455]
[New LWP 26476]
[New LWP 32442]
[Thread debugging using libthread_db enabled]
Using host libthread_db library "/lib/x86_64-linux-gnu/libthread_db.so.1".
0x00007fd755d345d9 in __GI__poll (fds=0x7fd72b82a3a0, nfds=5, timeout=-1) at ../sysd
eps/unix/sysv/linux/poll.c:29
29      ../sysdeps/unix/sysv/linux/poll.c: No such file or directory.
Saved corefile firegmail.dmp.19622
root@kali:~#
```

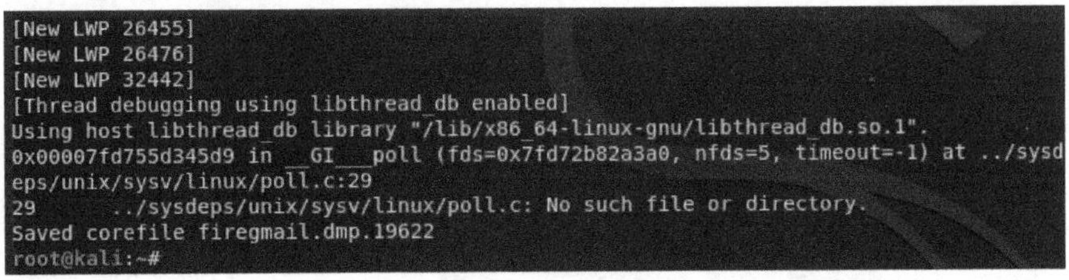

Figure 8.42 – Output of the gcore option

4. To analyze the saved process dump, run the following command:

```
strings -el firegmail.dmp.19622
```

The command is shown in the following image:

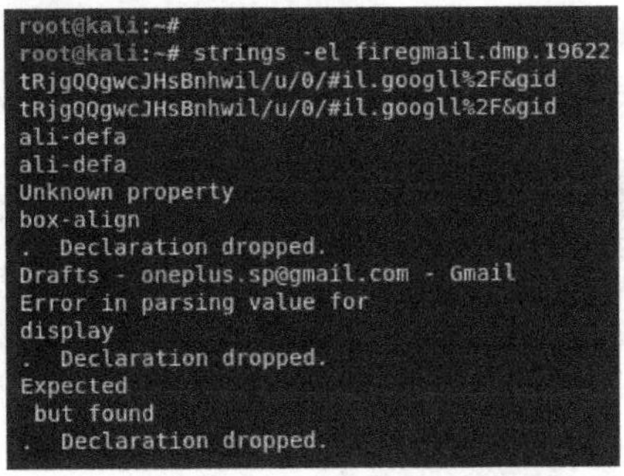

```
root@kali:~#
root@kali:~# strings -el firegmail.dmp.19622
tRjgQQgwcJHsBnhwil/u/0/#il.googll%2F&gid
tRjgQQgwcJHsBnhwil/u/0/#il.googll%2F&gid
ali-defa
ali-defa
Unknown property
box-align
.  Declaration dropped.
Drafts - oneplus.sp@gmail.com - Gmail
Error in parsing value for
display
.  Declaration dropped.
Expected
 but found
.   Declaration dropped.
```

Figure 8.43 – Process dump analysis

Scrolling through the output, you will be able to see the email you logged into, along with the number of unread emails in the inbox:

```
Inbox (163) - oneplus.sp@gmail.com - Gmail
Transferring data from ssl.gstatic.com
dealcabby
vertical
rgb(44, 44, 44)
Wayback Machine
https://web.archive.org/web/*/facebook
Wayback Machine
https://web.archive.org/web/*/facebook
```

Figure 8.44 – Gmail inbox details

5.   To verify, I'll click on the Gmail tab in Firefox and click on an email in my inbox. I can now see that there's 162 unread emails in the inbox, which means the `pgdmail` output was accurate. (There were 163 unread emails in the inbox but I clicked on an email from `www.academia.edu` to be able to continue with the following example):

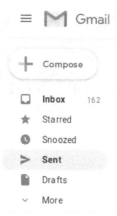

Figure 8.45 – Snippet of the Gmail mailbox

I can also see a link from one of the emails I just clicked on from `www.academia.eu`:

```
mousedown
activate
rgb(44, 44, 44)
https://www.academia.edu/t/a-NhRrtx9-n65JS/resource/work/40004849/WINDS_OF_CHANGE_The_Challenge_of_Mod
ernity_in_the_Middle_East_and_North_Africa_2019_Foreword_Chapters_6_8_11_
github - Google Search
https://www.google.com/search?q=github&ie=utf-8&oe=utf-8&client=firefox-b-ab
```

Figure 8.46 – Snippet of the pdgmail analysis

Here's a screen shot of the actual email subject in Gmail:

Figure 8.47 – Screenshot of the Gmail inbox

I can also see that the mail compartments/categories were also found:

```
      Declaration dropped.
https://mail.google.com/mail/u/0/#drafts
https://mail.google.com/mail/u/0/#sent
https://mail.google.com/mail/u/0/#snoozed
https://mail.google.com/mail/u/0/#snoozed
https://mail.google.com/mail/u/0/#sent
https://mail.google.com/mail/u/0/#drafts
Error in parsing value for
display
      Declaration dropped.
```

Figure 8.48 – Snippet of the pdgmail analysis output

Pdgmail has also found artifacts relating to www.20minutemail.com where I signed up for a temporary email account earlier:

```
20 minute mail - Temporary E-Mail 10 Minute and more - temp mail, fake email
http://www.20minutemail.com/
20 minute mail - Temporary E-Mail 10 Minute and more - temp mail, fake email
http://www.20minutemail.com/
20 minute mail - Temporary E-Mail 10 Minute and more - temp mail, fake email
http://www.20minutemail.com/
20 minute mail - Temporary E-Mail 10 Minute and more - temp mail, fake email
http://www.20minutemail.com/
20 minute mail - Temporary E-Mail 10 Minute and more - temp mail, fake email
http://www.20minutemail.com/
20 minute mail - Temporary E-Mail 10 Minute and more - temp mail, fake email
http://www.20minutemail.com/
20 minute mail - Temporary E-Mail 10 Minute and more - temp mail, fake email
http://www.20minutemail.com/
Snoozed
```

Figure 8.49 – Pdgmail artifact analysis output

It also showed the search entry on www.netcraft.com, where I previously did a DNS search for the www.certifiedhacker.com:

```
https://searchdns.netcraft.com/?host=www.certifiedhacker.com&x=2&y=6
https://searchdns.netcraft.com/?host=www.certifiedhacker.com&x=2&y=6
Unknown property
-moz-border-radius
.  Declaration dropped.
39/5
```

Figure 8.50 – DNS search details revealed in the analysis output

This concludes our usage of pdgmail, which we used to explore Gmail artifacts on a live Linux system, which would be stored within the browser cash within memory. Although the examples and screenshots were based on a sample email that I used, feel free to try this using your own email within Kali Linux.

Summary

This was quite an exciting chapter. We discovered communications services, devices, ports, and protocols using Nmap and p0f and then jumped into ransomware analysis using Volatility to discover the origin of the WannaCry cryptoworm on an infected system's memory dump. Finally, we did an analysis of the swap file using swap_digger, mimipenguin, and pdgmail.

In the next chapter, we'll use Autopsy and The Sleuth Kit to analyze an imaged drive and also compare Autopsy for Linux and Windows.

Section 4: Automated Digital Forensic Suites

In our final section, we look at various tools that focus on entire forensic investigative processes, as well as tools for network capture analysis.

This part comprises the following chapters:

- *Chapter 9, Autopsy*
- *Chapter 10, Analysis with Xplico*
- *Chapter 11, Network Analysis*

9
Autopsy

Autopsy and The Sleuth Kit, both created by Brian Carrier, go hand in hand. The Sleuth Kit is a powerful suite of CLI forensic tools, whereas Autopsy is the GUI that sits on top of The Sleuth Kit and is accessed through a web browser. The Sleuth Kit supports disk image file types including RAW (DD), EnCase (.01), and the **Advanced Forensic Format** (**AFF**).

The topics that we will cover in this chapter include the following:

- Introduction to Autopsy
- The sample image file used in Autopsy
- Digital forensics with Autopsy

Introduction to Autopsy

Autopsy offers GUI access to a variety of investigative command-line tools from The Sleuth Kit, including file analysis, image and file hashing, deleted file recovery, and case management, among other capabilities. Autopsy can be problematic when installing but, fortunately for us, comes built into Kali Linux and is also very easy to set up and use.

The sample image file used in Autopsy

The image file used for analysis is publicly available for download at `http://downloads.digitalcorpora.org/corpora/scenarios/2009-m57-patents/usb/`.

The file we will be working with is **terry-work-usb-2009-12-11.E01**, as in the following screenshot:

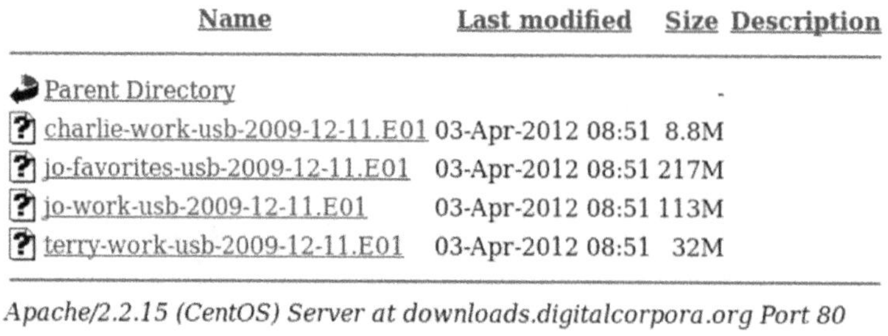

Name	Last modified	Size	Description
📚 Parent Directory		-	
⍰ charlie-work-usb-2009-12-11.E01	03-Apr-2012 08:51	8.8M	
⍰ jo-favorites-usb-2009-12-11.E01	03-Apr-2012 08:51	217M	
⍰ jo-work-usb-2009-12-11.E01	03-Apr-2012 08:51	113M	
⍰ terry-work-usb-2009-12-11.E01	03-Apr-2012 08:51	32M	

Apache/2.2.15 (CentOS) Server at downloads.digitalcorpora.org Port 80

Figure 9.1 – Snippet of the sample evidence files at digitalcorpora.org

> **Tip:**
>
> Be sure to note the location of the downloaded sample file, as this will be required later on.
>
> When investigating hard drives and devices, be sure to always follow proper acquisition procedures and use a write blocker to avoid tampering with original evidence.

Digital forensics with Autopsy

Now that we have our sample image file downloaded (or perhaps even a forensically acquired image of our own), let's proceed with the analysis using the Autopsy browser by first getting acquainted with the different ways to start Autopsy.

Although the Autopsy browser is based on The Sleuth Kit, features of Autopsy differ when using the Windows version compared to the Linux version. Some of the official features offered by The Sleuth Kit and Autopsy 2.4 in Kali Linux include the following:

- **Image analysis**: Analyze directories and files including sorting files, recovering deleted files, and previewing files.

- **File activity timelines**: Create timelines based on the timestamps of files, when they were written, accessed, and created.

- **Image integrity**: Create MD5 hashes of the image file used, as well as individual files.

- **Hash databases**: Match the digital hashes or fingerprints of unknown files (such as suspected malicious `.exe` files) against those in the **NIST National Software Reference Library (NSRL)**.

- **Events sequencer**: Display events sorted by date and time.

- **File analysis**: Analyze the entire image file to display directory and file information and contents.

- **Keyword search**: Allows searching using keywords and predefined expression lists.

- **Metadata analysis**: Allows the viewing of metadata details and structures of files that are essential for data recovery.

- **Parsing data and indexing**: Places a virtual mask over the actual evidence. This allows views for investigators to run queries without altering the "source data" or evidence.

- **Report generating**: Allows the compilation of findings into a user-friendly report.

The Sleuth Kit uses CLI tools to perform the following tasks:

- Find and list allocated and unallocated (deleted) files, and even files hidden by rootkits.

- Reveal NTFS **Alternate Data Streams (ADS)**, where files can be concealed within other files.

- List files by type.

- Display metadata information.

- Timeline creation.

Autopsy can be run from a live CD/USB in forensic mode, as part of a live analysis in live mode, or it can be used on a dedicated machine to investigate analysis in dead mode.

Starting Autopsy

Let's look at the different ways in which we can start Autopsy within Kali Linux:

1. Autopsy can be started in two ways. The first uses the **Applications** menu by clicking on **Applications | 11 - Forensics | autopsy**:

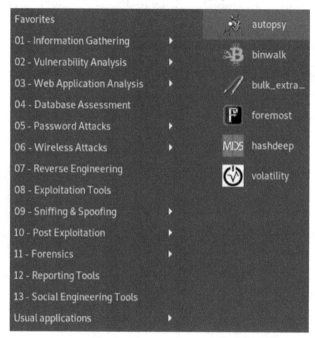

Figure 9.2 – Kali Linux Forensics menu

Alternatively, we can click on the **Show applications** icon (the last item in the side menu), type autopsy into the search bar at the top-middle of the screen, and then click on the **autopsy** icon:

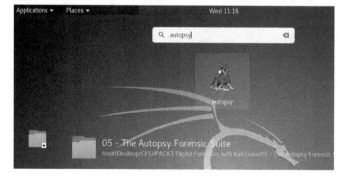

Figure 9.3 – Searching for Autopsy in Kali

Once the **autopsy** icon is clicked, a new Terminal is opened showing the program information along with the connection details for opening `Autopsy Forensic Browser`.

In the following screenshot, we can see that the version number is listed as 2.24, with the path to the `Evidence Locker` folder as `/var/lib/autopsy`:

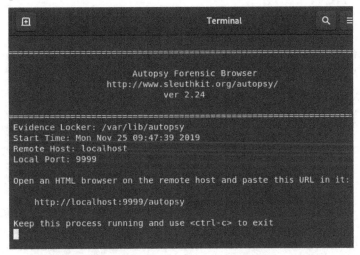

Figure 9.4 – Starting Autopsy in Kali

2. To open the Autopsy browser, position the mouse over the link in the Terminal, then right-click and choose **Open Link,** as in the following screenshot:

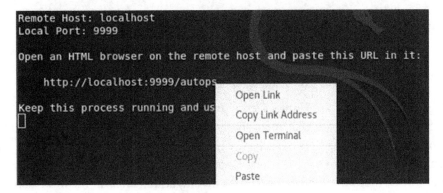

Figure 9.5 – Autopsy web address

> **Important note:**
> Alternatively, you can copy and paste the following link into the browser:
> `http://localhost:9999/autopsy`.

Creating a new case

To create a new case, follow the given steps:

1. When **Autopsy Forensic Browser** opens, investigators are presented with three options: **OPEN CASE**, **NEW CASE**, and **HELP**.

2. Click on **NEW CASE**:

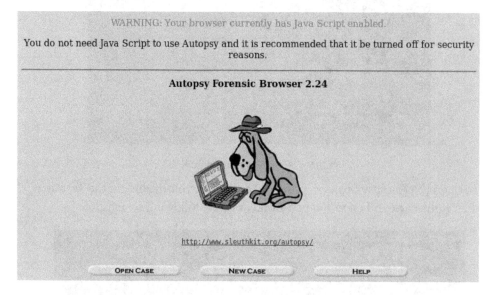

Figure 9.6 – Autopsy forensic browser interface

3. Enter the details for **Case Name**, **Description**, and **Investigator Names**. Documentation is a critical element in digital forensics where case management is concerned and all aspects of each case must be properly documented. For **Case Name**, I've entered `Terry_USB` as it closely matches the image name (`terry-work-usb`) that we will be using for this investigation. Once all the information is entered, click **NEW CASE**:

CREATE A NEW CASE

1. **Case Name:** The name of this investigation. It can contain only letters, numbers, and symbols.

Terry_USB

2. **Description:** An optional, one line description of this case.

USB drive - Terry X

3. **Investigator Names:** The optional names (with no spaces) of the investigators for this case.

a.	Shiva Parasram -CFSI	b.	
c.		d.	
e.		f.	
g.		h.	
i.		j.	

NEW CASE   CANCEL   HELP

Figure 9.7 – Creating a new case

Important note:

Several investigator name fields are available as there may be instances where several investigators are working together.

---

4. The locations of the case directory and configuration file are displayed and shown as **created**. It's important to take note of the case directory location, as in the screenshot: **Case directory (/var/lib/autopsy/Terry_USB/) created**. Click **ADD HOST** to continue:

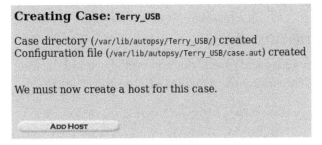

Creating Case: Terry_USB

Case directory (/var/lib/autopsy/Terry_USB/) created
Configuration file (/var/lib/autopsy/Terry_USB/case.aut) created

We must now create a host for this case.

ADD HOST

Figure 9.8 – Adding the evidence file

5. Enter the details for **Host Name** (the name of the computer being investigated) and the description of the host.

6. The following are optional settings:

    (a) Time zone: Defaults to local settings if not specified.

    (b) Timeskew Adjustment: Adds a value in seconds to compensate for time differences.

    (c) Path of Alert Hash Database: Specifies the path of a created database of known bad hashes.

    (d) Path of Ignore Hash Database: Specifies the path of a created database of known good hashes, similar to the NIST NSRL:

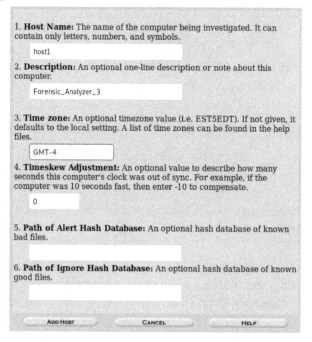

Figure 9.9 – New case details

7. Click on the **ADD HOST** button to continue.

8. Once the host is added and directories are created, we add the forensic image we want to analyze by clicking the **ADD IMAGE** button:

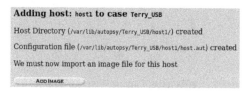

Figure 9.10 – Adding the evidence image

9. Click on the **ADD IMAGE FILE** button to add the image file:

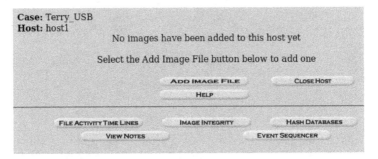

Figure 9.11 – Adding the evidence file (continued)

10. To import the image for analysis, the full path must be specified. On my machine, I've saved the image file to the default `Downloads` folder. As such, the location of the file is `/root/Downloads/terry-wor-usb-2009-12-11.E01`:

> **Important note:**
> For the import method, we choose **Symlink**. This way, the image file can be imported from its current location (`Downloads`) to the evidence locker without the risks associated with moving or copying the image file.

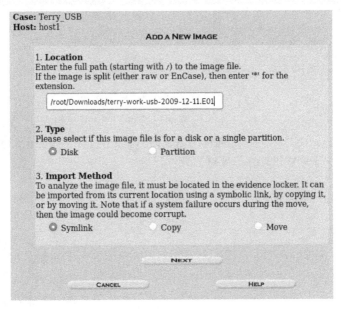

Figure 9.12 – Evidence file import method details

11. Upon clicking **Next**, the **Image File Details** are displayed:

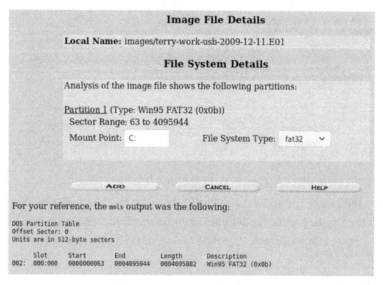

Figure 9.13 – Image file details

12. Click on the **ADD** button to continue:

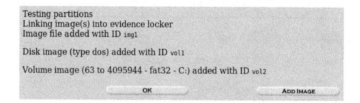

Figure 9.14 – Volume image details

13. Click **OK**.

14. At this point, we're just about ready to analyze the image file. Be sure to select the **C:/** option and then click on **ANALYZE**:

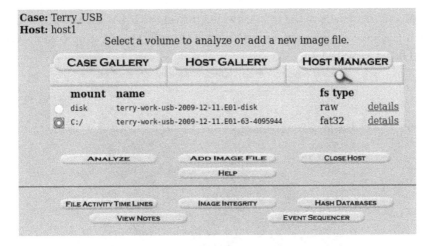

Figure 9.15 – Volume analysis details

Analysis using Autopsy

Now that we've created our case, added host information with appropriate directories, and added our acquired image, we get to the analysis stage:

1. After clicking on the **ANALYZE** button (see the previous screenshot), we're presented with several options, in the form of tabs, with which to begin our investigation:

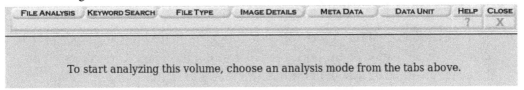

Figure 9.16 – Volume analysis options

2. Let's look at the details of the image by clicking on the **IMAGE DETAILS** tab. In the following screenshot, we can see the **Volume ID** and the operating system (**OEM Name**) listed as **BSD 4.4**:

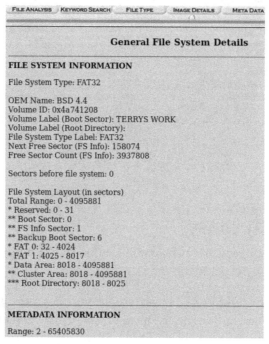

Figure 9.17 – Filesystem details

3. Next, we click on the **FILE ANALYSIS** tab. This opens in file browsing mode, which allows the examination of directories and files within the image. Directories within the image are listed by default in the main view area:

Del	Type dir / in	Name	Written	Accessed	Created	Size	UID	GID	Meta
			Error Parsing File (Invalid Characters?):						
			v/v 65405830: $OrphanFiles 0000-00-00 00:00:00 (UTC) 0000-00-00						
			00:00:00 (UTC) 0000-00-00 00:00:00 (UTC) 0000-00-00 00:00:00 (UTC) 0 0						
			0						
v/v		$FAT1	0000-00-00 00:00:00 (UTC)	0000-00-00 00:00:00 (UTC)	0000-00-00 00:00:00 (UTC)	2044416	0	0	65405828
v/v		$FAT2	0000-00-00 00:00:00 (UTC)	0000-00-00 00:00:00 (UTC)	0000-00-00 00:00:00 (UTC)	2044416	0	0	65405829
v/v		$MBR	0000-00-00 00:00:00 (UTC)	0000-00-00 00:00:00 (UTC)	0000-00-00 00:00:00 (UTC)	512	0	0	65405827
r/r		. .Trashes	2009-11-17 10:47:46 (GMT)	2009-11-17 00:00:00 (GMT)	2009-11-17 10:47:47 (GMT)	4096	0	0	5
r/r		. M57biz.jpg	2009-11-17 10:49:24 (GMT)	2009-11-17 00:00:00 (GMT)	2009-11-17 10:49:25 (GMT)	4096	0	0	17
r/r		. patentauto.py	2009-11-17	2009-11-17	2009-11-17	4096	0	0	54

Figure 9.18 – File analysis output

In file browsing mode, directories are listed with the current directory specified as C:/.

As seen in the previous screenshot, for each directory and file there are fields that show when the item was **WRITTEN**, **ACCESSED**, **CHANGED**, and **CREATED**, along with its **SIZE** and metadata:

(a) WRITTEN: The date and time the file was last written to

(b) ACCESSED: The date and time the file was last accessed (only the date is accurate)

(c) CREATED: The date and time the file was created

(d) META: Metadata describing the file and information about the file

If we scroll down a bit, we can see carved items listed in red, which are deleted files:

✓	d / d	/sevevlsc/	2009-11-17 10:48:38 (GMT)	2009-11-17 00:00:00 (GMT)	2009-11-17 10:48:38 (GMT)	0	0	0	10
	d / d	.Spotlight-V100/	2009-11-17 10:47:46 (GMT)	2009-11-17 00:00:00 (GMT)	2009-11-17 10:47:47 (GMT)	4096	0	0	13
	d / d	.Trashes/	2009-11-17 10:47:46 (GMT)	2009-11-17 00:00:00 (GMT)	2009-11-17 10:47:47 (GMT)	4096	0	0	8
✓	d / d	9/8421 /	2009-11-20 10:59:48 (GMT)	2009-11-20 00:00:00 (GMT)	2009-11-20 10:59:47 (GMT)	0	0	0	85
✓	d / d	189812 /	2009-11-20 11:33:04 (GMT)	2009-11-20 00:00:00 (GMT)	2009-11-20 11:33:03 (GMT)	0	0	0	67
✓	d / d	457281 /	2009-11-20 11:06:04 (GMT)	2009-11-20 00:00:00 (GMT)	2009-11-20 11:06:02 (GMT)	0	0	0	66
✓	d / d	461531 /	2009-11-20 10:49:32 (GMT)	2009-11-20 00:00:00 (GMT)	2009-11-20 10:49:30 (GMT)	0	0	0	63
✓	r / r	54403 F30	2009-11-20 10:31:36 (GMT)	2009-11-20 00:00:00 (GMT)	2009-11-20 10:31:34 (GMT)	0	0	0	61
✓	d / d	634466 /	2009-11-20 10:51:54 (GMT)	2009-11-20 00:00:00 (GMT)	2009-11-20 10:51:53 (GMT)	0	0	0	64
	d / d	Log/	2009-12-07 08:05:22 (GMT)	2009-12-07 00:00:00 (GMT)	2009-12-07 08:05:20 (GMT)	643072	0	0	72

Figure 9.19 – Deleted items displayed in the analysis output

If we scroll even further, we can see that there is an installer (**vnc-4_1_3-x86_win32.exe**) file for VNC, which was possibly downloaded to use on another machine as this OS is not Windows.

There is also a keylogger installation file (**xpadvancedkeylogger.exe**) listed in red, meaning it was deleted:

	r / r	urlstime_machine.txt	2009-11-16 10:22:50 (GMT)	2009-11-24 00:00:00 (GMT)	2009-11-16 10:22:51 (GMT)	1538990	0	0	20
	r / r	vnc-4_1_3-x86_win32.exe	2008-10-15 17:14:08 (GMT)	2009-12-07 00:00:00 (GMT)	2008-10-15 17:14:08 (GMT)	741744	0	0	75
	r / r	webauto.py	2009-11-16 14:23:38 (GMT)	2009-11-24 00:00:00 (GMT)	2009-11-14 17:39:19 (GMT)	2237	0	0	6
✓	r / r	xpadvancedkeylogger.exe	2009-12-03 09:40:44 (GMT)	2009-12-07 00:00:00 (GMT)	2009-12-03 09:41:16 (GMT)	1580600	0	0	70

Figure 9.20 – Keylogger executable file listed in the output

For integrity purposes, MD5 hashes of all files can be made by clicking on the
GENERATE MD5 LIST OF FILES button:

Figure 9.21 – MD5 generation options

This generates a text file of the files and their hashes:

```
MD5 Values for files in C:/ (terry-work-usb-2009-12-11.E01-63-4095944)

d41d8cd98f00b204e9800998ecf8427e  -    TERRYS WORK (Volume Label Entry)
5ecad39c470178e1b0ef93e534b60fda  -    ._.Trashes
ce3231180e69f5a56c16459da0f1d531  -    webauto.py
8ad51236530591ff2a9e84a15bd89ed1  -    M57biz.jpg
7e777ea21c6763c62518c304ca5d4ce1  -    ._M57biz.jpg
64ee6fb48ca85ce93df69bb7941a4b54  -    urlstime_machine.txt
4ee3e80d4fa851aca7ec2bb40b9b77c3  -    ._urlstime_machine.txt
5170ec45ba4ed423ffed57b431a1fe4f  -    ._webauto.py
d72b25eccfe732030000ddde08335191  -    urlspersona.txt
5e1783e9f289ece7d6d9c3952f38b1d1  -    ._urlspersona.txt
95fa678acc9369d89a4513a0b8e4b26d  -    urlspatents.txt
5e9fc9d520c0acf4b4ca1ec77f80325f  -    ._urlspatents.txt
31262fcf2a6d69d3bacb7574fc9e0445  -    urlscryptography.txt
341e85a6854a69687facfdbffd18afac  -    ._urlscryptography.txt
02fcfbd3f7b2b021bec1d27250a832d0  -    urlscopyright.txt
d4799d3877f0867c5b21f1217284aa05  -    ._urlscopyright.txt
35c3cd97833a1be73d974f4798bcbff7  -    patentauto.py
071a9abef36c665a4dc480098d974ff4  -    ._patentauto.py
934541851380f404a8efb659003c6ad7  -    patentterms.txt
b02a2a4b05e80a81e38fcf8bccef1d1b  -    ._patentterms.txt
55f9facaec8cf1d1bf1f8c04f3d287a4  -    R54402.EXE
790856e8ae34f0ac3eb40e031cf7a47a  -    vnc-4_1_3-x86_win32.exe
```

Figure 9.22 – Screenshot of individually generated hashes

Investigators can also make notes about files, times, anomalies, and so on by
clicking on the **ADD NOTE** button:

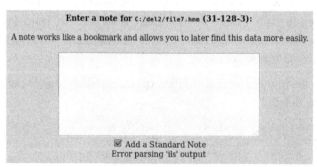

Figure 9.23 – Note entry field

4. The left pane contains four main features that we will be using:

    (a) Directory Seek: Allows the searching of directories

    (b) File Name Search: Allows the searching of files by Perl expressions or filenames

(c) **ALL DELETED FILES**: Searches the image for deleted files

(d) **EXPAND DIRECTORIES**: Expands all directories for easier viewing of contents:

Figure 9.24 – File search options

5. By clicking on **EXPAND DIRECTORIES,** all contents are easily viewable and accessible within the left pane and main window. The + next to a directory indicates that it can be further expanded to view subdirectories (++) and their contents:

Figure 9.25 – File directory menu

6. To view deleted files, we click on the **ALL DELETED FILES** button in the left pane. Deleted files are marked in red and also adhere to the same format of **WRITTEN**, **ACCESSED**, **CHANGED**, and **CREATED** times.

From the following screenshot, we can see that the image contains a number of deleted files:

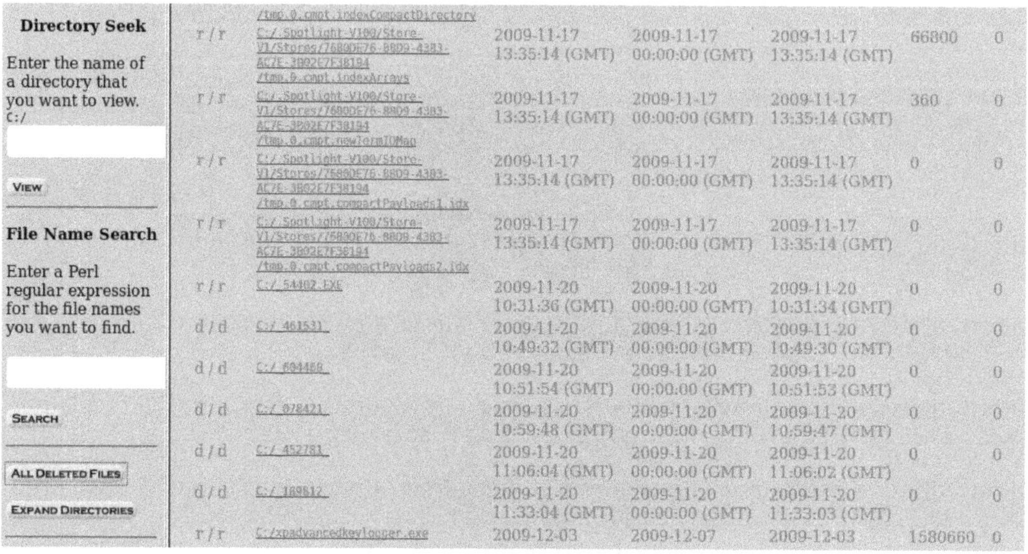

Figure 9.26 – Deleted files

7. We can also view more information about this file by clicking on its **META** entry. By viewing the metadata entries of a file (the last column on the right), we can also view the hexadecimal entries for the file, which may give the true file extension, even if the extension was changed:

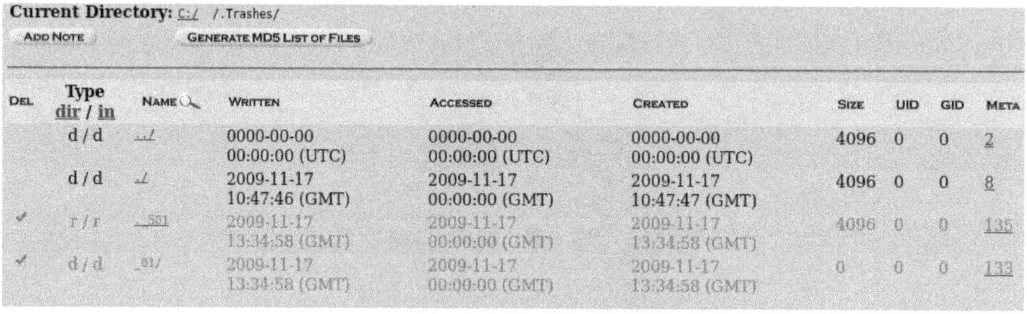

Figure 9.27 – File meta data

In the preceding screenshot, we can see that the first deleted file, named ._501, has a metadata/directory entry number of **135**. Click on **135** to view the metadata information:

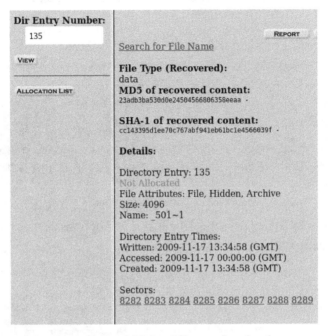

Figure 9.28 – Additional file metadata details

Under the **Sectors** section, click on the first and second sectors (**8282** and **8283**) to view the ASCII content information of the file:

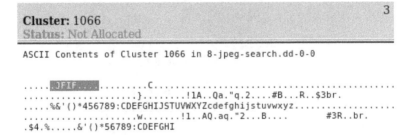

Figure 9.29 – ASCII content information

We can see several instances of JPG and .JFIF, which is an abbreviation for **JPEG File Interchange Format**. This means that the file is an image file.

Sorting files

Inspecting the metadata of each file may not be practical with large evidence files. For such an instance, the **FILE TYPE** feature can be used. This feature allows the examination of existing (allocated), deleted (unallocated), and hidden files:

1. To begin the sorting process, click on the **FILE TYPE** tab:

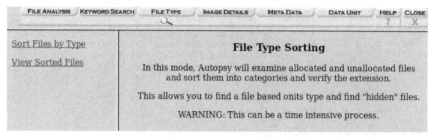

Figure 9.30 – File sorting options

2. Click **Sort Files by Type** (leave the default-checked options as they are) and then click **OK** to begin the sorting process:

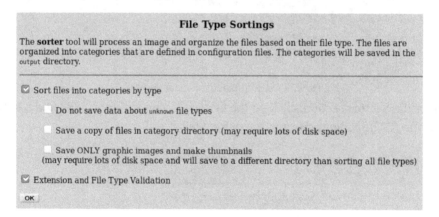

Figure 9.31 – File sorting category types

This may take a while. Allow The Sleuth Kit to process and sort through the files automatically for us:

Analyzing "/var/lib/autopsy/Terry_USB/host1/images/terry-work-usb-2009-12-11.E01"
Loading Allocated File Listing

Figure 9.32 – File sorting process

Once the sorting is complete, a results summary is displayed:

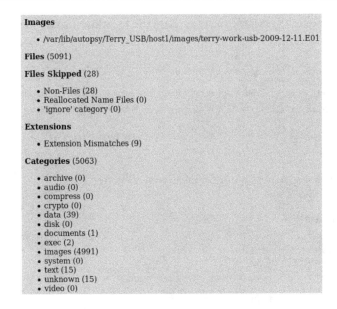

Images

- /var/lib/autopsy/Terry_USB/host1/images/terry-work-usb-2009-12-11.E01

Files (5091)

Files Skipped (28)

- Non-Files (28)
- Reallocated Name Files (0)
- 'ignore' category (0)

Extensions

- Extension Mismatches (9)

Categories (5063)

- archive (0)
- audio (0)
- compress (0)
- crypto (0)
- data (39)
- disk (0)
- documents (1)
- exec (2)
- images (4991)
- system (0)
- text (15)
- unknown (15)
- video (0)

Figure 9.33 – File sorting output

3. To view the sorted files, we must manually browse to the location of the output folder, as Autopsy 2.4 does not support the viewing of sorted files. To reveal this location, click on **View Sorted Files** in the left pane:

Sort Files by Type

View Sorted Files

Figure 9.34 – Viewing Sorted Files

Sorted files can be viewed by opening the file at /var/lib/autopsy/Terry_ USB/host1/output/sorter-vol2/index.html:

> **Tip:**
> The output folder's location will vary depending on the information
> specified by the user when first creating the case, but can usually be found at
> /var/lib/autopsy/<case name>/<host name>/output/
> sorter- vol#/index.html.

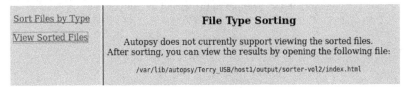

Figure 9.35 – Link to sorted files

4. To open the index.html file output, paste the location into a new tab in the browser:

Figure 9.36 – HTML file output listing sorted files

5. Click on the **documents** category:

documents Category

C:/Log/Thumbs.db
Composite Document File V2 Document, Cannot read section info
Image: /var/lib/autopsy/Terry_USB/host1/images/terry-work-usb-2009-12-11.E01 Inode: 2371853

Figure 9.37 – Snippet of the sorted documents

6. Click on the **exec** category:

exec Category

C:/R54402.EXE
    PE32 executable (GUI) Intel 80386, for MS Windows
    Image: /var/lib/autopsy/Terry_USB/host1/images/terry-work-usb-2009-12-11.E01 Inode: 62

C:/vnc-4_1_3-x86_win32.exe
    PE32 executable (GUI) Intel 80386, for MS Windows
    Image: /var/lib/autopsy/Terry_USB/host1/images/terry-work-usb-2009-12-11.E01 Inode: 75

Figure 9.38 – Snippet of the sorted EXE files

7. Click on the **images** category:

images Category

C:/M57biz.jpg
    JPEG image data, JFIF standard 1.01, resolution (DPI), density 150x150, segment length 16, Exif Standard: [TIFF image data,
    big-endian, direntries=4, xresolution=62, yresolution=70, resolutionunit=2], baseline, precision 8, 1650x1275, components 3
    Image: /var/lib/autopsy/Terry_USB/host1/images/terry-work-usb-2009-12-11.E01 Inode: 15

C:/Log/2009-12-03_00036d9f_big.jpg
    JPEG image data, JFIF standard 1.01, resolution (DPI), density 96x96, segment length 16, baseline, precision 8, 800x600,
    components 3
    Image: /var/lib/autopsy/Terry_USB/host1/images/terry-work-usb-2009-12-11.E01 Inode: 4235

C:/Log/2009-12-03_00036d9f_small.jpg
    JPEG image data, JFIF standard 1.01, resolution (DPI), density 96x96, segment length 16, baseline, precision 8, 150x110,
    components 3
    Image: /var/lib/autopsy/Terry_USB/host1/images/terry-work-usb-2009-12-11.E01 Inode: 4239

C:/Log/2009-12-03_0005425f_big.jpg
    JPEG image data, JFIF standard 1.01, resolution (DPI), density 96x96, segment length 16, baseline, precision 8, 800x600,
    components 3
    Image: /var/lib/autopsy/Terry_USB/host1/images/terry-work-usb-2009-12-11.E01 Inode: 4243

C:/Log/2009-12-03_0005425f_small.jpg
    JPEG image data, JFIF standard 1.01, resolution (DPI), density 96x96, segment length 16, baseline, precision 8, 150x110,
    components 3
    Image: /var/lib/autopsy/Terry_USB/host1/images/terry-work-usb-2009-12-11.E01 Inode: 4247

C:/Log/2009-12-03_0007171f_big.jpg
    JPEG image data, JFIF standard 1.01, resolution (DPI), density 96x96, segment length 16, baseline, precision 8, 800x600,
    components 3
    Image: /var/lib/autopsy/Terry_USB/host1/images/terry-work-usb-2009-12-11.E01 Inode: 4251

Figure 9.39 – Snippet of the sorted image files

As we've seen, Autopsy, as used in Linux environments, is a simple open source tool for analyzing forensic images and carving various artifacts such as deleted images, videos, and documents. The sorting feature can also assist with documentation as it provides details of carved data, including data paths. As with any good tool, you can also return to any case and continue with your investigations and analysis, as detailed in the next section.

Reopening cases in Autopsy

Cases are usually ongoing and can easily be restarted by starting Autopsy and clicking on **OPEN CASE**:

Figure 9.40 – Autopsy forensic browser options

In **CASE GALLERY**, be sure to choose the correct case name and, from there, continue your examination:

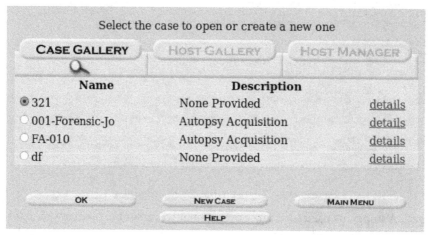

Figure 9.41 – Case gallery options

That's it for using Autopsy in Kali Linux. Let's now look at using Autopsy in Windows.

Autopsy in Windows

Autopsy for Windows comes as a full GUI application. Currently in version 4.13, Autopsy is very simple and user-friendly.

It can be downloaded from the Autopsy website at `https://www.autopsy.com/download/` and is available in 32- and 64-bit versions. The installation is simple and just requires the user to click the **Next** button until completed:

1. To open Autopsy in Windows, double-click the Autopsy icon on the desktop:

Figure 9.42 – Autopsy desktop icon in Windows

2. Once the modules have loaded, you are prompted to choose between creating a new case and opening previous cases. Click on **New Case**:

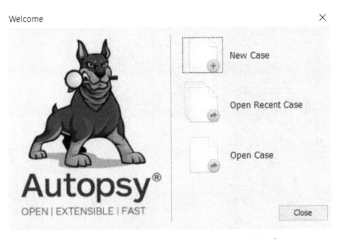

Figure 9.43 – Autopsy welcome screen in Windows

3. We'll be analyzing the same `terry-usb-work` file we used previously in this chapter. Fill in the details and click on **Next**:

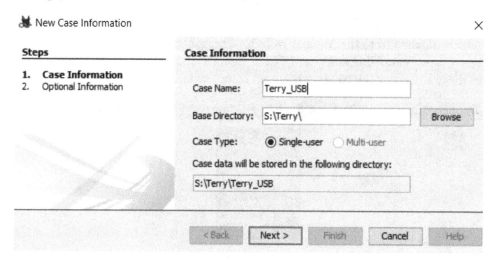

Figure 9.44 – Case information details

4. Fill in the optional details and click on **Finish**:

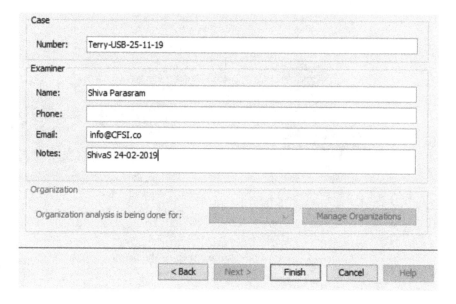

Figure 9.45 – Case information details (continued)

5.   Select the **Disk Image or VM File** option and click on **Next**:

Figure 9.46 – Data source selection options

6.   Browse to the data source file, select your time zone, and click **Next**:

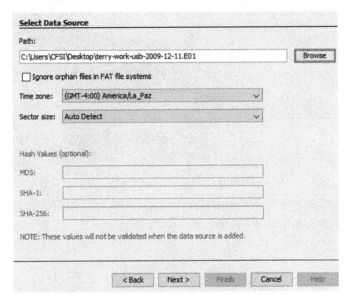

Figure 9.47 – Data source selection details

7. Next, we configure the ingest modules, which allow quick big data analysis against each data source. The ingest modules can also be downloaded on mobile memory and other types of advanced analysis. More information on the ingest modules can be found at `https://sleuthkit.org/autopsy/docs/user-docs/4.5.0/ingest_page.html`.

    Leave the checked options for the ingest modules as they are and click on **Next**:

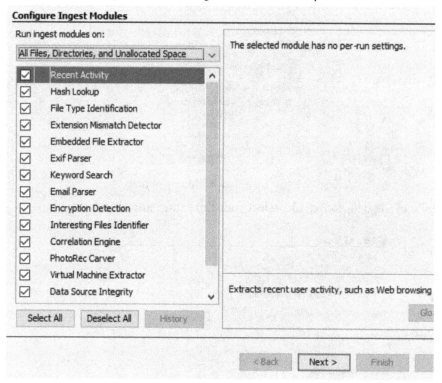

Figure 9.48 – Configuring ingest modules

8. The data source will be added, and you can now click on **Finish**. This imports the image and begins analyzing the files within:

Figure 9.49 – Autopsy interface with data sources loaded

9.   We can click on the + signs in the left menu to expand on the artifact categories, which allows us to view images, documents, deleted files, and emails discovered within the data source:

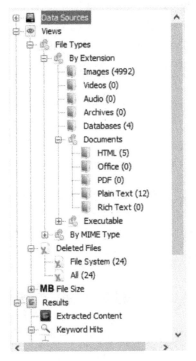

Figure 9.50 – Data source pane expanded

10. Expand the **File Types** category, then expand **By Extension** and click on **Images**. This shows us the 4,992 images that were carved from the image by Autopsy:

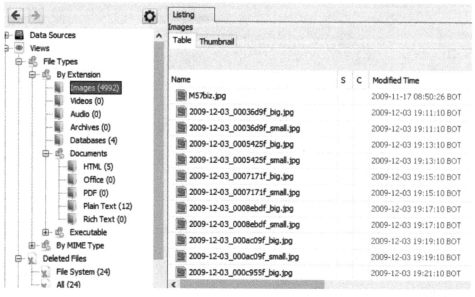

Figure 9.51 – Images carved by Autopsy

11. Clicking on **Deleted Files** and then **All**, we can see all the deleted files, including the deleted `keylogger` file that we also found in the older Linux 2.4 version:

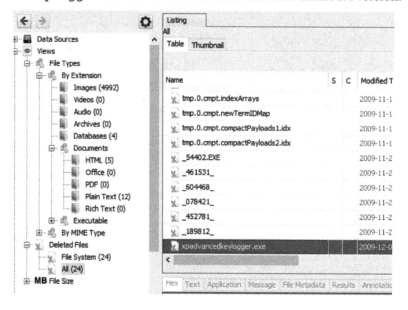

Figure 5.52 – Deleted files carved by Autopsy in Windows

As we can see, Autopsy for Windows is much easier to use and may for some users, seem like the better option. Keep exploring the categories in Autopsy to see whether you can find any evidence of theft or stolen items.

Summary

In this chapter, we looked at forensics using the Autopsy Forensic Browser with The Sleuth Kit. Compared to individual tools, Autopsy has case management features and supports various types of file analysis, searching, and the sorting of allocated, unallocated, and hidden files. Autopsy can also perform hashing on the file and directory levels to maintain evidence integrity. We also compared Autopsy for Linux and Windows to view the differences. It's up to you to decide which one you prefer to work with. We will now move on to the **Digital Forensic Framework (DFF)**, which, like Autopsy, allows us to perform file carving and analysis on forensic images.

10
Analysis with Xplico

Xplico is an open source, GUI **Network Forensics Analysis Tool (NFAT)** that focuses on extracting artifacts from network and internet captures.

Captures of network and internet traffic are obtained directly in Xplico using its live acquisition feature but can also be done using tools within Kali Linux, such as Wireshark and Ettercap. These network acquisition files are saved as .pcap or **packet capture** files, which are then uploaded to Xplico and decoded automatically using its IP decoder and decoder manager components.

In this chapter, we'll cover the following topics:

- Installing Xplico in Kali Linux
- Starting Xplico in DEFT Linux
- Packet capture analysis using Xplico
- Network activity analysis using Xplico

Software requirements

Should you run into difficulties updating Kali Linux or running Xplico (which happens sometimes), consider downloading and running DEFT Linux 8.2 in a virtual environment. Beginners may find that Xplico may be easier to work with in DEFT Linux as there are GUI menu items to start the Apache and Xplico services options, whereas these have to be typed into the Terminal in Kali Linux.

> **Important note:**
> DEFT Linux 8.2 can be downloaded from `https://na.mirror.garr.it/mirrors/deft/iso/`.

Installing Xplico in Kali Linux

First, let's update Kali Linux and also install the Forensic metapackage for Kali Linux. Kali metapackages allow the user to install required tools of the same category, such as wireless, vulnerability assessment, and forensic tools.

For more information on installing various, or all, metapackages and the list of tools within each package, visit this link: `https://tools.kali.org/kali-metapackages`.

Here's a screenshot of some of the forensic tools within the forensics metapackage:

kali-tools-forensics: Forensic tools - Live & Offline

afflib-tools	parted	volatility
apktool	pasco	wce
autopsy	pdf-parser	wireshark
binwalk	pdfid	xplico
bulk-extractor	pdgmail	yara
cabextract	pev	libaff4-utils
chkrootkit	polenum	exifprobe
creddump	pst-utils	ext3grep
dc3dd	python-capstone	ext4magic
dcfldd	python-distorm3	forensic-artifacts
ddrescue	python-peepdf	forensics-colorize
dumpzilla	radare2	gpart
edb-debugger	radare2-cutter	grokevt
ewf-tools	recoverjpeg	lime-forensics
exiv2	recstudio	mac-robber
extundelete	reglookup	md5deep
fcrackzip	regripper	metacam
firmware-mod-kit	rifiuti	myrescue
flasm	rifiuti2	nasty
foremost	rkhunter	neopi
galleta	safecopy	plaso

Figure 10.1 – List of forensic tools available in the forensics metapackage for Kali

To run the update and install the forensics metapackage, type the following command into a Terminal:

```
sudo apt update && sudo install kali-linux-forensics
```

The following output is displayed after running the preceding command:

```
root@kali:~# sudo apt update && sudo install kali-linux-forensics
Hit:1 http://kali.download/kali kali-rolling InRelease
Reading package lists... Done
Building dependency tree
Reading state information... Done
```

Figure 10.2 – Installing the kali-linux-forensics metapackage

At some point, you will be prompted to press *Y* (yes) to continue downloading and installing the updates:

```
After this operation, 15.4 MB of additional disk space will be used.
Do you want to continue? [Y/n] y
Get:1 http://kali.download/kali kali-rolling/main amd64 lame amd64 3.100-2+b1 [280 kB]
Get:2 http://kali.download/kali kali-rolling/main amd64 php7.3-readline amd64 7.3.10-1+b1 [12.2 kB]
Get:3 http://kali.download/kali kali-rolling/main amd64 php7.3-opcache amd64 7.3.10-1+b1 [183 kB]
Get:4 http://kali.download/kali kali-rolling/main amd64 php7.3-mysql amd64 7.3.10-1+b1 [119 kB]
Get:5 http://kali.download/kali kali-rolling/main amd64 php7.3-json amd64 7.3.10-1+b1 [18.8 kB]
Get:6 http://kali.download/kali kali-rolling/main amd64 libapache2-mod-php7.3 amd64 7.3.10-1+b1 [1,355 kB]
Get:7 http://kali.download/kali kali-rolling/main amd64 php7.3-cli amd64 7.3.10-1+b1 [1,406 kB]
Get:8 http://kali.download/kali kali-rolling/main amd64 php7.3-common amd64 7.3.10-1+b1 [946 kB]
Get:9 http://kali.download/kali kali-rolling/main amd64 php7.3-sqlite3 amd64 7.3.10-1+b1 [26.1 kB]
Get:10 http://kali.download/kali kali-rolling/main amd64 php-sqlite3 all 2:7.3+69 [5,996 B]
Get:11 http://kali.download/kali kali-rolling/main amd64 librecode0 amd64 3.6-24 [531 kB]
Get:12 http://kali.download/kali kali-rolling/main amd64 recode amd64 3.6-24 [188 kB]
Get:13 http://kali.download/kali kali-rolling/main amd64 libsox3 amd64 14.4.2+git20190427-1+b1 [264 kB]
Get:14 http://kali.download/kali kali-rolling/main amd64 libsox-fmt-alsa amd64 14.4.2+git20190427-1+b1 [51
5 kB]
```

Figure 10.3 – Forensics metapackage installation process

Now, we can install Xplico by typing `apt install xplico`.

The following output is displayed after running the preceding command:

```
root@kali:~# apt install xplico
Reading package lists... Done
Building dependency tree
Reading state information... Done
The following packages were automatically installed and are no longer required:
  girl.2-clutter-gst-3.0 girl.2-gtkclutter-1.0 tpm2-abrmd tpm2-tools
Use 'apt autoremove' to remove them.
The following additional packages will be installed:
  lame libapache2-mod-php7.3 libndpi2.6 librecode0 libsox-fmt-alsa
  libsox-fmt-base libsox3 php-sqlite3 php7.3-cli php7.3-common php7.3-json
  php7.3-mysql php7.3-opcache php7.3-readline php7.3-sqlite3 recode sox
Suggested packages:
  lame-doc php-pear libsox-fmt-all
The following NEW packages will be installed:
  lame libndpi2.6 librecode0 libsox-fmt-alsa libsox-fmt-base libsox3
  php-sqlite3 php7.3-sqlite3 recode sox xplico
The following packages will be upgraded:
  libapache2-mod-php7.3 php7.3-cli php7.3-common php7.3-json php7.3-mysql
  php7.3-opcache php7.3-readline
```

Figure 10.4 – Installing Xplico in Kali Linux

During the installation, you'll also be prompted to press *Y* to continue installing the required files:

Figure 10.5 – Xplico installation process continued

After the installation is complete, we can verify that it has been installed and also view the options within Xplico by typing xplico -h.

This command also shows the version of Xplico. In this instance, we can see that we have installed and are running Xplico v1.2.2:

Figure 10.6 – Xplico help options

Lastly, before we get to the Xplico web GUI, we'll have to start the `apache2` and `xplico` services from the Terminal by typing the following two commands:

- `service apache2 start`
- `service xplico start`

The commands are shown in the following screenshot:

```
root@kali:~# service apache2 start
root@kali:~# service xplico start
root@kali:~#
```

Figure 10.7 – Starting apache2 services

A browser window opens immediately with the following URL:

`localhost:9876/users/login`

If the browser does not open automatically, you can open a browser and enter the following URL into the address bar: `localhost:9876`.

Starting Xplico in DEFT Linux 8.2

Should you find great difficulty in installing Xplico, another option would be to use DEFT Linux 8.2, which can be run either as a live OS or as a virtual host. This process is not as in-depth as installing Kali Linux (as covered in *Chapter 2, Installing Kali Linux*) because DEFT can be used as a live forensic acquisition distribution.

You can download DEFT 8.2 from `https://na.mirror.garr.it/mirrors/deft/iso/`, then open VirtualBox, click **New**, and enter the following details:

- **Name**: `Deft 8.2`
- **Type**: `Linux`
- **Version**: `Ubuntu (64-bit)`

The following figure shows the options selected:

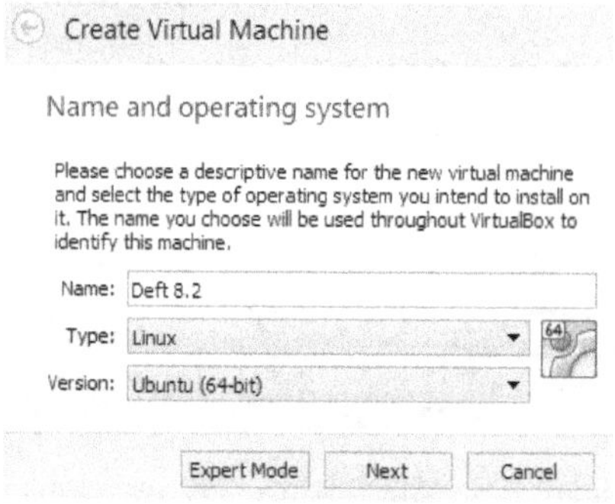

Figure 10.8 – DEFT Linux virtual machine details

Now, after filling in the appropriate information, follow these steps:

1. Assign four or more GBs of RAM.

2. Leave the default option of **Create a virtual hard disk now** and click **Create**.

3. Leave the default option of **VDI (VirtualBox Disk Image)** and click **Next**.

4. Leave the default option of **Dynamically allocated**, click **Next**, and click on **Create**.

5. Click the green start arrow on the **VirtualBox Manager** screen to start the virtual machine.

When prompted to **Select start-up disk**, click the browse-folder icon and browse to the downloaded DEFT Linux 8.2 ISO image, then click **Start**:

Figure 10.9 – Selecting the DEFT Linux image in VirtualBox

This brings the user to the DEFT splash screen. Select **English** for your language and select **DEFT Linux 8 live**:

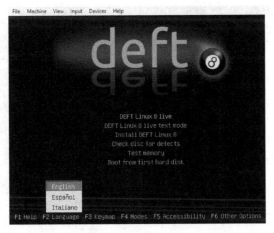

Figure 10.10 – DEFT Linux boot menu

After DEFT Linux boots and loads the desktop, click the DEFT menu button in the lower-left corner, then click the **Service** menu, and then click **Apache start**. Repeat this process to get to the **Service** menu and then click **Xplico start**:

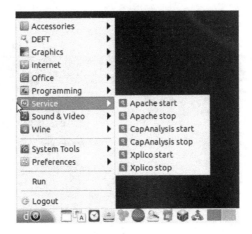

Figure 10.11 – DEFT Linux Xplico menu

Finally, start Xplico by clicking the DEFT button, then go to the **DEFT** menu, go across to **Network Forensics**, and click **Xplico**:

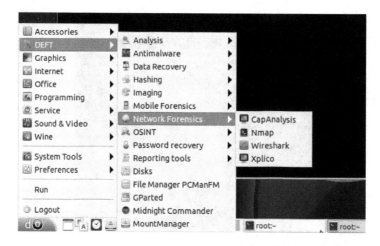

Figure 10.12 – Network Forensics menu

This brings us to the very same Xplico web interface GUI that is also available in Kali Linux:

Figure 10.13 – Xplico web interface

Once you have Xplico installed and running using either Kali Linux or DEFT Linux, we can now move on to analyzing packet capture (.pcap) files to find various artifacts.

Packet capture analysis using Xplico

The protocols that we can investigate using Xplico include, but are not limited to, the following:

- **Transmission Control Protocol (TCP)**
- **User Datagram Protocol (UDP)**
- **Hypertext Transfer Protocol (HTTP)**
- **File Transfer Protocol (FTP)**
- **Trivial FTP (TFTP)**
- **Session Initiation Protocol (SIP)**
- **Post Office Protocol (POP)**
- **Internet Map Access Protocol (IMAP)**
- **Simple Mail Transfer Protocol (SMTP)**

Data contained in network and internet packet captures, and even live acquisition, can contain artifacts such as the following:

- HTTP traffic, such as websites browsed
- Email
- Facebook chats
- **Real-time transport protocol (RTP)** and **Voice over Internet Protocol (VoIP)**
- Printed files

> **Important note:**
> Traffic encrypted using **Secure Sockets Layer (SSL)** cannot currently be viewed with Xplico.

Specialized commercial tools, such as FTK, EnCase, and Belkasoft, may have to be purchased to view encrypted traffic. It should also be noted that the unauthorized capturing of data packets may violate company policies and may also be illegal in many countries. I urge you to only capture data on networks that you have been given explicit written permission to do so for, as long as it does not violate company, state, and country laws.

Whether you're using Kali Linux or DEFT Linux, for this chapter we will be using publicly available sample packet capture (.pcap) files, which can be downloaded at http://wiki.xplico.org/doku.php?id=pcap:pcap.

The files needed are as follows:

- **DNS**
- **MMS**
- **Webmail: Hotmail/Live**
- **HTTP (web)**
- **SIP example 1**

We will also require an SMTP sample file, available from the Wireshark sample captures page at https://wiki.wireshark.org/SampleCaptures.

HTTP and web analysis using Xplico

In this exercise, we will upload the following **HTTP (web)** sample packet capture file: xplico.org_sample_capture_web_must_use_xplico_nc.cfg.pcap.

For this HTTP analysis, we will use Xplico to search for artifacts associated with the HTTP protocol, such as URLs, images from websites, and possible browser-related activities.

Once Xplico has been started, log in using the following credentials:

- **Username**: xplico
- **Password**: xplico

We then choose **New Case** from the menu on the left and select the **Uploading PCAP capture file/s** button as we will be uploading files and not performing live captures or acquisition. For each case, we must also specify a case name:

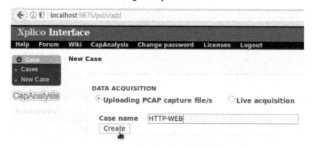

Figure 10.14 – Data acquisition details

In the previous screenshot, I have entered HTTP-WEB for **Case name**. Click **Create** to continue. The case **HTTPWEB** has now been created. Click **HTTPWEB** to continue to the **Session** screen:

Figure 10.15 – Case list details

Now, we create a new session for this instance of our case by clicking the **New Session** option in the menu to the left:

Figure 10.16 – Xplico cases menu

We give our session a name and click **Create** to continue:

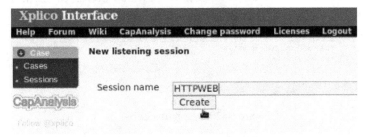

Figure 10.17 – Session name details

Our new session has been created with the name **HTTPWEB**:

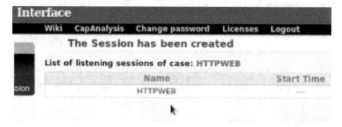

Figure 10.18 – Newly created session

Once our case and session details have been entered, we are presented with the main Xplico interface window, which displays the various categories of possible artifacts found after our .pcap file has been uploaded and decoded, including the **HTTP**, **DNS**, **Webmail**, and **Facebook** categories:

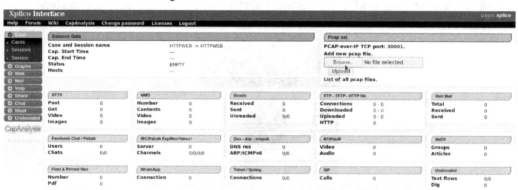

Figure 10.19 – Xplico interface

To upload our .pcap file, click the **Browse...** button in the **Pcap set** area to the top right, choose the downloaded .pcap file (xplico.org_sample_capture_web_must_ use_xplico_nc.cfg.pcap), and then click the **Upload** button to begin the decoding process in Xplico:

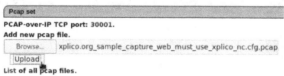

Figure 10.20 – pcap uploading

The decoding process can take a while depending on the size of the .pcap file as this process decodes the .pcap file into easily searchable categories within Xplico. Once finished, the **Status** field in the **Session Data** area reads **DECODING COMPLETED** and also displays the details of the case and session name and the start and end times:

Figure 10.21 – Session data details

After the decoding is completed, the results are then displayed in the various category areas. In the following screenshot, we can see that there is an entry in the **Undecoded** category under **Text flows**:

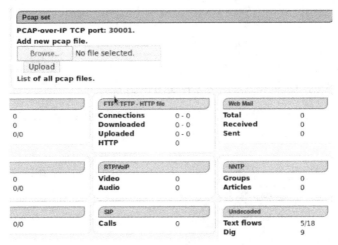

Figure 10.22 – Decoded pcap results

To analyze the decoded results, we use the menu to the extreme left of the Xplico interface. Seeing that we have results listed in the **Undecoded** category, click **Undecoded** in the menu, which expands into the **TCP-UDP** and **Dig** sub-menus. Click the **TCP-UDP** sub-menu to explore further:

Figure 10.23 – Xplico menu

The **TCP-UDP** option reveals the destination IP, port, date and time, duration of connection, and an info file with more details. The destination IP entries marked in red can be clicked on and also explored further:

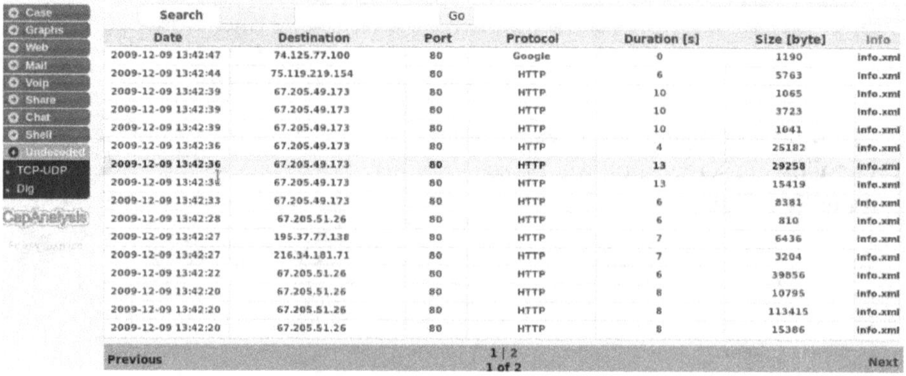

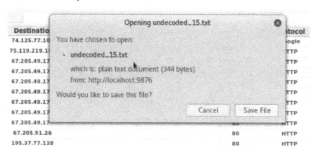

Figure 10.24 – TCP-UDP artifacts

If we click the first destination IP entry, 74.125.77.100, we are prompted to save the information details of this entry in a text file:

Figure 10.25 – Saving details to a text file

To view the contents of the file, we can either open it directly from the saved location or use the cat command to display the contents within a Terminal by typing cat/root/Downloads/undecoded_15.txt:

Figure 10.26 – Viewing the text file in the Terminal

The results displayed in the previous Terminal window show that a `.gif` image was viewed or downloaded on `Wed, 09 Dec 2009`.

We can also click the **info.xml** link under the **Info** column to obtain more information:

Protocol	Duration [s]	Size [byte]	Info
Google	0	1190	info.xml pcap
HTTP	6	5763	info.xml
HTTP	10	1065	info.xml
HTTP	10	3723	info.xml

Figure 10.27 – .xml files containing more information

info.xml shows the source and destination IP addresses and port numbers. We can now explore all the destination IP addresses and their respective `info.xml` files to gather more information for our case:

Figure 10.28 – Contents of the .xml file

Let's go back to the **Undecoded** menu on the left and click the **Dig** sub-menu to explore our capture file further:

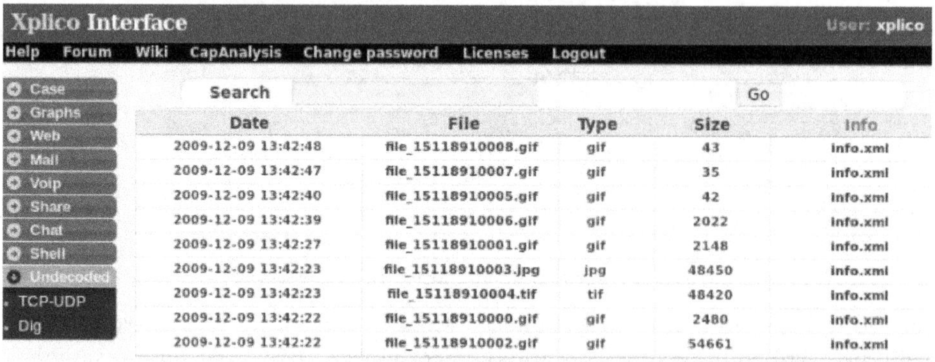

Figure 10.29 – Undecoded menu

In the previous screenshot, the **Dig** sub-menu reveals several image artifacts in the form of .gif, .tif, and .jpg formats, along with the dates viewed through an HTTP connection.

The images should be viewed and documented as part of our case findings:

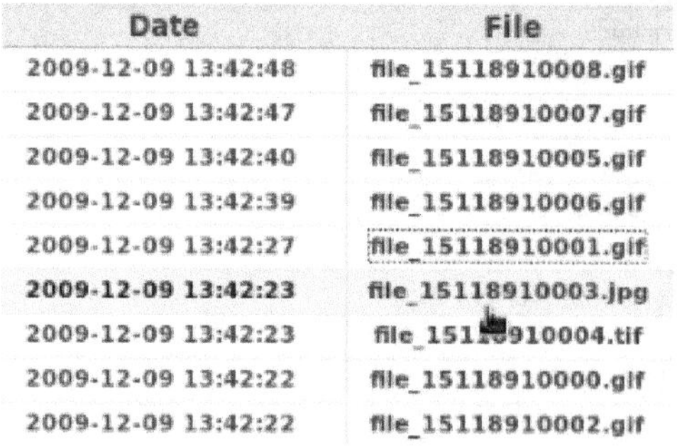

Date	File
2009-12-09 13:42:48	file_15118910008.gif
2009-12-09 13:42:47	file_15118910007.gif
2009-12-09 13:42:40	file_15118910005.gif
2009-12-09 13:42:39	file_15118910006.gif
2009-12-09 13:42:27	file_15118910001.gif
2009-12-09 13:42:23	file_15118910003.jpg
2009-12-09 13:42:23	file_15118910004.tif
2009-12-09 13:42:22	file_15118910000.gif
2009-12-09 13:42:22	file_15118910002.gif

Figure 10.30 – Dig sub-menu

This covers HTTP analysis using Xplico. Let's now download and analyze a VoIP .pcap file in the next section.

VoIP analysis using Xplico

Many organizations, and even regular end users, have implemented or used **Voice over IP** (**VoIP**) solutions, mainly to reduce costs in voice and multimedia communication sessions that would have otherwise required the use of paid telephone lines. To use VoIP services, we must use the **Session Initiation Protocol** (**SIP**).

For this exercise, we will be using the SIP example 1 (`freeswitch4560_tosipphone_ok.pcap`) packet capture file to analyze VoIP services, if there are any.

As with our previous HTTP web analysis, a new case and session must be created with the relevant details for this new case:

- **Case name**: `SIP_Analysis`
- **Session name**: `Sip_File`

Once the case and session has been created, browse to the `.pcap` file to be uploaded (`freeswitch4560_tosipphone_ok.pcap`) and click **Upload** to begin the decoding process:

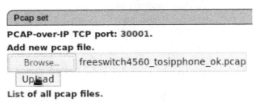

Figure 10.31 – PCAP upload

After the file has been decoded, we can see that there are **2** results listed in the **Calls** category in the lower-right corner:

Figure 10.32 – SIP results

To begin exploring and analyzing the details of the VoIP calls, click the **Voip** option on the menu to the left:

Figure 10.33 – SIP menu

Clicking the **Sip** sub-menu, we are presented with the details of the calls. We can see that calls were made from "Freeswitch" <sip:5555551212@192.168.1.111> to Freeswitch <sip:5555551212@192.168.1.112>:

From	To	Duration
"FreeSwitch" <sip:5555551212@192.168.1.111>	<sip:6580@192.168.1.12>	0:0:19
"FreeSwitch" <sip:5555551212@192.168.1.111>	<sip:6580@192.168.1.12>	0:0:0

Figure 10.34 – SIP results

Click on the duration details (0:0:19) to analyze and explore further:

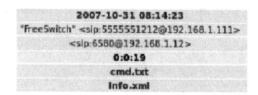

Figure 10.35 – Call duration details

Let's first click on cmd.txt to view the information file and log:

Figure 10.36 – Call details

In the previous screenshot, we can see details of the numbers in conversation, date, time, and duration. There is also an option to play the conversations on either end:

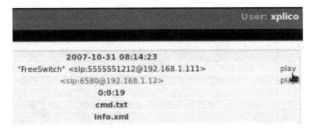

Figure 10.37 – Play option for calls

Using Xplico, we discovered phone numbers and IP addresses by analyzing the SIP protocol. Let's now move on to email analysis.

Email analysis using Xplico

Emails use different protocols to send and receive emails depending on the method used for sending, receiving, and storing/accessing emails. The three protocols used are as follows:

- **SMTP**

- **Post Office Protocol (POP3)**

- **IMAP4**

SMTP uses port 25 and is used for sending emails.

POP3 uses port 110 and is used to retrieve emails by downloading them from the email server to the client. Microsoft Outlook is an example of a POP3 client.

IMAP4 uses port 143 and is similar to POP3 in that it retrieves emails but leaves a copy of the email on the server and can be accessed anywhere through a web browser, commonly referred to as webmail. Gmail and Yahoo are examples of webmail.

For this exercise, we will be using two sample files.

The first file is the **Webmail: Hotmail / Live** .pcap file (xplico.org_sample_capture_webmail_live.pcap), which can be downloaded from http://wiki.xplico.org/doku.php?id=pcap:pcap.

The second is the smtp.pcap file, which can be downloaded from https://wiki.wireshark.org/SampleCaptures.

For the analysis of the first `.pcap` file (**Webmail: Hotmail / Live**), I've created a case with the following details:

- **Case name**: `Webmail_Analysis`

- **Session name**: `WebmailFile`

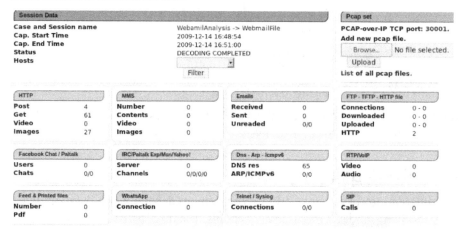

Figure 10.38 – Webmail analysis results

If we take a closer look at the decoded results, we can see that we now have several populated categories, including the HTTP, DNS -ARP - ICMP v6, and FTP - TFTP - HTTP files:

- The **HTTP** category:

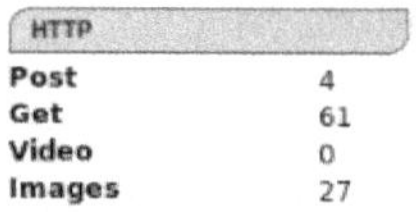

HTTP	
Post	4
Get	61
Video	0
Images	27

Figure 10.39 – HTTP results

- The **Dns - Arp - Icmpv6** category:

Dns - Arp - Icmpv6	
DNS res	65
ARP/ICMPv6	0/0

Figure 10.40 – DNS, ARP, and Icmp results

- The **FTP - TFTP - HTTP** file:

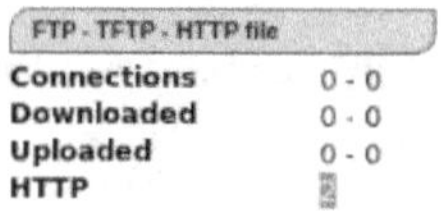

FTP - TFTP - HTTP file	
Connections	0 - 0
Downloaded	0 - 0
Uploaded	0 - 0
HTTP	2

Figure 10.41 – FTP, TFTP, and HTTP results

Now that we have an idea of what artifacts exist, let's now use the menu on the left-hand side to analyze the results further.

Clicking the **Graphs** menu on the left displays domain information, including the hostname, **Canonical Name** (**CName**) entries, IP addresses of the host, and also the info.xml files for each entry, for more detailed information about the source and address:

Host	CName	IP	Info
spe.atdmt.com	spe.atdmt.com.edgesuite.net	194.224.66.90	info.xml pcap
rmd.atdmt.com	rmd.atdmt.com.edgesuite.net	194.224.66.83	info.xml
rmd.atdmt.com	rmd.atdmt.com.edgesuite.net		info.xml
spe.atdmt.com	spe.atdmt.com.edgesuite.net		info.xml
ads2.msads.net	msnads.vo.msecnd.net		info.xml
ads2.msads.net	msnads.vo.msecnd.net	65.54.81.78	info.xml

Figure 10.42 – Host Cname and IP details

The info.xml file (as in the following screenshot) for the first entry (spe.atdmt.com) reveals that a local IP (ip.src) of 10.0.2.15 is connected to the host with an IP (ip.dst) of 194.179.1.100 (also illustrated in the **IP** field of the preceding screenshot):

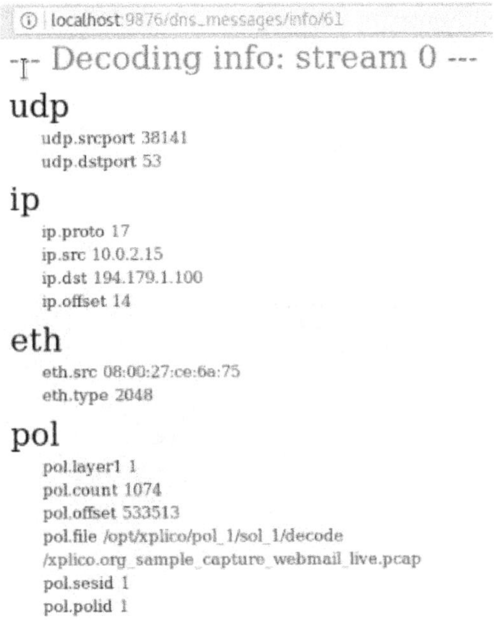

Figure 10.43 – info.xml details

Next, we move on to the **Web** menu and scroll down to the **Site** sub-menu. A list of web pages visited is displayed along with the date and time that each was accessed. We can see that the first three entries belong to the `mail.live.com` domain and the fourth and fifth to `msn.com`:

For a complete view of html page set your browser to use Proxy,

Search:

Date	
2009-12-14 16:51:00	sn118w.snt118.mail.live.com/im/pages/ToastMini.aspx
2009-12-14 16:50:56	sn118w.snt118.mail.live.com/im/pages/BuddyList.aspx
2009-12-14 16:50:56	sn118w.snt118.mail.live.com/im/pages/ToastFull.aspx
2009-12-14 16:50:51	a.rad.msn.com/ADSAdClient31.dll?GetSAd=&DPJS=4&PN=MSFT&ID=C9F912A
2009-12-14 16:50:51	rad.msn.com/ADSAdClient31.dll?GetSAd=&DPJS=4&PN=MSFT&ID=C9F912A3
2009-12-14 16:50:51	view.atdmt.com/D5I/iview/136566009/direct;wi.160;hi.600/01?click=
2009-12-14 16:50:50	sn118w.snt118.mail.live.com/im/pages/im.aspx
2009-12-14 16:50:49	sn118w.snt118.mail.live.com/mail/InboxLight.aspx?n=1641341718
2009-12-14 16:50:49	sn118w.snt118.mail.live.com/default.aspx?n=424857020
2009-12-14 16:50:09	ad.doubleclick.net/adi/N4022.iges.msn.es/B4123425.3;sz=300x250;ord=1165

Figure 10.44 – Web results

We can examine the first **Site** entry by clicking on **info.xml**. Under the **http** section, we can see that the Mozilla Firefox browser was used and the `sn118w.snt118.mail.live.com` host accessed:

Figure 10.45 – info.xml details

Close the `info.xml` file and select the **Image** button, then click **Go** to display any i images found:

Figure 10.46 – info.xml display options

The **Image** search results display several images and icons found. Click through the list to view the images:

Date	Url
2009-12-14 16:50:50	h.msn.com/c.gif?RF=&PI=7324&DI=5707&S=96690&cb=1260823850606
2009-12-14 16:50:49	sn118w.snt118.mail.live.com/favicon.ico
2009-12-14 16:50:47	c.live.com/c.gif?NC=31263&NA=1149&PS=97598&PI=94811&DI=13263&TP=spaces.live.com-&GT1=;
2009-12-14 16:50:47	msnportal.112.2o7.net/b/ss/msnspacesus/1/H.6-pdv-2/s2517528184171?[AQB]&ndh=1&t=14/11/2009%2021%3A50%3A4
2009-12-14 16:50:41	shared.live.com/7E81kqTseEOmzDIpeFPS8g/Web/images/profile_24x24.gif
2009-12-14 16:50:41	shared.live.com/7E81kqTseEOmzDIpeFPS8g/Web/images/wlmessenger_24x24.gif
2009-12-14 16:50:22	msnportal.112.2o7.net/b/ss/msnspacesus/1/H.6-pdv-2/s28172311985137?AQB=1&pccr=true&vidn=2593528605162659-
2009-12-14 16:50:17	c.live.com/c.gif?NC=31263&NA=1149&PS=97596&PI=94811&DI=13263&TP=spaces.live.com-&GT1=;&MUID=DEF4FE7FA
2009-12-14 16:50:15	p.live.com/p.aspx?CI=8000&PN=Live.Profile&U=e8d1303a3a49e367&MS=&X=7xpv%2bVOHwReigUjw9mhB2it3rCQ%3d
2009-12-14 16:50:15	img.wlxrs.com/$live.controls.images/h/s3.png

Search: Web URLs: ⚪ Html ⦿ Image

Figure 10.47 – Image results list

We can also view the found images by returning to the **Web** menu to the left and then clicking the **Images** sub-menu. This presents us with a graphical grouping of the images, with links to their respective pages also:

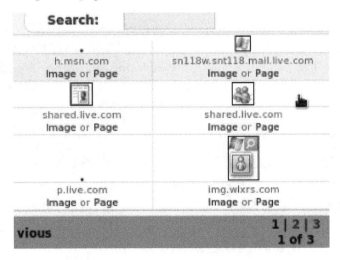

Figure 10.48 – Image and icon previews

Moving down the main menu to the left, click the **Share** menu and then click the **HTTP file** sub-menu. Here, we are presented with two items, which we can investigate further by clicking on their `info.xml` files:

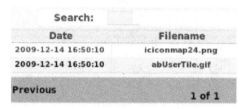

Figure 10.49 – HTTP results

By clicking on the `info.xml` file of `abUserTile.gif`, we can see that this was accessed from the `194.224.66.18` host:

Figure 10.50 – info.xml file details

In the **Undecoded** menu and **HTTP** sub-menu, we also have the HTTP information about the `194.224.66.19` destination IP. Try exploring this further by clicking on the `info.xml` file:

Date	Destination	Port	Protocol	Duration [s]
2009-12-14 16:49:13	194.224.66.19	80	HTTP	96

Previous   1 of 1

Figure 10.51 – Destination IP info

Let's now delve a bit further into email analysis by performing an SMTP analysis.

SMTP exercise using a Wireshark sample file

For this example, we will use the SMTP sample capture file downloaded from the Wireshark samples link at the beginning of this section.

I've created a case with the following details, as in the **Session Data** section of the following screenshot:

- **Case name**: SMTP

- **Session name**: SMTPfile

Looking at the lower-right corner of the screen, we can see that there is an item in the **Unreaded** field of the **Emails** category:

Figure 10.52 – Unread emails results

Knowing that we are analyzing and investigating emails, we can go directly to the **Mail** menu and the **Email** sub-menu on the left side of the interface. This shows us that an email with no subject was sent by gurpartap@patriots.in to raj_deo2002in@ yahoo.co.in. Click on the **-(no subject)-** field to examine the email further:

Subject	Sender	Receivers	Size
-(no subject)-	gurpartap@patriots.in	raj_deol2002in@yahoo.co.in	14544

1 of 1

Figure 10.53 – Unread emails

After clicking on the **-(no subject)-** field, we can now see the contents of the email:

Figure 10.54 – Unread email content

This concludes our email and SMTP analysis of the `.pcap` file. Let's now download and analyze another `.pcap` file to discover any network activity.

Network activity analysis exercise

Putting it all together, we can download a PCAP file from `https://wiki.xplico.org/doku.php?id=pcap:pcap` named `SAMPLE OF ALL PROTOCOLS SUPPORTED IN XPLICO 0.6.3`. This `.pcap` file can also be downloaded directly from `https://wiki.xplico.org/lib/exe/fetch.php?media=pcap:xplico.org_sample_capture_protocols_supported_in_0.6.3.pcap.bz2`.

Some browsers may prompt you with a privacy warning, as in the following screenshot, due to the sample files being hosted on an older site:

Figure 10.55 – Security exception

Click on the **Advanced** button and then click on **Proceed to wiki.xplico.org (unsafe)** at the bottom of the page, as in the following screenshot. The site is safe, just a bit dated, and does not use SSL:

Figure 10.56 – Xplico.org safety exception

The downloaded file can be compressed by right-clicking on the file and selecting **Extract Here**.

We can start a new case analysis by clicking on **New Case**, giving the case a name, and then clicking on **Create**, as we've previously done in this chapter:

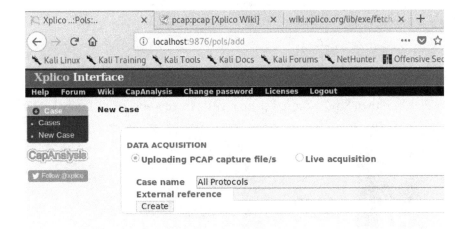

Figure 10.57 – PCAP upload interface

Follow the same procedure that we've done so far to upload the `xplico.org_sample_capture_protocols_supported_in_0.6.3.pcap` file:

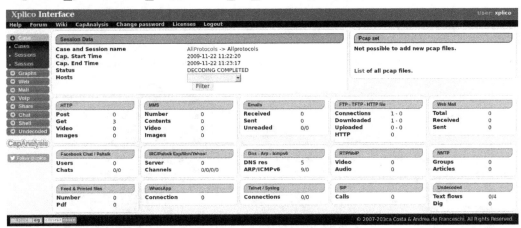

Figure 10.58 – Xplico interface

Although it's hard to see in the preceding screenshot, here's a list of the number of items found:

HTTP:

- **Get** – 3

FTP - TFTP - HTTP file:

- **Connections** – 1
- **Downloaded** – 1

DNS – Arp - Icmpv6

- **DNS res** – 5

- **ARP/ICMPv6** – 9 / 0

Clicking on **Web** and then **Site** in the left pane reveals three websites, as informed by the **HTTP Get** section:

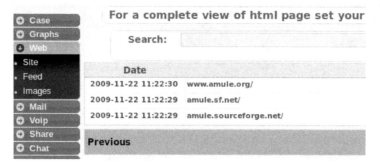

Figure 10.59 – Web results

Click on www.amule.org to visit the site in a new window:

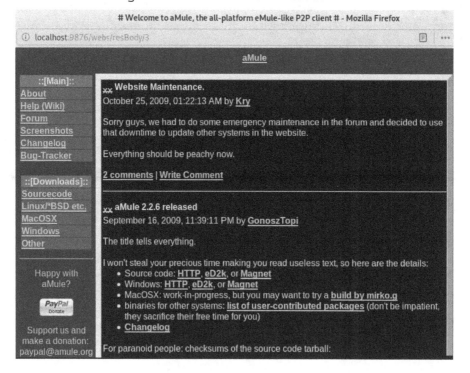

Figure 10.60 – aMule website

aMule was a popular **Peer-to-Peer** (**P2P**) client for downloading content. `Sourceforge.net` is also a popular site for downloading software. Most likely, the user visited these sites to download the `Amule.exe` program.

Under the **Share** menu in the left pane, click on **Ftp**:

Figure 10.61 – FTP results

We see that there was an FTP session by looking at the URL `ftp://ftp.debian.org:21`.

Next to the **Url** column, there is a **User** column and a **Download** column, and there is an entry of **anonymous**, meaning that the user logged in using the `anonymous` username and downloaded one file.

To see these details, we can also click on the **Url** name:

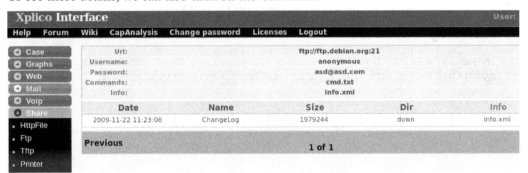

Figure 10.62 – Url details

We can see that the user logged in with the password `asd@asd.com`. We can see these passwords because the FTP session is not secure and both usernames and passwords are sent in plaintext because they are not encrypted.

Click on the `cmd.txt` file to view the user's activities during the session:

```
220 ftp.debian.org FTP server
USER anonymous
331 Please specify the password.
PASS asd@asd.com
230 Login successful.
SYST
215 UNIX Type: L8
PORT 172,26,0,21,228,22
200 PORT command successful. Consider using PASV.
LIST
150 Here comes the directory listing.
drwxr-xr-x    8 1176     1176         4096 Nov 22 15:50 debian
226 Directory send OK.
CWD debian
250 Directory successfully changed.
PORT 172,26,0,21,214,239
200 PORT command successful. Consider using PASV.
LIST
150 Here comes the directory listing.
-rw-r--r--    1 1176     1176         1062 Sep 04 18:54 README
-rw-r--r--    1 1176     1176         1290 Dec 04  2000 README.CD-manufacture
-rw-r--r--    1 1176     1176         2583 Sep 04 18:53 README.html
-rw-r--r--    1 1176     1176       131846 Nov 16 01:54 README.mirrors.html
-rw-r--r--    1 1176     1176        69595 Nov 16 01:54 README.mirrors.txt
drwxr-xr-x   11 1176     1176         4096 Sep 04 18:54 dists
drwxr-xr-x    4 1176     1176         4096 Nov 22 14:01 doc
drwxr-xr-x    3 1176     1176         4096 Nov 22 15:25 indices
-rw-r--r--    1 1176     1176      6605062 Nov 22 15:26 ls-lR.gz
-rw-r--r--    1 1176     1176       181759 Nov 22 15:26 ls-lR.patch.gz
drwxr-xr-x    5 1176     1176         4096 Dec 19  2000 pool
drwxr-xr-x    4 1176     1176         4096 Nov 17  2008 project
drwxr-xr-x    2 1176     1176         4096 Feb 07  2009 tools
226 Directory send OK.
CWD dists
250 Directory successfully changed.
PORT 172,26,0,21,190,170
200 PORT command successful. Consider using PASV.
LIST
150 Here comes the directory listing.
lrwxrwxrwx    1 1176     1176            4 Feb 09  2009 Debian4.0r8 -> etch
lrwxrwxrwx    1 1176     1176            5 Feb 14  2009 Debian5.0.3 -> lenny
-rw-r--r--    1 1176     1176          534 Sep 04 18:54 README
drwxr-sr-x    5 1176     1176         4096 May 23  2009 etch
drwxr-xr-x    5 1176     1176         4096 May 23  2009 etch-m68k
drwxr-sr-x    5 1176     1176       110592 Nov 22 15:16 etch-proposed-updates
drwxr-sr-x   19 1176     1176         4096 Nov 22 15:17 experimental
drwxr-xr-x    5 1176     1176         4096 Sep 04 21:11 lenny
```

Figure 10.63 – cmd.txt content

We can also click on the `info.xml` file to view the connection information:

--- Decoding info: stream 0 ---

tcp
    tcp.srcport 40667
    tcp.dstport 21
    tcp.clnt 1
    tcp.lost 0
    tcp.syn 0

ip
    ip.proto 6
    ip.src 172.26.0.21
    ip.dst 130.89.149.226
    ip.offset 14

eth
    eth.src 00:80:5a:4f:2d:59
    eth.type 2048

Figure 10.64 – info.xml details

This brings us to the end of our network analysis section. Feel free to capture and create your own `.pcap` files for analysis with Xplico.

Summary

I hope you enjoyed the exercises in this chapter as much as I did. Xplico can be used in Kali Linux and also DEFT Linux, should you have any difficulty in installing it within Kali Linux. As we have seen and practiced in this chapter, Xplico can be used for HTTP, VoIP, email, and network analysis, but can also perform MMS, DNS, Facebook, and WhatsApp chat analysis. I encourage you to try to download and analyze more sample files from the Xplico and Wireshark sample capture pages to become more familiar with analysis and examination using Xplico.

Let's move on to the final chapter now, where we'll delve even further into network analysis using more tools.

11
Network Analysis

We're at the last chapter now but, instead of slowing things down, I believe in finishing strong. Let's have a go at some network forensics.

We've done quite a bit of acquisition and analysis thus far, including hard drive, storage, RAM, and swap file analysis to acquire, document, and analyze evidence in the hopes of finding or recovering artifacts. Let's go a step further by analyzing protocols and network communication as they may also be useful artifacts that can aid us in our investigations.

Seeing that some incidents and crimes occur over the internet, or even a **Local Area Network (LAN)**, capturing and analyzing network traffic should be an essential part of our investigative process. Packet captures can be used to reveal artifacts that may help us to better understand an incident, point to its origin, and even, in some cases, assist in extending the scope of the investigation if it is suspected that the incident may not be an isolated one.

In this chapter, we'll first capture packets with Wireshark in Kali Linux and then proceed with network and packet analysis tools to examine packet capture (.pcap) files.

In this chapter, we'll cover the following topics:

- Capturing packets using Wireshark
- Analyzing packet captures using NetworkMiner
- **Packet capture (PCAP)** analysis with **PcapXray**
- Online PCAP analysis

Let's get started!

Capturing packets using Wireshark

Wireshark is a very popular and well-known tool used for network and packet analysis and troubleshooting. It comes pre-installed in Kali Linux and is relatively straightforward to use once you have an idea about filters, protocols, and color codes.

If you're new to the Wireshark protocol analyzer and packet analysis, you can find some great tutorials online, including the official documentation at `https://www.wireshark.org/docs/wsug_html_chunked/ChapterCapture.html`.

Before we begin using Wireshark, let's see what our network interfaces are first. We'll need to specify the interface we want to begin capturing packets on when we start Wireshark. To get information on your interfaces in Kali Linux, open Terminal and type `ifconfig`:

```
root@kali:~# ifconfig
eth0: flags=4163<UP,BROADCAST,RUNNING,MULTICAST>  mtu 1500
        inet 172.16.79.94  netmask 255.255.0.0  broadcast 172.16.255.255
        inet6 fe80::a00:27ff:fe7c:8e8e  prefixlen 64  scopeid 0x20<link>
        ether 08:00:27:7c:8e:8e  txqueuelen 1000  (Ethernet)
        RX packets 25  bytes 2474 (2.4 KiB)
        RX errors 0  dropped 0  overruns 0  frame 0
        TX packets 18  bytes 2418 (2.3 KiB)
        TX errors 0  dropped 0 overruns 0  carrier 0  collisions 0

lo: flags=73<UP,LOOPBACK,RUNNING>  mtu 65536
        inet 127.0.0.1  netmask 255.0.0.0
        inet6 ::1  prefixlen 128  scopeid 0x10<host>
        loop  txqueuelen 1000  (Local Loopback)
        RX packets 40  bytes 2116 (2.0 KiB)
        RX errors 0  dropped 0  overruns 0  frame 0
        TX packets 40  bytes 2116 (2.0 KiB)
        TX errors 0  dropped 0 overruns 0  carrier 0  collisions 0

root@kali:~# 
```

Figure 11.1 – Viewing the network adapter configurations

In the previous screenshot, the `ifconfig` command displays the output for two interfaces. The interface I'll be using is my Ethernet interface, listed as **eth0**, and there is also the loopback interface, listed as **lo**.

Important note

If you're using a wireless **Network Interface Card** (**NIC**) to capture interfaces, it will be listed as **wlan0**.

Now that we know which of our interfaces we'll be using to capture packets and sniff the network with, we can start Wireshark by typing `wireshark` in the Terminal:

Figure 11.2 – Starting Wireshark in Kali

You can also run Wireshark by clicking on **Applications | 09 - Sniffing & Spoofing | wireshark**:

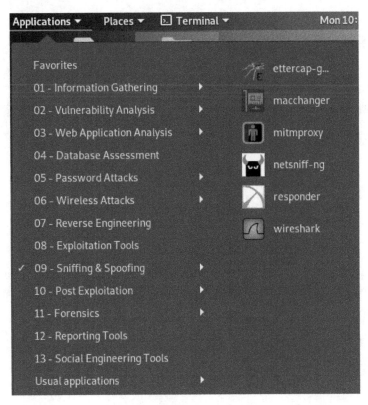

Figure 11.3 – Finding Wireshark in the Sniffing & Spoofing menu

As mentioned previously, when Wireshark runs, we'll need to select an interface to begin capturing packets on. In this instance, my **eth0** interface is highlighted, but be sure to select the interface you will be working with to capture packets:

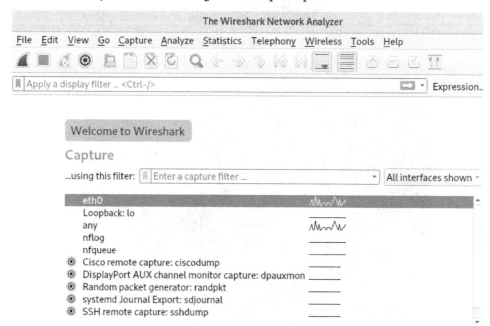

Figure 11.4 – Adapter selection in Wireshark

Once the interface is selected, we can begin the packet capture process by either clicking on the blue shark fin icon or by clicking on **Capture | Start**:

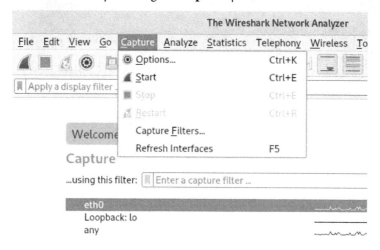

Figure 11.5 – Starting the packet capture in Wireshark

The packet capture process automatically begins after clicking on the button to start capturing:

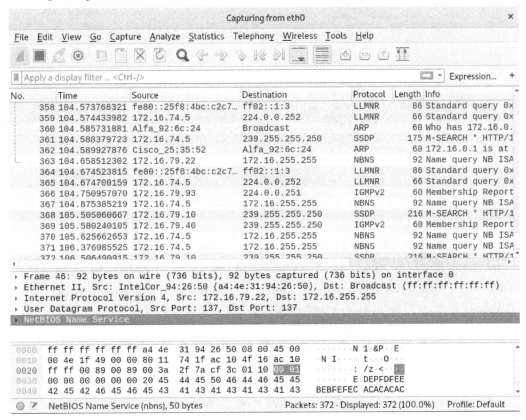

Figure 11.6 – Packet capture in Wireshark

In the previous screenshot, we can see that Wireshark organizes the display into three sections, with the main section at the top containing rows populated with **Source**, **Destination**, **Protocol**, and other information, all color-coded.

To stop the capture, click on the stop button at the top (the red square):

Figure 11.7 – Start and stop packet capture icons in the Wireshark menu

Be sure to save the packet capture file by clicking on **File | Save As**:

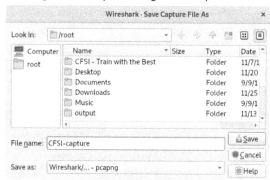

Figure 11.8 – Saving the .pcap file

We can also use specific Wireshark filters to sort the data, thereby presenting a logical and simpler view of the packets.

Common Wireshark filters can be found at `https://www.networkdatapedia.com/single-post/2019/01/29/Top-10-Wireshark-Filters`.

To set a filter for packets with a particular source or destination IP address, we use the `ip.addr==a.b.c.d` format, for example, `ip.addr==172.16.79.21`:

Figure 11.9 – Filtering by IP address

To set a filter for a specific TCP port, we can use the `tcp.port==` `filter` format, for example, `tcp.port==443`:

Figure 11.10 – Filtering by port

To set a filter that searches for a specific word, string, or even user, use the `frame contains` filter. For example, I've visited a website (`www.malware-traffic-analysis.net`) that hosts sample PCAP files of malware infections and downloaded a sample PCAP file. To search for the word `malware`, I'll use the `frame contains malware` filter:

No.	Time	Source	Destination	Protocol	Length	Info
183	15.530022860	172.16.79.94	8.8.8.8	DNS	84	Standard que
184	15.530177746	172.16.79.94	8.8.8.8	DNS	84	Standard que
186	15.619137254	8.8.8.8	172.16.79.94	DNS	159	Standard que
187	15.627999736	8.8.8.8	172.16.79.94	DNS	159	Standard que
188	15.629640271	172.16.79.94	8.8.8.8	DNS	84	Standard que
189	15.629956679	172.16.79.94	8.8.8.8	DNS	84	Standard que
190	15.705055792	8.8.8.8	172.16.79.94	DNS	159	Standard que
191	15.707594288	8.8.8.8	172.16.79.94	DNS	159	Standard que
593	18.633612929	172.16.79.94	8.8.8.8	DNS	92	Standard que
604	18.734664576	8.8.8.8	172.16.79.94	DNS	108	Standard que
605	18.734752687	172.16.79.94	8.8.8.8	DNS	92	Standard que
614	18.821576709	8.8.8.8	172.16.79.94	DNS	162	Standard que
622	18.907861584	172.16.79.94	166.78.135.34	TLSv1.2	583	Client Hello
623	18.999808412	166.78.135.34	172.16.79.94	TLSv1.2	1514	Server Hello

Figure 11.11 – Filter by frame containing text

To set a filter to view a conversation between two IPs, we use the format `ip.addr==a.b.c.d && ip.addr==w.x.y.z`, for example, `ip.addr==172.16.79.94 && ip.addr==172.16.0.1`:

No.	Time	Source	Destination	Protocol	Length	Info
368	105.372189167	172.16.79.94	172.16.0.1	UDP	74	50365 → 3343
369	105.372228883	172.16.79.94	172.16.0.1	UDP	74	39880 → 3343
370	105.372265338	172.16.79.94	172.16.0.1	UDP	74	46656 → 3343
371	105.372303402	172.16.79.94	172.16.0.1	UDP	74	59728 → 3344
372	105.372343141	172.16.79.94	172.16.0.1	UDP	74	57163 → 3344
373	105.372400321	172.16.79.94	172.16.0.1	UDP	74	33207 → 3344
374	105.372462245	172.16.79.94	172.16.0.1	UDP	74	51231 → 3344
375	105.372515914	172.16.79.94	172.16.0.1	UDP	74	57708 → 3344
376	105.372555133	172.16.79.94	172.16.0.1	UDP	74	48775 → 3344
377	105.372592562	172.16.79.94	172.16.0.1	UDP	74	33870 → 3344
378	105.372621374	172.16.79.94	172.16.0.1	UDP	74	44736 → 3344
379	105.372652997	172.16.79.94	172.16.0.1	UDP	74	36525 → 3344
380	105.372680860	172.16.79.94	172.16.0.1	UDP	74	58197 → 3344
381	105.374653767	172.16.0.1	172.16.79.94	ICMP	70	Destination

Figure 11.12 – Filter by IP conversation

You can find more information on Wireshark filters here:

`https://wiki.wireshark.org/DisplayFilters`

Let's move on to automated packet capture display and analysis using NetworkMiner.

NetworkMiner

Analyzing captured data from Wireshark can be a bit of a challenge to people who may be new to the protocol analyzer, as it requires knowledge of protocols and filters and the ability to follow data streams (all of which becomes easier with practice).

NetworkMiner is an easy-to-use packet capture viewer, which some users may find easier to use than Wireshark for packet capture analysis as it extracts and sorts the found data into categories of hosts (with operating system fingerprinting), files, images, messages, sessions, and more by parsing the `.pcap` file.

NetworkMiner comes in a free version as well as a paid Professional version and can be installed on Windows and Linux. You can visit the official website for NetworkMiner at `https://www.netresec.com/?page=NetworkMiner`.

Installing NetworkMiner in Kali Linux is straightforward. Open a new Terminal and type the following command to download the `.zip` file:

```
wget www.netresec.com/?download=NetworkMiner -O /tmp/nm.zip
```

The following screenshot shows the output of the command:

```
root@kali:~# wget www.netresec.com/?download=NetworkMiner -O /tmp/nm.zip
--2019-08-15 10:05:24--  http://www.netresec.com/?download=NetworkMiner
Resolving www.netresec.com (www.netresec.com)... 195.74.38.16
Connecting to www.netresec.com (www.netresec.com)|195.74.38.16|:80... connected.
HTTP request sent, awaiting response... 301 Moved Permanently
Location: https://www.netresec.com/?download=NetworkMiner [following]
--2019-08-15 10:05:25--  https://www.netresec.com/?download=NetworkMiner
Connecting to www.netresec.com (www.netresec.com)|195.74.38.16|:443... connected
.
HTTP request sent, awaiting response... 200 OK
Length: 2183693 (2.1M) [application/octet-stream]
Saving to: '/tmp/nm.zip'

/tmp/nm.zip         100%[===================>]   2.08M   624KB/s    in 3.4s

2019-08-15 10:05:29 (624 KB/s) - '/tmp/nm.zip' saved [2183693/2183693]
```

Figure 11.13 – Downloading NetworkMiner to Kali

After downloading, we'll need to unzip the file by typing the following:

```
unzip /tmp/nm.zip -d /opt/
```

The following screenshot shows the output of the command:

```
root@kali:~# unzip /tmp/nm.zip -d /opt/
Archive:   /tmp/nm.zip
   creating: /opt/NetworkMiner_2-4/
   creating: /opt/NetworkMiner_2-4/AssembledFiles/
   creating: /opt/NetworkMiner_2-4/AssembledFiles/cache/
   creating: /opt/NetworkMiner_2-4/Captures/
  inflating: /opt/NetworkMiner_2-4/ChangeLog
   creating: /opt/NetworkMiner_2-4/CleartextTools/
  inflating: /opt/NetworkMiner_2-4/CleartextTools/all-words.txt
   creating: /opt/NetworkMiner_2-4/Fingerprints/
  inflating: /opt/NetworkMiner_2-4/Fingerprints/dhcp.xml
  inflating: /opt/NetworkMiner_2-4/Fingerprints/etter.finger.os
  inflating: /opt/NetworkMiner_2-4/Fingerprints/mac-ages.csv
  inflating: /opt/NetworkMiner_2-4/Fingerprints/oui.txt
  inflating: /opt/NetworkMiner_2-4/Fingerprints/p0f.fp
  inflating: /opt/NetworkMiner_2-4/Fingerprints/p0f.fp.netsa
  inflating: /opt/NetworkMiner_2-4/Fingerprints/p0fa.fp
  inflating: /opt/NetworkMiner_2-4/Fingerprints/tcp.xml
   creating: /opt/NetworkMiner_2-4/Images/
  inflating: /opt/NetworkMiner_2-4/Images/abb.png
  inflating: /opt/NetworkMiner_2-4/Images/android.jpg
  inflating: /opt/NetworkMiner_2-4/Images/arrow_incoming.jpg
  inflating: /opt/NetworkMiner_2-4/Images/arrow_outgoing.jpg
  inflating: /opt/NetworkMiner_2-4/Images/arrow_received.jpg
  inflating: /opt/NetworkMiner_2-4/Images/arrow_sent.jpg
  inflating: /opt/NetworkMiner_2-4/Images/broadcast.jpg
```

Figure 11.14 – Unzipping the NetworkMiner file

We then change to the NetworkMiner 2-4 directory by typing the following command:

```
cd opt/NetworkMiner_2-4/
```

We then run the `ls` command to view the files within the directory and ensure that `NetworkMiner.exe` exists:

```
root@kali:/opt# cd NetworkMiner_2-4
root@kali:/opt/NetworkMiner_2-4# ls
AssembledFiles    CleartextTools    NetworkMiner.exe        PacketParser.dll
Captures          Fingerprints      networkminericon.ico
ChangeLog         Images            NetworkWrapper.dll
```

Figure 11.15 – Viewing the contents of the Network Miner directory

We'll also need to assign various file permissions by typing the following three commands:

- `chmod +x NetworkMiner.exe`
- `chmod -R go+w AssembledFiles/`
- `chmod -R go+w Captures/`

We must then run the `mono NetworkMiner.exe` file, which is used to run .NET applications:

```
root@kali:~# cd /opt/NetworkMiner_2-4/
root@kali:/opt/NetworkMiner_2-4# chmod +x NetworkMiner.exe
root@kali:/opt/NetworkMiner_2-4# chmod -R go+w AssembledFiles/
root@kali:/opt/NetworkMiner_2-4# chmod -R go+w Captures/
root@kali:/opt/NetworkMiner_2-4# mono NetworkMiner.exe
bash: mono: command not found
```

Figure 11.16 – Assigning permissions to NetworkMiner dependencies

If you're presented with an error when attempting to run the `mono` command, open a new Terminal tab and run `apt-get install mono-complete`. Press *Y* to continue when prompted:

```
root@kali:/opt/NetworkMiner_2-4#  apt-get install mono-complete
Reading package lists... Done
Building dependency tree
Reading state information... Done
The following packages were automatically installed and are no longer required:
  acccheck dh-python geoip-database-extra libappindicator1 libavcodec57
  libavfilter6 libavformat57 libavresample3 libavutil55 libbabeltrace-ctf1
  libcamel-1.2-60 libcdio17 libcue1 libdbusmenu-gtk4 libedataserver-1.2-22
  libedataserverui-1.2-1 libfile-copy-recursive-perl libgcab-1.0-0
  libhttp-parser2.7.1 libindicator7 libisl15 libjs-openlayers libllvm5.0
  liblouis14 libmagickcore-6.q16-5 libmagickcore-6.q16-5-extra
  libmagickwand-6.q16-5 libnfs8 libpoppler73 libpostproc54 libqgis-core2.18.17
  libqgis-gui2.18.17 libqgis-networkanalysis2.18.17 libqgispython2.18.17
  libradare2-2.4 libswresample2 libswscale4 libsynctex1 libtcl8.5 libtk8.5
  libwireshark10 libwiretap7 libwscodecs1 libwsutil8 libx265-146 openjdk-9-jdk
  openjdk-9-jdk-headless openjdk-9-jre python-imaging python-unicodecsv
  python3-configargparse python3-editorconfig python3-flask
  python3-itsdangerous python3-jsbeautifier python3-pyinotify
  python3-simplejson python3-werkzeug tk8.5
```

Figure 11.17 – Installing mono

The following prompt appears. Select **<Yes>** to restart services during package upgrades without asking. This may take up to 5 minutes or more depending on your connection speed and the RAM assigned to Kali Linux:

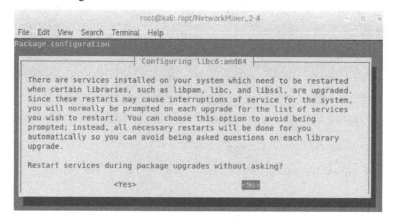

Figure 11.18 – Restart services prompt

Once completed, you are returned to the `NetworkMiner` folder:

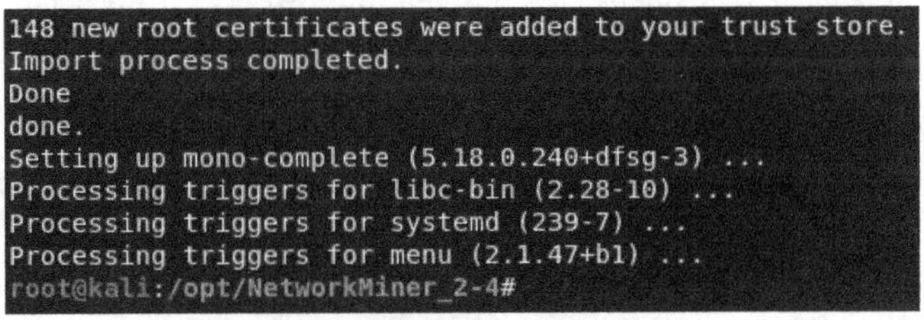

Figure 11.19 – Process status

Finally, run `mono NetworkMiner.exe` again, which will now open the NetworkMiner application:

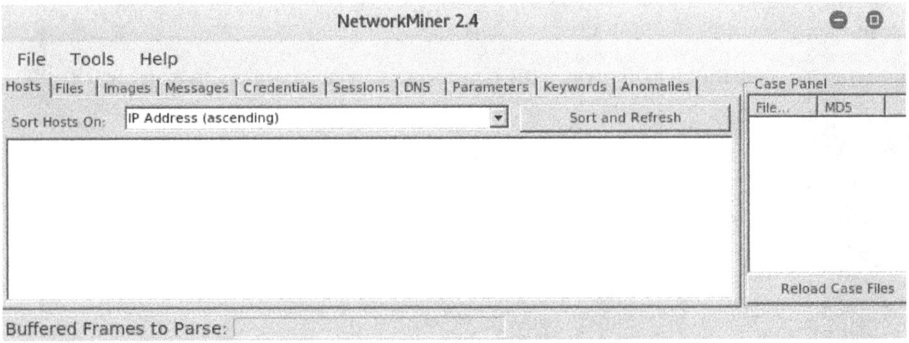

Figure 11.20 – The NetworkMiner interface

To view further documentation and videos and to get access to sample PCAP files, visit this link:

`https://www.netresec.com/?page=Resources`

For this analysis, we'll be using the PCAP from the following link, which you can download and save to your Kali Linux machine:

`http://wiki.xplico.org/lib/exe/fetch.php?media=pcap:xplico.org_sample_capture_protocols_supported_in_0.6.3.pcap.bz2`

This file was previously downloaded for use with **Xplico,** so you may already have it in your `Downloads` folder.

I've decided to use this file not only because we downloaded it for analysis with Xplico in *Chapter 10, Analysis with Xplico,* but also to view the differences between Xplico and NetworkMiner by also opening the PCAP file in Xplico.

I've already downloaded and extracted the file to my `Downloads` folder. In the **NetworkMiner** program, click on **File** and **Open** and browse to the `xplico. org_sample_capture_protocols_supported_in_0.6.3.pcap` file in the `Downloads` folder (or wherever you may have downloaded the file to). Click on the `.pcap` file and then click **Open**:

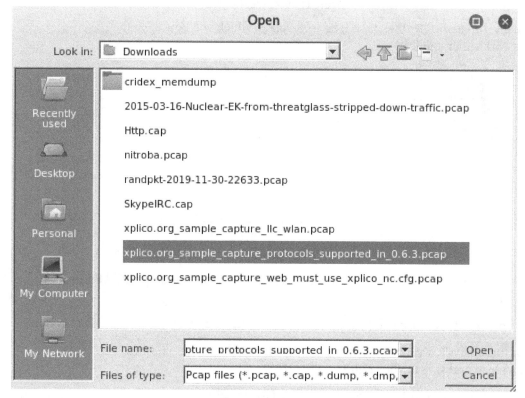

Figure 11.21 – Opening the .pcap file

After clicking on **Open**, NetworkMiner loads and parses the file and categorizes the findings:

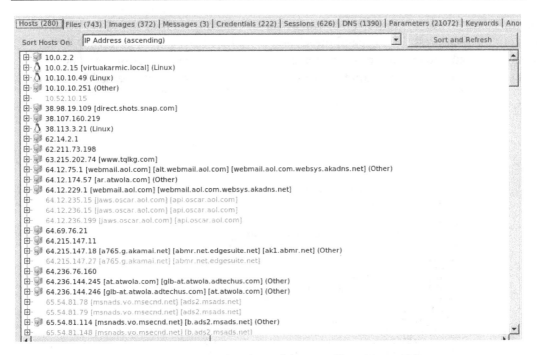

Figure 11.22 – Automated analysis of the .pcap file in NetworkMiner

At first glance, we are presented with information about devices in the **Hosts** tab. The .pcap files contain several hits per category:

- **Hosts** – 280

- **Files** – 743

- **Images** – 372

- **Messages** – 3

- **Credentials** – 222

- **Sessions** – 626

- **DNS** – 1390

- **Parameters** – 21072

In the **Hosts** tab, details for each host can be seen by clicking on the expand (+) button next to the IP address. Let's expand the second IP address (10.0.2.15) to view the details. We can also expand the other items, such as **OS**, **Outgoing sessions**, and host details, to see all the information that NetworkMiner has automatically parsed for us:

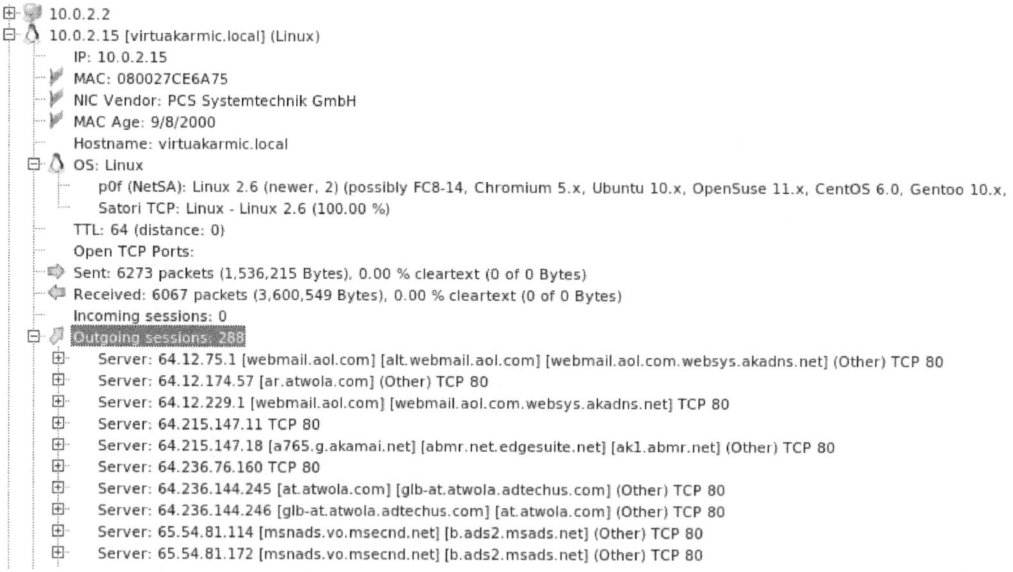

```
⊞ 🖳 10.0.2.2
⊟ △ 10.0.2.15 [virtuakarmic.local] (Linux)
        IP: 10.0.2.15
     ⍓ MAC: 080027CE6A75
     ⍓ NIC Vendor: PCS Systemtechnik GmbH
     ⍓ MAC Age: 9/8/2000
        Hostname: virtuakarmic.local
  ⊟ △ OS: Linux
            pOf (NetSA): Linux 2.6 (newer, 2) (possibly FC8-14, Chromium 5.x, Ubuntu 10.x, OpenSuse 11.x, CentOS 6.0, Gentoo 10.x,
            Satori TCP: Linux - Linux 2.6 (100.00 %)
        TTL: 64 (distance: 0)
        Open TCP Ports:
     ⇨ Sent: 6273 packets (1,536,215 Bytes), 0.00 % cleartext (0 of 0 Bytes)
     ⇦ Received: 6067 packets (3,600,549 Bytes), 0.00 % cleartext (0 of 0 Bytes)
        Incoming sessions: 0
  ⊟ 🗐 Outgoing sessions: 288
     ⊞    Server: 64.12.75.1 [webmail.aol.com] [alt.webmail.aol.com] [webmail.aol.com.websys.akadns.net] (Other) TCP 80
     ⊞    Server: 64.12.174.57 [ar.atwola.com] (Other) TCP 80
     ⊞    Server: 64.12.229.1 [webmail.aol.com] [webmail.aol.com.websys.akadns.net] TCP 80
     ⊞    Server: 64.215.147.11 TCP 80
     ⊞    Server: 64.215.147.18 [a765.g.akamai.net] [abmr.net.edgesuite.net] [ak1.abmr.net] (Other) TCP 80
     ⊞    Server: 64.236.76.160 TCP 80
     ⊞    Server: 64.236.144.245 [at.atwola.com] [glb-at.atwola.adtechus.com] (Other) TCP 80
     ⊞    Server: 64.236.144.246 [glb-at.atwola.adtechus.com] [at.atwola.com] (Other) TCP 80
     ⊞    Server: 65.54.81.114 [msnads.vo.msecnd.net] [b.ads2.msads.net] (Other) TCP 80
     ⊞    Server: 65.54.81.172 [msnads.vo.msecnd.net] [b.ads2.msads.net] (Other) TCP 80
```

Figure 11.23 – Hosts tab in NetwokMiner

In the preceding screenshot, we can see details such as the MAC address, NIC manufacturer, OS (Linux), open ports, and outgoing sessions to servers and websites.

In the **Files** tab, there are several hundred entries (743 of them). Click on the **Files** tab. We can see several entries and file types (.html, .css, .jpeg, and so on). We can also open these links and view the files. Right-click on the Bienvenido.html file and select **Open file**:

40	jav.SAXParserFactory.html	html	1 157 B 200.57.7.194 [200.57.7.194] (Windows)
157	jav.SAXParserFactory[1].html	html	1 157 B 200.57.7.194 [200.57.7.194] (Windows)
181	jav.SAXParserFactory[2].html	html	1 157 B 200.57.7.194 [200.57.7.194] (Windows)
242	jav.SAXParserFactory[3].html	html	1 157 B 200.57.7.194 [200.57.7.194] (Windows)
260	jav.SAXParserFactory[4].html	html	1 157 B 200.57.7.194 [200.57.7.194] (Windows)
290	jav.SAXParserFactory[5].html	html	1 157 B 200.57.7.194 [200.57.7.194] (Windows)
409	jav.SAXParserFactory[6].html	html	1 157 B 200.57.7.194 [200.57.7.194] (Windows)
969	jav.SAXParserFactory[7].html	html	1 157 B 200.57.7.194 [200.57.7.194] (Windows)
1819	jav.SAXParserFactory[8].html	html	1 157 B 200.57.7.194 [200.57.7.194] (Windows)
2740	jav.SAXParserFactory[9].html	html	1 157 B 200.57.7.194 [200.57.7.194] (Windows)
3236	jav.SAXParserFactory[10].html	html	1 157 B 200.57.7.194 [200.57.7.194] (Windows)
4041	jav.SAXParserFactory[11].html	html	1 157 B 200.57.7.194 [200.57.7.194] (Windows)
4257	jav.SAXParserFactory[12].html	html	1 157 B 200.57.7.194 [200.57.7.194] (Windows)
11291	index.html	html	291 B 216.34.181.96 [amule.sf.net] [amule.sourceforg..
11304	index.html	html	15 091 B 85.14.219.10 [rabbithole.amule.org] [www.amul..
11452	ChangeLog		1 979 243 B 130.89.149.226 [ftp.debian.org]
13791	Bienvenido.html		
13791	Bienvenido.eml		
13905	n27037696386_93806		
13905	testingYah.eml		
13915	index.html		w.xplico.org]
13938	scheme.css		w.xplico.org]
13941	jquery.ifixpng.js		w.xplico.org]
13935	style.css.php.html		w.xplico.org]
13944	jquery.js		w.xplico.org]
13963	style.css.php.452AE84		w.xplico.org]
14053	bullet_sidebars_hide.png	png	226 B 67.205.51.26 [xplico.org] [www.xplico.org]

Menu overlay:
- Open file
- Open folder
- Calculate MD5 / SHA1 / SHA256 hash
- Auto-resize all columns
- OSINT hash lookup isn't available in the free version
- Sample submision isn't available in the free version

Figure 11.24 – Opening files within the File tab

This opens the `.html` file in the browser:

Figure 11.25 – Web page preview

You can also do this for other files, such as the `.jpeg` files:

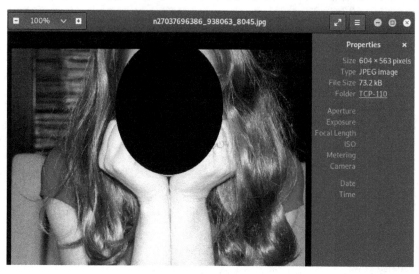

Figure 11.26 – Viewing an image file

Click on the **Images** tab. In this scenario, NetworkMiner has found 372 images, most with previews. You can let the mouse hover over an entry to see more information about the image, such as the **Source** and **Destination** IP addresses. You can also right-click on the image and choose **Open Image** to view it:

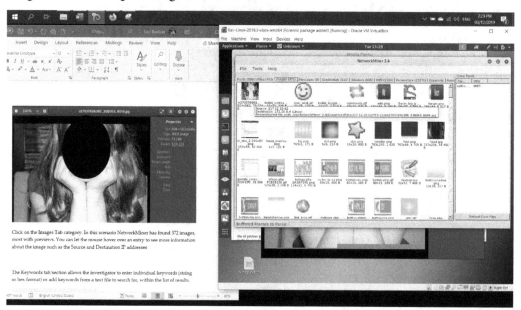

Figure 11.27 – Contents within the Images tab

In the **Messages** tab, there are three messages that show the source and destination hosts as well as the sender and recipient of the message/email if we scroll to the right:

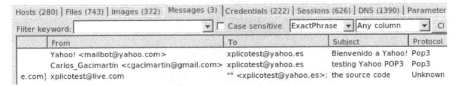

From	To	Subject	Protocol
Yahoo! <mailbot@yahoo.com>	xplicotest@yahoo.es	Bienvenido a Yahoo!	Pop3
Carlos_Gacimartin <cgacimartin@gmail.com>	xplicotest@yahoo.es	testing Yahoo POP3	Pop3
e.com] xplicotest@live.com	"" <xplicotest@yahoo.es>;	the source code	Unknown

Figure 11.28 – Email messages

In the **Credentials** tab, we find some very interesting artifacts. This tab shows the client and server IP, OS type, protocol, and any associated usernames and passwords that may have been used in that session, which are most likely unencrypted plain-text passwords:

Client	Server	Protocol	Username	Password
200.57.7.204 (Windows)	200.57.7.194 [200.57.7.194]	HTTP Cookie	JSESSIONID=1s6ylq2znjyl5	N/A
200.57.7.194 [200.57.7.1...	200.57.7.197	SNMPv2c	SNMP community	public
200.57.7.197	200.57.7.194 [200.57.7.194] (Windows)	SNMPv2c	SNMP community	public
200.57.7.205	10.52.10.15	SNMPv1	SNMP community	public
200.57.7.205 (Windows)	216.136.173.10 (FreeBSD)	POP3	ecortones	cortone$
200.57.7.205 (Windows)	200.73.183.213 (Cisco)	POP3	gmanriquez@IPvision.com.ar	gonzal0
200.57.7.205 (Windows)	200.73.183.213 (Cisco)	POP3	ecortones@telesmart.com.ar	gonzal0
172.26.0.21 (Linux)	85.14.219.10 [rabbithole.amule.org] [www.amul...	HTTP Cookie	PHPSESSID=697698db39b462b88f1865e03f500fb...	N/A
172.26.0.21 (Linux)	130.89.149.226 [ftp.debian.org]	FTP	anonymous	asd@asd.com
172.26.0.4 (Linux)	38.113.3.21 (Linux)	POP3	xplicotest@HotPOP.com	kebab1
172.26.0.4 (Linux)	217.12.10.62	POP3	xplicotest@yahoo.es	kebablover
172.26.0.4 (Linux)	67.205.51.26 [www.xplico.org]	HTTP Cookie	wassup_screen_res=1680x1050	N/A
172.26.0.4 (Linux)	67.205.51.26 [xplico.org] [www.xplico.org]	HTTP Cookie	wassup=ZWNmZGUyNWMwOWVjYzhkMDNmNjN...	N/A

Figure 11.29 – Credentials tab

The **Sessions** tab shows the sessions between devices at the time of the packet capture:

Frame nr.	Client host	C. port	Server host	S. port	Protocol (app
14579	172.26.0.4 (Linux)	45442	76.74.254.121 [stats.wordpress.com]	80	Http
14581	172.26.0.4 (Linux)	45444	76.74.254.121 [stats.wordpress.com]	80	Http
14606	172.26.0.4 (Linux)	39670	93.184.220.20 [s.wordpress.com]	80	Http
14613	172.26.0.4 (Linux)	45446	76.74.254.121 [stats.wordpress.com]	80	Http
14625	172.26.0.4 (Linux)	45448	76.74.254.121 [stats.wordpress.com]	80	Http
14631	172.26.0.4 (Linux)	45449	76.74.254.121 [stats.wordpress.com]	80	Http
14696	172.26.0.4 (Linux)	49201	87.248.109.251 [add.my.yahoo.com]	80	Http
14697	172.26.0.4 (Linux)	56341	74.125.77.104 [images.l.google.com] [images.g...	80	Http
14712	172.26.0.4 (Linux)	56003	209.85.227.104 [www.google.com]	80	Http
14704	172.26.0.4 (Linux)	43808	66.235.112.64 [www.bloglines.com]	80	Http
14713	172.26.0.4 (Linux)	45447	76.74.254.121 [stats.wordpress.com]	80	Http
14738	172.26.0.4 (Linux)	43214	76.74.255.123 [gacimartin.com]	80	Http
14760	172.26.0.4 (Linux)	56156	74.125.79.191 [thrillingwonder.blogspot.com] [...	80	Http
14767	172.26.0.4 (Linux)	50198	74.125.77.121 [www.darkroastedblend.com]	80	Http
14808	172.26.0.20 (Linux)	37508	74.125.165.84 [safebrowsing-cache.google.com]	80	
14814	172.26.0.20 (Linux)	37510	74.125.165.84 [safebrowsing-cache.google.com]	80	
14834	172.26.0.4 (Linux)	41178	161.184.245.22 [www3.telus.net]	80	Http
14846	172.26.0.4 (Linux)	56159	74.125.79.191 [thrillingwonder.blogspot.com] [...	80	Http
14847	172.26.0.4 (Linux)	56160	74.125.79.191 [thrillingwonder.blogspot.com] [...	80	Http
14848	172.26.0.4 (Linux)	56161	74.125.79.191 [thrillingwonder.blogspot.com] [...	80	Http
14849	172.26.0.4 (Linux)	50590	208.122.7.98 [cache.blogads.com]	80	Http
14870	172.26.0.4 (Linux)	41500	93.188.130.83 [www.lijit.com]	80	Http
14895	172.26.0.4 (Linux)	41503	93.188.130.83 [www.lijit.com]	80	Http
14893	172.26.0.4 (Linux)	50592	208.122.7.98 [cache.blogads.com]	80	Http

Figure 11.30 – Sessions tab

The **Keywords** tab/section allows the investigator to enter individual keywords (in the string or hex format) or add keywords from a text file to search for within the list of results. If using keywords, you may have to start over by specifying a keyword list or file and then re-opening the .pcap file in NetworkMiner:

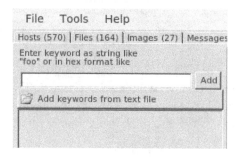

Figure 11.31 – Keywords search tab

As we can see, NetworkMiner is a powerful packet capture analyzer, which makes analysis much easier for investigators and networking personnel by automatically parsing and categorizing the information found in a .pcap file.

Packet capture analysis with PcapXray

Much like NetworkMiner, PcapXray is another powerful and comprehensive packet capture analysis tool. Some of the main features of this tool are the identification of malicious, web, and even Tor traffic, and covert communication.

Let's install PcapXray by cloning it from GitHub by typing the following command in the Terminal. As usual, I've changed my directory to Desktop. Cloning PcapXray to your desktop will take some time as the file is 115 MB in size:

```
git clone https://github.com/Srinivas11789/PcapXray.git
```

The following screenshot shows the output of the command:

```
root@kali:~# cd Desktop
root@kali:~/Desktop# git clone https://github.com/Srinivas11789/PcapXray.git
Cloning into 'PcapXray'...
remote: Enumerating objects: 145, done.
remote: Counting objects: 100% (145/145), done.
remote: Compressing objects: 100% (105/105), done.
remote: Total 1681 (delta 74), reused 98 (delta 39), pack-reused 1536
Receiving objects: 100% (1681/1681), 115.74 MiB | 347.00 KiB/s, done.
Resolving deltas: 100% (954/954), done.
root@kali:~/Desktop#
```

Figure 11.32 – Cloning PcapXray to the Desktop

Next, we need to install `python3-pip` to ensure that pip version 3 will be available to install any requirements.

Let's begin by installing Python by running this command in the terminal:

```
apt install python3-pip
```

The following screenshot shows the output of the command:

Figure 11.33 – Installing the Python package

Once Python is installed, run the following command to install the python3-tk package:

```
apt install python3-tk
```

The following screenshot shows the output of the command:

Figure 11.34 – Installing the python3-tk package

Now, let's install the **Graph Visualization Software (graphviz)** by typing the following command:

```
apt install graphviz
```

The following screenshot shows the output of the command:

Figure 11.35 – Installing graphviz

Let's install the final Python dependency by running the following command:

`apt install python3-pil python3-pil.imagetk.`

The following screenshot shows the output of the command:

```
root@kali:~# apt install python3-pil python3-pil.imagetk
Reading package lists... Done
Building dependency tree
Reading state information... Done
```

Figure 11.36 – Installing the final Python dependencies

Now, change to the `PcapXray` directory and show the contents of the directory:

```
root@kali:~/Desktop# cd PcapXray
root@kali:~/Desktop/PcapXray# ls
_config.yml  Dockerfile  logo.png    requirements.txt  Samples  Test
Design       LICENSE     README.md   run.sh            Source
root@kali:~/Desktop/PcapXray#
```

Figure 11.37 – Contents of the PcapXray directory

There's a `requirements.txt` file present, which means that we'll need to install certain requirements by typing `pip3 install -r requirements.txt`:

```
root@kali:~/PcapXray# pip3 install -r requirements.txt
Collecting scapy (from -r requirements.txt (line 4))
  Downloading https://files.pythonhosted.org/packages/52/e7/464079606a9cf97ad049
36c52a5324d14dae36215f9319bf3faa46a7907d/scapy-2.4.3.tar.gz (905kB)
    100% |                              | 911kB 119kB/s
Collecting pyshark (from -r requirements.txt (line 5))
  Downloading https://files.pythonhosted.org/packages/b9/b0/ef87c71f7937ea812494
4b2081210f9df10e47d2faa57d7c30d3e12af064/pyshark-0.4.2.9-py3-none-any.whl
Collecting ipwhois (from -r requirements.txt (line 12))
```

Figure 11.38 – Installing additional requirements

Finally, to run PcapXray, run the following command, which opens the PcapXray GUI:

```
python3 Source/main.py
```

The following screenshot shows the output of the command:

```
root@kali:~/PcapXray# python3 Source/main.py

DevTools listening on ws://127.0.0.1:56530/devtools/browser/
7fd3e620-90cf-4237-9ae9-58a5b5fe6477
```

Figure 11.39 – Starting PcapXray

Using the PcapXray GUI is simple. We capture our traffic or download the `.pcap` file for analysis, specify the paths for the `.pcap` file and `output` folder, and then click **Analyze!**.

Let's first download a file to analyze from `https://www.malware-traffic-analysis.net/2019/07/19/index.html`

2019-07-19 - TRAFFIC ANALYSIS EXERCISE - SO HOT RIGHT NOW

ASSOCIATED FILES:

- Zip archive of the pcap: **2019-07-19-traffic-analysis-exercise.pcap.zip**   21 MB (20,969,562 bytes)

  - 2019-07-19-traffic-analysis-exercise.pcap   (26,347,323 bytes)

Figure 11.40 – Screenshot of the sample file download page

Click on the `2019-07-19-traffic-analysis-exercise.pcap.zip` file to download it and then extract it so that we can begin the analysis. If asked for a password when extracting, type `infected`.

We can now get back to the PcapXray GUI and browse to the extracted `.pcap` file and also specify an output directory:

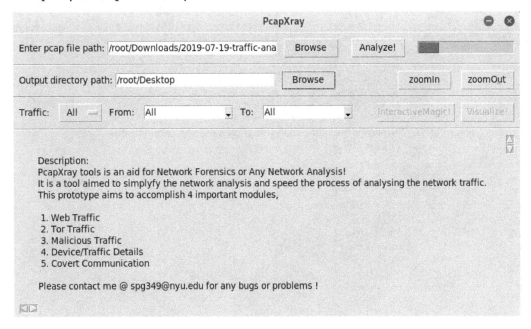

Figure 11.41 – PcapXray .pcap upload interface

Click on the **Analyze!** button, which will then take a while to perform the analysis. You should then be able to click on the **Visualize!** button when it becomes available. Although it's a bit hard to see in the previous screenshot, it analyzes the traffic between the source and destinations:

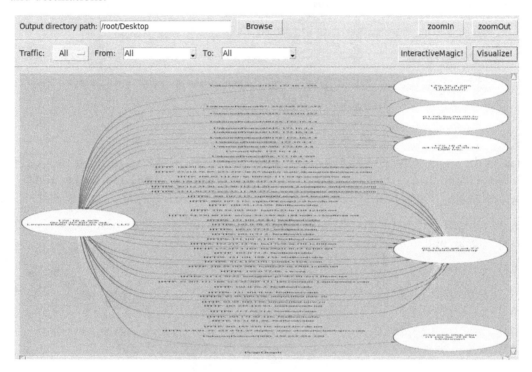

Figure 11.42 – Display of the traffic analysis between the source and destinations

Click on the **InteractiveMagic!** button to see a different view of the devices and their relations to each other:

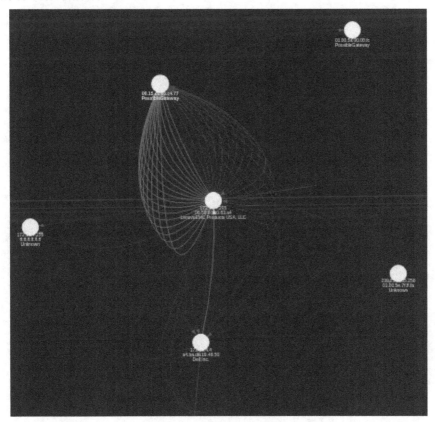

Figure 11.43 – InteractiveMagic feature

These views can help pinpoint which devices were in communication with each other, whether legitimately or covertly, and help with incident analysis.

We can also narrow down our view by clicking on the **All** button in the menu above the traffic visualization and choosing which type of traffic we'd like to view:

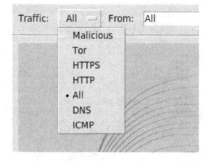

Figure 11.44 – Traffic visualization options

Click on **Malicious** and then click on the **Visualize!** button again:

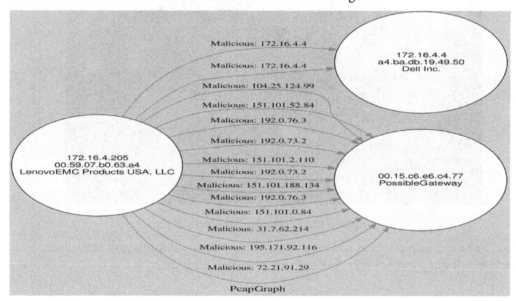

Figure 11.45 – Malicious traffic timeline details

Here, we can actually see traffic labeled as **Malicious** and the IPs and gateway addresses associated with the communicating devices. If we change the **Traffic** view to **HTTPS** and then click on the **Visualize!** button again, we can also see the HTTPS web traffic and thereby begin putting together or recreating the scenario between the malware, devices, and web traffic at the time of capture.

Online PCAP analysis

We've come to the last topic and the last lab in this book. This one is also a fully automated tool for PCAP analysis and is done online using **PacketTotal**: www.packettotal.com.

PacketTotal is completely free and is, quite simply, where a user can visit the site and either drag a file or click on the **upload** button to upload and analyze a .pcap file. The only restriction is that there is a limit of 50 MB on .pcap file uploads:

Drag .pcap files here or click to upload.

(Accepts .pcap and .pcapng files. Limit 50 MB.)

Figure 11.46 – PacketTotal.com .pcap upload page

Click on **upload** and browse to the very same file we just analyzed using PcapXray (2019-07-19-traffic-analysis-exercise.pcap) and then click on **Open**. You'll have to click on the **I'm not a robot** checkbox to continue before clicking on the **Analyze** button:

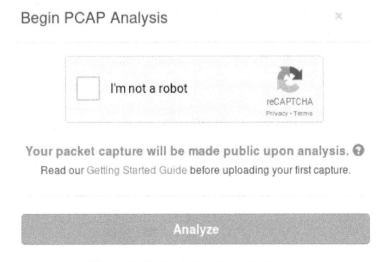

Figure 11.47 – PacketTotal security feature

Once the analysis is complete, PacketTotal gives a very detailed view of the traffic captured. Notice the categories at the top (**Malicious Activity**, **Suspicious Activity**, **Connections**, and various protocols):

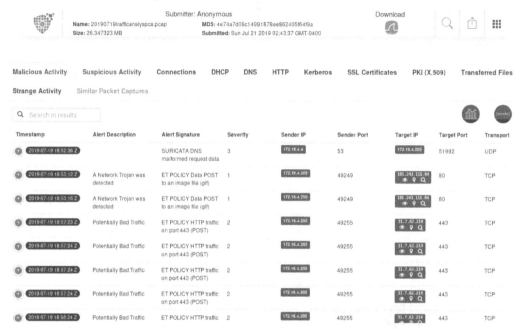

Figure 11.48 – PacketTotal analysis results

Let's click on **Malicious Activity** first:

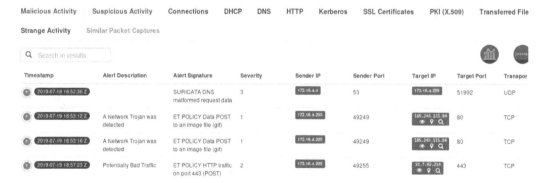

Figure 11.49 – Malicious activity

We can see that a network Trojan was detected, with a sender IP of 172.16.4.4.

Click on **Suspicious Activity** next:

Figure 11.50 – Suspicious Activity

Here, we can see the connection ID, along with the sender and target IPs, to get more information on the 172.16.4.205 IP address.

Feel free to continue your analysis on PacketTotal and the other tools using the freely available PCAP files at https://www.malware-traffic-analysis.net/index.html and https://www.malware-traffic-analysis.net/training-exercises.html.

Reporting and presentation

Throughout this chapter and the entire book, you will have referred to various steps, screenshots, and even several best practices from ENISA, ACPO, and the SWGDE. It's of the utmost importance to document all the steps in an investigation, not only to be able to recreate and verify your results but also to present your findings within a formal report that may be used in court.

In a professional and unbiased manner, your findings must be presented in layman's terms that can be understood by non-technical persons, such as lawyers, managers, businesspersons, accountants, and others who may not be familiar with forensic processes and terms in any way whatsoever.

Here are some links that may be useful in creating and presenting your findings in a report:

- Intro to Report Writing for Digital Forensics: `https://www.sans.org/blog/intro-to-report-writing-for-digital-forensics/`

- NIST 800-86, Guide to Computer and Network Data Analysis: `https://www.hsdl.org/?view&did=460595`

- An actual forensics examination report: `http://www.rnyte-cyber.com/uploads/9/8/5/9/98595764/exampledigiforensicsrprt_by_ryan_nye.pdf`

Summary

You made it! This was our last chapter. You're now capable of creating your own `.pcap` files using Wireshark and you can also choose a tool or, as I do, use all the tools from this chapter to gather as much information as possible when performing network forensics using Wireshark, NetworkMiner, PcapXray, and PacketTotal.

I hope you enjoyed this book and found it useful in your investigations. Should you have any questions or need advice, feel free to add me on LinkedIn and send a message, at `https://tt.linkedin.com/in/shiva-parasram-87a66564`.

Other Books You May Enjoy

If you enjoyed this book, you may be interested in these other books by Packt:

Learn Kali Linux 2019

Glen D. Singh

ISBN: 978-1-78961-180-9

- Explore the fundamentals of ethical hacking

- Learn how to install and configure Kali Linux

- Get up to speed with performing wireless network pentesting

- Gain insights into passive and active information gathering

- Understand web application pentesting

- Decode WEP, WPA, and WPA2 encryptions using a variety of methods, such as the fake authentication attack, the ARP request replay attack, and the dictionary attack

Mastering Kali Linux for Advanced Penetration Testing - Third Edition

Vijay Kumar Velu, Robert Beggs

ISBN: 978-1-78934-056-3

- Configure the most effective Kali Linux tools to test infrastructure security
- Employ stealth to avoid detection in the infrastructure being tested
- Recognize when stealth attacks are being used against your infrastructure
- Exploit networks and data systems using wired and wireless networks as well as web services
- Identify and download valuable data from target systems
- Maintain access to compromised systems
- Use social engineering to compromise the weakest part of the network - the end users

Leave a review - let other readers know what you think

Please share your thoughts on this book with others by leaving a review on the site that you bought it from. If you purchased the book from Amazon, please leave us an honest review on this book's Amazon page. This is vital so that other potential readers can see and use your unbiased opinion to make purchasing decisions, we can understand what our customers think about our products, and our authors can see your feedback on the title that they have worked with Packt to create. It will only take a few minutes of your time, but is valuable to other potential customers, our authors, and Packt. Thank you!

Index